NO
BIG
DEAL

NO BIG DEAL

Mark Fidrych
and
Tom Clark

J.B. Lippincott Company
Philadelphia and New York

To all my fans

Acknowledgments

When we started this book, Mark Fidrych wanted to call it "How They Made Me" in acknowledgment of his gratitude to everyone who helped him along the way. Their names are on the pages that follow; they'll know who they are; without them, this book wouldn't have existed.

In addition, special thanks are owed to Gerry McCauley, Dock Ellis, Mel Berger, Steve Pinkus, Hal Middlesworth, John Kinney, and Angelica Clark, all of whom helped considerably and without whom, again, there'd be no book.

T.C.

Copyright © 1977 by Mark Fidrych and Tom Clark
All rights reserved
First edition
9 8 7 6 5 4 3 2 1
Printed in the United States of America

U.S. Library of Congress Cataloging in Publication Data

Fidrych, Mark.
 No big deal.

 SUMMARY: An interview with Mark Fidrych in which he discusses his life and his baseball career.
 1. Fidrych, Mark. 2. Baseball players—United States—Biography.
[1. Fidrych, Mark. 2. Baseball players] I. Clark, Tom, birth date joint author. II. Title.
GV865.F426A36   796.357′092′2   [B] [92] 77-8651
ISBN-0-397-01233-0

Contents

Introduction   *13*

PART ONE: MY FIRST TIME OUT IN LIFE

1. *When They Took Our Woods Away, We Knew How*
   the Indians Felt   *23*
2. *I Can't See Looking at a Gas Station Job the Rest of*
   My Life   *35*
3. *School Wasn't My Bag*   *42*
4. *I Just Played the Game, I Didn't Pay Much Attention*
   to It   *48*
5. *The Scout That Signed Me Saw Me Throw One Pitch*   *57*
6. *My First Time Out in Life (Bristol, 1974)*   *65*
7. *I Made Them Drop Me Off at the End of My Street*
   (Lakeland, 1975)   *85*
8. *A Whole Other Relief in Your Life*
   (Montgomery/Evansville, 1975)   *94*
9. *Throw a Guy into a Winning Atmosphere, He's*
   Gonna Win   *105*

PART TWO: THIS YEAR I WAS THE MAGNET

10. *How Many Games Will They Give Me?*   *127*
11. *A Town Reunion in the Men's Room at Fenway*
    Park   *142*
12. *Those Ballplayers, They Really Know That I Like to*
    Play Ball (The All-Star Game)   *156*
13. *I Get in a Bad Train of Atmosphere in Cleveland*   *169*

14. The Girls Really Do Sit Down in the Halls and Wait for You   *186*

15. When You Get Down to Real Life, the Bird Was Just a Symbol   *197*

16. The Agents Throw the Million Dollar Man in My Face   *215*

17. I Get the Man of the Year Award and Live to Tell It   *231*

Epilogue   *244*

Appendix A: Detroit Tigers' 1976 Roster   *248*

Appendix B: Mark Fidrych's record in organized baseball   *249*

Appendix C: Mark Fidrych—1976, Game-by-Game   *250*

Appendix D: A Pitchers' Efficiency Rating System for the American League, 1976   *251*

An eight-page section of photographs follows Part One

"I've never seen anything like this in all my twenty-eight years in baseball."—Don Zimmer, manager, Boston Red Sox

"In all my years in baseball, I've never seen anything like it. I don't think even Walter Johnson started this fast."—Ralph Houk, manager, Detroit Tigers

"He's the most exciting thing I've ever seen. I've seen Tommy Seaver go out and mow 'em down, but I've never seen anybody electrify the fans like this."—Rusty Staub, outfielder, Detroit Tigers

"Babe Ruth didn't cause this much excitement in his brightest day."—Paul Richards, manager, Chicago White Sox

"On June 28 I had the pleasure of watching one of the greatest baseball games in many years. It was on Monday Night Baseball television and not so much for the game itself but for watching a kid named Mark Fidrych pitching for the Detroit Tigers against the New York Yankees.

"The man they called 'Bird' was a joy to watch. He talked to the baseball, he congratulated his fellow players on practically every play, he was as jubilant as a teenager. He was refreshing. And he can pitch!

"As a tribute to him, all of the more than 47,000 fans would not leave the park until he came out of the dugout to tip his cap. Now if only the agents don't get hold of him and ruin him as they have so many others."—Sam Epstein, Sunnyvale, California (letter to *The Sporting News,* August 7, 1976).

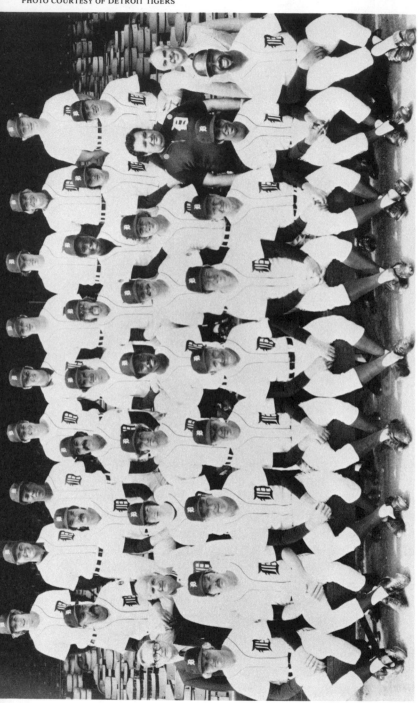

1976 Detroit Tigers. "The way I look at it, Detroit has treated me so well, I just say I ain't gonna move from 'em. Until they tell me to go." Front row: Dan Meyer, Chuck Scrivener, Jim Hegan, Dick Tracewski, Ralph Houk, Fred Gladding, Joe Schultz, Jerry Manuel, Willie Horton. Second row: Dr. Clarence Livingood, Trainer Bill Behm, Batboy Tim Lennon, John Wockenfuss, Ron LeFlore, Milt May, Gary Sutherland, Equipment Manager Jack Hand, Traveling Secretary Vince Desmond. Third row: John Hiller, Ray Bare, Aurelio Rodriguez, Bill Laxton, Bruce Taylor, Ben Oglivie, Tom Veryzer, Vern Ruhle. Back row: Mark Fidrych, Bill Freehan, Alex Johnson, Jim Crawford, Joe Coleman, Dave Roberts, Steve Grilli, Mickey Stanley, Rusty Staub.

Introduction

Of Dizzy Dean's crazy starburst on the American scene in 1932, it has been said, he "realized the American dream at a time when most Americans had abandoned it. The country wanted entertainment more than it wanted inspiration, and he filled the need." If Dizzy filled that need in 1932, Mark Fidrych did so equally in 1976. Ol' Diz, though, never drew crowds like these. In a year made glum in the ballyards by high-up lawsuits and grabby agents, empty pennant races and a runaway World Series, Mark Fidrych made people laugh and feel happy, forty and fifty thousand at a time. For that, the people who run the game forgave him everything. Even if they thought he was a little insane, they loved him. In 1976 Mark Fidrych hit baseball with a pie in the face containing money.

Looking for Mark Fidrych in a crowd of baseball people is like looking for an ocean liner in your backyard. If he's there, you'll find him instantly. I didn't have any trouble finding him. I went to the baseball people and there he was, ragged, splendid, wild, sticking out of the expectable heraldry of the national pastime like a gigantic puce-and-mauve sore thumb rampant on a field of snow-white jock straps. ("If you're gonna stick out," Mark later expounded apropos of his inability to blend at high-class social functions, "stick out!")

My conversations with Mark were recorded in the Los Angeles Hilton during the week of baseball's winter meetings, December 4–9, 1976. Mark was in Los Angeles at the request (and expense) of the Tigers, who'd flown him out so that he could receive a hastily instituted Man of the Year award from the National Association of Professional Baseball Leagues. (Mark later confided to me that the nature and purpose of the award hadn't been explained to him, and that the whole idea of receiving it had given him at least one sleepless night before his arrival in California.) At the Hilton, it was clear as soon as you hit the main lobby that baseball was holding up Mark Fidrych as its number-one selling point for the first year of America's third century. A Lord Fauntleroy-style airbrush head-and-shoulders poster portrait of Mark in Tiger red-white-and-blue, complete with apple-pie grin and halo of golden curls, decorated a pillar between the escalator and the main desk, where it couldn't be missed. In style this work reminded me of Russian patriotic art of the forties, as did two other posters, farther down the row of pillars. These depicted (1) Cub outfielder Rick Monday rescuing an American flag from lighter-fluid arsonists at Dodger Stadium and (2) Hank Aaron and Babe Ruth floating in the sky above a kid batting on a sandlot.

The scene under these idealistic posters looked like so much business as usual, at first. One could casually observe the lobby intercourse and assume it had been this way since time began. There was the ceaseless babble of wheeling-dealing, job hunting, buying and selling. One could stand behind a newspaper and eavesdrop on industry social climbers who had the lift-off of great high-jumpers. (Brown Suit intercepts Bob Feller in the lobby. "Hi there, Robert, how ya doin'?" "Yayup, jes' hangin' around, havin' a few beers," twangs Feller, bored. His eyes flick past Brown Suit, scan the lobby. "See ya later, keed.") But all these things you'd no doubt run into at *any* trade convention. For make no mistake, fans, except for a sprinkling of famous faces this could have been a bunch of rug salesmen from Ogden and Kankakee and Utica, getting together for the yearly expense-account bash.

Rug salesmen, or you name it. The hail-fellow tone, the half-smashed jolliness, the sense of satisfaction for owed favors paid for that hangs over each conversational tableau like a solid zone—all these things could probably be found equally at any annual gathering of Jaycees or admen or police chiefs. But here, even though the ubiquitous open-bar hospitality suites (run by leagues, ball clubs, card and bat and glove firms) keep everybody nicely oiled, the lobby banter has a dissonant air, which you only notice after you've been listening for a few hours. Then the conviviality begins to sound subtly forced. Much of the talk is doubtless as it always has been—gravel-voiced baseball lifers benignly exchanging news and comparing notes over bourbon and cigars ("Course what *I* do with these new uniforms today, I *cold* wash 'em—sixty-five washings, they still hold up like new") or in offhandedly brutal phrases throwing away actual lives ("Back when that pitching coach from Chicago ruined Darold Knowles' arm. . . ." "So-and-so said, I'll give you four warm bodies for your third baseman. . . ."). But this time, you start to sense, the gossip has this slightly desperate tone, like so much high-pitched whistling in the dark.

Taking place in 1976, the year of Jerry Kapstein and the free agent, this set of baseball meetings has a special milestone-ish *angst* of its own, the sport having developed a belatedly realistic concern for its own future that even a handshake and a nod from Hammerin' Hank or Stan the Man can't dispel. This winter of 1976, baseball is finally hearing some heavy shock waves through the sand it's had its head in for years. Those waves, of course, are being made by the dreaded free agents, who in one month of sustained plunder have notably depleted several of the richer owners' pockets and severely damaged most of the game's traditional assumptions about salary ratio, team identification, player freedom, and God knows what else. Having been tortured by the sight of the Hamburger Man, Ray Kroc, kicking up three million for two ballplayers; and having suffered while the Golden Cowboy, Gene Autry, threw down six mil for three; and having gasped as the Highest Roller, George Steinbrenner, dropped *five* mil on the table for a thirty-year-old outfielder and a pitcher with a record of brilliance alternating with disability—after the pain of all that, what joy can there be in the executive heart to learn of the daily gossip? How indeed can it provoke true gladness then to hear that Bob Cluck is the Astros' new minor league director? Or that the Expos have hired Harry Bright as their Northern California scout? Or that Connie Ryan is the Rangers' new third-base coach? Or that the Red Sox have peddled Bobby Heise to Kansas City? Or that the Rawlings Big Stick Award will be presented to club secretary Alice Neighbors of the Tulsa Oilers? This year all those familiar songs have a hollow ring. The ordinary owner shuffles his feet and thinks of other things. So the Twins announced that Del Wilber will be managing at Tacoma? But what with things the way they are these days, who's to say there'll *be* a Tacoma next year? Or even a Twins? (Sound funny? Maybe, but do you think Minnesota's Calvin Griffith laughed when he found out the Red Sox—whose '77 payroll averages $100,000 per man—would pay his twenty-two-grand relief pitcher, Bill Campbell, a cool million?)

And will there *be* a minor leagues for Tacoma to be in, five years from today? Don't bet on it, say the vibes in the lobby. Okay, so the Orioles laid in a new supply of windbreakers for their farm teams, and the Yankees renewed their working agreement with Winter Haven. Okay, so Bucky Buchheister of Cedar Rapids has been named Executive of the Year in the Midwest League. How can these facts lighten the mind of the lifetime baseball man who picks up his morning paper and reads with disbelief of Reggie Jackson's new $7,000 nutria fur coat, his $65,000 maroon Rolls-Royce Corniche, his quarter interest in a San Francisco Porsche agency, an investment of "several hundred thousand dollars"? Before long, Reggie will be able to buy the Twins, and Tacoma too. These days, who needs a Midwest League or a Winter Haven to bring up players somebody else can snatch away from you with one wave of a King Kong-size check?

"An incredible exercise in egotism," Bill Veeck calls the free-agent draft. Talking to the L.A. *Times,* Veeck says his fellow owners "paid ridiculous sums to feed their egos."

So the normal orders of business don't seem to be the true subjects of these lobby conversations. Between each sentence uttered about third-base coaches and Gulf Coast scouts, there is a silent telepathic message of anxiety, apprehension, doubt. What will happen next? Will Bowie Kuhn boot Ted Turner out of the owners' sandbox because Ted wined and dined Gary Matthews before he signed him? Will Bowie lose his shirt, starch collar and all, to Charley Finley's lawyers? Bowie himself, papal, bilious, steps cautiously from a sleek black limo on Wilshire and enters by a side door, his lunch heavy under his belt, his aides glancing from side to side, Secret Service style, ever vigilant for signs of behavior detrimental to our national sport.

The reporters are dying to get the word from Bowie on who, in the long run, is going to pay for all those little rare animals that are keeping Reggie Jackson's back warm. Will it be the fans who have to underwrite it all? But after next year, when this year's flock of twenty free agents expands to two hundred, will the fans still care? Will they know who's playing for who? Will they want to pay that extra fifty cents in ticket prices it costs you when your team buys a Sal Bando? When is enough enough? Bowie, Bowie, tell us if you know!

To which Bowie responds with a few cool remarks about how good the Reds/Yankees World Series TV ratings were, and how there were 3,054 stolen bases in the big leagues last year, and how a recent "influx of new stars" leaves him feeling "bullish on baseball's future." At the top of his influx list he names Mark "The Bird" Fidrych and smiles complacently. Everyone bows three times in the direction of the nearest dollar, giving the Commissioner a chance to change the subject.

Nine floors (and it might as well be nine miles, for all the interest he took in it) above all this, shoeless, in denim cut-offs and a T-shirt from an auto body shop, and ensconced in a tiny room with a partially amputated view of the Harbor Freeway's glimmering eastward sprawl, this broad-shouldered, blue-eyed twenty-two-year-old pitcher with a headful of blond curls, a Polish name, a Massachusetts accent, a hummingbird's metabolism, and the protruding beak, spindly legs, and rolling, splayfooted gait of a famous children's television character, kept his wastebasket full of iced Coors and his mind 100 percent off the trials and tribulations and hustles of the suit-and-tie set down below. Mark Fidrych, with one big-league season under his wing and the baseball world at his feet, was spending his first day and night in Los Angeles doing exactly what he'd done most of the days and nights he'd spent on the road over the past six months—exactly nothing.

Once you got to the ninth floor, Room 957 was made easy to locate by the loud rock music coming through the door and wafting down the corridor. (Mark's constantly got something cooking on his stereo tape deck: homemade or store-bought cassettes of the Jefferson Starship, The Eagles, Bad Company, New Riders of the Purple Sage, Stevie Wonder, Peter Frampton, or his favorite group, The Grateful Dead.) When I came in, Mark swooped over to his wastebasket cooler, reached in, and held out a beer to me in one extraordinarily large hand. Then he fell back on the messed-up sheets and launched into a plaintive description of the inadequacy of his room (he didn't care for the narrow twin beds and was considering a plan that involved consolidating them) and of the instructions he'd been given for the upcoming awards banquet ("They want me to wear a *tuxedo,* man—y'see, they want me to *change!*"). Behind him, Grace Slick of the Starship shrieked about tearing down the walls. Our marathon interview was done in this room.

Our first order of work was to turn the volume down. Then, for five days and with only occasional interruptions, we talked. I'd brought a detailed file of notes and questions, but it was rarely of use. Interviewing Mark is like being thrown into the water at an early age. You learn how to float in time, then you take a few strokes, then you're in the swim of it. The swim of this interview was oceanic. His thoughts and responses moved in large wavelike periods (he called them trains of thought), and as interviewer it was the best I could do to hang on. I tried to guide him through the story in clock time, from beginning to end. But I lost that battle in the first round!

Mark's replies to my questions were often stories. Those trains of thought—those nonstop, headlong, run-on, animated, disjunctive rambles into personal history and perception—make up the largest part of this book. Every bit of Mark Fidrych's fame as a talker is justified. Once under way, he is boundless. ("He was liable to say any damn thing that came into his mind," said one of his minor league managers.) His statements possess, if not total adherence to the rules of textbook English, then certainly a bull's-eye-perfect intuitive grammar and logic. His stories are tracer patterns of a na(t)ive intelligence at work. "Everybody can see the enthusiasm in Mark," Rusty Staub testified. And a blind man could hear it. I found the incantatory onrush of the Fidrych speaking style to be both irresistible and inseparable from the content of his stories, and in transcribing his words I've tried at all costs to retain that style. With a story, he doesn't so much tell it as swarm around it, covering the ground with the verbal thoroughness of a lock-er-room Gertrude Stein.

Aside from an afternoon off to party with baseball friends in Fullerton, and another for Mark to visit William Morris's offices in Beverly Hills, and a couple of hours of wedged-in shut-eye, we worked day and night on this project from Saturday to Wednesday. Mark finished up his obligations to baseball by starring at the award banquet on Tuesday night and picking up his slightly hincty trophy. On Wednesday I flew back to Northern California, Mark flew back to Detroit, and in the ensuing weeks we communicated by phone cross-country while I typed up the tapes, sifted out repetitive material, and put the rest into what felt like a natural narrative order. That order's a reconstruction, but where possible it keeps to the order of real time (childhood, adolescence, maturity). Where the context and flow of the conversations demanded it, I've taken minor liberties with chronology so as to preserve Mark's major themes.

A final note on the editing—the words you find here are the actual ones that were said. As Mark said when we discussed the issue of honesty in this book, "Why give them a false atmosphere?" I've kept to this principle of truthfulness, believing it to be the best way to go. To replace Mark's actual diction and syntax with simulated ones seemed a bad idea in theory and turned out to be impossible in practice. Because where his language is raw or halting, it's always expressive in being so. He came into the big leagues with the utter ingenuousness of the parabolic rookie (the "busher" of Lardner's *You Know Me Al*) and to this day retains it. He hasn't yet learned the kind of "couth" that counterfeits actual thoughts and feelings with acceptable clichés at appropriate moments. Again Rusty Staub was right when he said about Mark's exuberance, "None of it is contrived." If there's one thing Mark fails in, it's contrivance. To alter his book at those points where the language seemed rough or contorted would have been to take away the unselfconscious directness that makes the feel of his speech so unique. In the interest of the emotional accuracy and sheer presence I found therein, I chose to preserve the real thing the way it came rolling off his tongue.* And, reader, to trust in your sympathetic understanding.

After all, as I told Mark, that's what moms are for.

Tom Clark
Bolinas, California
January 20, 1977

---

*My decision, however, wasn't final, and in the production of the book alterations *were* made (in the interests of good taste and brevity) by Mark's agents and the publisher. ("My agent went through it," Mark said in describing his original manuscript to *Rolling Stone*, "and said there were too many swears in it.")

ONE: MY FIRST TIME OUT IN LIFE

1 When They Took Our Woods Away, We Knew How the Indians Felt

We Sat Down for a Week and Made Our Own Field

T. What kind of a town is Northboro? I mean, to grow up in, as opposed to another one?

M. Well, I wouldn't know what it's like to grow up in another town. I just grew up in that town. But I'll clue ya, I grew up in that town, and when I grew up—it's a whole different story, now. The whole town has changed, like. From what I can see. When I was a little kid, I used to go down and play whatever sport was goin' on. If football was goin' on, I mean after school, we'd be after school playin' football. Y'know? Or if it was basketball, we'd be out playin' basketball. Or baseball, we'd be playin' baseball. And like all the kids around my neighborhood played this. I mean everyone that I hung around with. Y'know, I mean, played it.

T. Same for me. That's all I did when I was a kid, played ball.

M. I mean, if you're around it, you're gonna do it, right? So then we played. And we made our own field, one time. I mean we sat down for like a week. I mean the parents are goin', Wow, we can't, y'know—like I went home and got a wheelbarrow from my dad, and a shovel, because he does concrete work. And he let me use them. He goes, Just make sure you bring 'em back. Another kid's father brought some junk down from, y'know, his work. I mean we all—all the kids got together that was in the field, like.

T. Near your house someplace?

M. Yeah! Oh, it was like, cut through two people's yards and I'm right there. So, like we made this field.

T.   What did you have to do? You mean flatten, level it?

M.   Oh, we did everything. We cut—we cut the infield, I mean we cut the base lines right down. And like we even made —we made the whole diamond! I mean, when we started, it was all like brush and shit. I mean it was—they said, my, uh, the parents said, Yeah, go ahead, try it, sure, you guys are gonna really fix it up. We're sittin' there, screw you, we're gonna fix it up! We even had a backstop, right?

T.   How old is this—like a bunch of six-, eight-year-olds? Ten-year-olds?

M.   Well, we mighta been about ten. Y'know, goin' up to fourteen.

T.   You didn't have a field to play in?

M.   Oh, we had a field to play on. But this was *our* field, now.

When You Hit a Home Run in
Left Field, the Neighbor Kept the Ball

T.   A field that no one could kick you off of, huh?

M.   Right. It was like—you'd go over to the school, someone else might be over there already playin'. And we can't play. So now we got our own designated field.

T.   For like you and your guys.

M.   Yeah. I mean, and whoever wanted to come down and play. We had—we started like a Little League, too, y'know? And stuff. And like one of the fathers once in a while would come down and be an umpire. And stuff like that. But if we took a picture of the beginning of it, and at the end—it was such an incredible thing. After we were all done—like everyone's sayin', Oh, it's done. And some other kid'll be goin', Nah, the mound's not done yet. I mean we were always trying to rush it. And finally we all got together, and this thing looked *nice.* I mean it was great. And then we only had one problem. That was, every time you hit a home run in left field, the neighbor would keep the ball.

T.   Keep the ball!

M.   Yeah, 'cause they had a fence around there. She just didn't like it, y'know?

T.   And she had windows?

M.   Yeah, she didn't like—we didn't break windows or anything. She just, the person just didn't like us climbin' her fence, and stuff like that. Y'know? But it was a good home-run fence. 'Cause it was pretty hard to hit it out. But yet, you got these guys that *could* jack it out. Y'know, the older guys.

T. You were mostly all right-handed hitters?

M. No, we had righties, lefties. Switch-hitters. Like the guy wanted to be a switch-hitter, he'd be a switch-hitter.

T. But you hit right-handed?

M. Mm-hmm.

T. Did you hit good?

M. Ah, I did all right. But I mean it was like—

T. But you used to play first base, and different positions?

M. Oh, I played every position. In baseball I've played every position, except in the major leagues. In high school, I played every position.

T. So you and your buddies built this field. Who were some of 'em?

M. Well, Ray Dumas, uh, what's his—his little brother, Kevin Dumas. And then there was Paul Beals, Jerry Beals. Paul McAfee, possibly Billy McAfee. Vic Porrea. Uh, David Moss, Donnie Moss. Uh, probably Jeff Berglund. Bobby Berglund, maybe. I mean, there was just, everyone just—a lot of kids just saw us makin' it, and then *they* started comin' in and helpin' too, just so they could play. We said, If you guys don't help, you guys aren't gonna play on our field.

T. Did your dad—

M. No, he didn't help. He just, they just—the parents, y'know? And one parent, like—it was hard to get a lawn mower. Y'know, Dad, can I borrow a lawn mower and bring it down there and mow the goddam'—he'd go, Hell, no, man, that blade's gonna end up like Swiss cheese! So finally this guy's father had an old horseshit lawn mower. He just had it sittin' downstairs. He goes, If you can get it runnin', take it. I don't give a shit what you do with it, I got another one. So we, everyone—y'know, we got one guy that could, that liked to work on that junk. And he worked on it. Like that was his job—he got it goin'. And *voom,* we had —mowin' the lawn and shit. I mean it wasn't *good* grass or anything. It was, y'know, dirt and—but still, we kept it cut. It was good. We had a mound. We had a good time, man. I'll never forget that. And now the field is still there. But it's not like it used to be, y'know? No one kept it up.

After We Grew Out of It, Our Field Broke Up and Got Old

T.   But it's still there?

M.   Yeah. After we grew out of it, y'know—it's like no one used it.

T.   What'd you call it?

M.   Huh?

T.   Did you have a name for it?

M.   No, we'd just call it our field.

T.   So you used to play until it got dark, in the summer? Fall, too?

M.   Oh, yeah. We'd play—like during the summer, we'd just have a scrub game. We'd say, All right, who wants to play? We'll be down there at ten o'clock. If we got enough guys, fine, y'know? If we didn't, we said, Let's goof around.

T.   These are kids you went to public school with?

M.   Yeah. Well, a lot of the kids—like you didn't go to their school. I mean they mighta been a little higher than you, or a little lower. I mean there was—there was no generation gap there. Like I coulda been ten years old, and one of the guys coulda been fifteen. Y'know? It was just somethin' like that.

T.   Did you go to public school?

M.   Oh, yeah.

T.   Was there a Catholic school around there, too?

M.   Where I was? No, you had to go to Worcester to get a Catholic school. Y'know? But it was like we all did it, and after it was done we just played. And then, say after two years it kinda wore out, because like now I couldn't go because I was playin' Little League baseball, y'know, like when *we* used to play. And then—and then other guys got older than high school now, and they didn't really wanna play. It just—y'know, everything, it just started breaking up, like. And then it finally broke up. And got old. Really, no one uses it now that I know of. But once in a while you used to see a little kid down there goofin' off. Kids, y'know? It was just weird. And like, they could've told us we couldn't do it. The town could've. Because we were on town property, just doin' it. 'Cause they had—they had swings there, and other things, y'know?

T.   Oh, it was a park.

M.   Yeah, it was like a little park. And like all houses all the way around it. And it was just this big dirt thing. We just made it. And it was good.

We Always Had Bats and Baseballs

T.   What did you do for equipment? Bats and balls?

M.   We always had bats and baseballs. That was no problem. Bats—it was easy, you'd go and steal 'em. Or just go borrow a ball here, and a ball and a bat there, or somethin'. Like they're playin' over here—at night or something'? Walk off with one, or some-thin'. It was always easy to get bats. My dad—he always got balls and bats for me. He's from—like he's a schoolteacher, right? So he'd come home with a ball, or a cracked bat, or somethin' like that.

My Parents

T.   Did your dad teach at Algonquin, the high school in Northboro? Or in grade school?

M.   No, elementary.

T.   Has he been doing that for—

M.   His life.

T.   His whole career?

M.   His whole life.

T.   Was he from Massachusetts, originally?

M.   Yeah. He's from Worcester.

T.   Your mother too?

M.   Yeah.

When They Bulldozed Our Underground Tree Fort and Took Our Woods Away, We Knew How the Indians Felt

T.   So your field broke up.

M.   Yeah, and then I started goin' into the *woods*, now. And we just goofed around. And then we started makin' *forts* in the woods, right? And then one time—we had a tree fort *under ground.* Right? We made a underground one? And like, we cut trees, and threw 'em on there. And all of a sudden we hear this motor noise. We go, Holy shit. We come out, What the hell is happening? The guy was bulldozin' us in! He was comin' by with a bulldozer, and he was yellin' at us, You guys get outa here! Y'know? And—because they were startin' to take all our land away, man, now! I mean we'd lose—we lost, we lost our woods. Since I grew up, every year we were losin' more and more. It was like the Indians, man. Here we are—we're deep in the woods where our parents couldn't see us. Like, if you went in. . . . But see, now gettin' back to that bulldozer scene, right? Where the guy, here he is, with a bulldozer. And he's just tellin' us, we gotta get outa there. And now our woods is gettin' taken. So now we're gettin' pushed back, and back. So like one treehouse we built deep in the woods, now you could see it from my friend's house, right?

T.   You mean it's all developed now?

M.   Yeah!

T.   In what, condos?

M.   No! Not condos—what're you, shittin' me? It's like, y'know, just houses—family houses. I mean, they just blew it all up, man. They just took all the woods. The woods isn't even there, now. There ain't—I betcha there aren't a hundred yards of woods now.

It's Not That Girls Weren't Allowed—There Were Just None Around

T.   So this is before you got into girls, or cars?

M.   That's before we even thought about girls! Y'know? I mean, shit.

T.   Keep the girls out of the tree fort, eh?

M.   No, it wasn't that.

T.   They didn't want to come, is probably closer.

M.   It was just—that's right. There was just none around. I mean we never really got into that. I don't think I really ever got into that scene where I'd say, No girls allowed in our tree fort.

T.   Well, you were used to having girls around since you had three sisters.

M.   Yeah, but they weren't . . . my sisters were just, y'know, sisters.

T.   Well, they must have had some friends.

M.   Yeah.

The Free Life Is Over Now

T.   You had a good time with all those tree forts.

M.   Heck, yeah.

T.   That's the time in life when you get into what you're doing, and nobody's . . .

M.   No one hassled us, man!

T.   And nobody's going to argue with you about it.

M.   No. We just—that was the free life, man! The free life is over now, man. When you—when your parents are supportin' you, that's the free life. Y'know? And when it stops, that's when it stops. Because I could go in the woods for eight hours. I'd get up at seven o'clock in the morning, go over and get a friend if we were gonna build a tree fort—we'd have, like five or six guys, and we'd just take off. Go in the woods and not come back until like four, or when it gets dark. Man, that's—you look at that now, you couldn't figure yourself doin' it, y'know. And like, my mother would never come out. She didn't worry about me, because she knew where I was. I said, I'm gonna be in the woods. Y'know? I would—if I wanted to go uptown, I told her, I'm goin' uptown. I told her where I was goin'. I didn't say, Well, I'm goin' *here* and then all of a sudden end up *there.* Nah, I told 'em where I was goin'.

T.   Your mom and dad sound all right.

M.   Yeah.

I'm Eight Years Old, Ma, I Want to Buy Some Weeds

M.   Then you get into the cigarette scene, man.

T.   Smokin' a few secret cigarettes.

M.   Yeah! Steal a pack from my dad. He quits, I'm goin', *Whoa,* I'm hurtin' now. Y'know? And then you go uptown, you steal it. And you go, *Wow,* y'know. And then you buy it once in a while. And then you got—it came up to where you hadda have your mother's consent, or your dad's consent, before you could buy cigarettes. That means you hadda steal it, now. Because you couldn't buy 'em, unless you had a note. And who the hell are you—I'm eight years old, Ma, give me a note, I wanna buy some weeds! It was just weird, cigarettes and shit.

By Eight O'clock You'd Get Your Six-pack

T.   What's the drinking age there, eighteen?

M.   Eighteen, now.

T.   Did you find older guys to buy it for you?

M.   Oh, shit, that was—

T.   Have any fake cards?

M.   No, I didn't have any fake cards. That's one thing. The guys—they wouldn't give you fake cards. Y'know, your friends uptown? The guy you knew, where you could get for five bucks an ABC card. Right? He wouldn't give it to you. He'd go, I'll buy the beer for you, I won't give you one. Y'know, he goes, he can —I got a way of gettin' 'em. But yet, he goes, You're too young right now. He goes, When you're eighteen, come hit me. But then it *changed* to eighteen, so I didn't have to worry about it. But shit, all you do is go up at six o'clock. We used to just go up at six at night. And by eight o'clock you'd at least get your six-pack, or whatever you wanted. I mean, one guy might be goin' in and buyin' twenty-five cases of beer!

T.   And then go drive around?

M.   Y'know, that one guy buys twenty-five cases of beer, and then we all meet at this one area. And he goes, All right, a six-pack to John, here, here's a six-pack for that, and that—aw, that guy was just like an adding machine. Y'know, he had a piece of paper. He had a pencil.

T.   They still do that?

M.   No, they don't do that any more.

T.   Town I live in, any time you go in the liquor store there's kids hangin' around outside asking you to buy beer.

M.   But now in that town, since it's eighteen you really don't need it, y'know? I mean most of the kids are gettin' served at sixteen.

We Threw Our Cans in One Big Pile

T.   So what'd you do once you got the beer?

M.   Yeah, we used to just drive around, and, uh—whatayacallit, park it here.

T.   What's there to do at night there? Just drive around?

M.   That's all we did.

T.   Drive-ins?

M.   No. We used to go to the drive-in. But we used to have this field, right? And we drove in to it. And like, it went for about a mile. And then it comes to an opening. And then go up to the right, over to this section. And up to the left, over to that section. And right in the middle, you'd have a big bonfire there.

T.   Nobody hassled you?

M.   No one hassled us, right? We'd just sit there and drink beer. Throw a big pile of beer cans right there. All have a big pile, right? And everyone used to just go up there—cars'd be open, music would be blastin', y'know? And shit. And no one hassled —you'd get there at eight, not probably leave until maybe one. Or twelve, y'know, depends on what time you hadda get home, right? And it was great.

Marlboro Comes After Don White

M.   And then all of a sudden, one time, me, Jerry Milano, and this kid Henry Gustafson that I'd just met from my next-door neighbor, right? We went over to their house on the Fourth of July, and he used to always come over, because they were cousins —and then he'd come over to my house, 'cause he had no one to hang around with. He was the only kid in his family. And so he used to come over. And then all of a sudden he came up, and we were sittin' in his car, and Jerry and I . . . I forget who the other kid was. It mighta been Peter Flanagan, maybe. He was in the back. Right? And we're just sittin' there. And just drinkin' a few beers, talkin', and I introduced him, y'know, and shit. And all of a sudden, we just look up. We're down in a gully, in the field that was off to the right before you get to the big main field. And all of a sudden, these people came runnin' over. *There they are, down here!* And I'm sittin' there—*Whoa!* Henry tries to start his car— flooded it, man! I mean, we was flippin', we didn't know *who* it was. They had sticks. All of a sudden one guy got right on the front of the car, big black guy, and goes, *Where is he? Which one of you guys is Don White?* I'm just goin', Aw—we had the windows and doors locked, we weren't about to do *nothin'*, man. He goes, *Open the fuckin' thing or I'll break the window!* Whoa!

Y'know, give 'em a *little* bit of an edge! And we—they started yellin' at us. *Where are you?* 'Cause Don White supposedly did something over in Marlboro—the town that this was. And these guys—there was about *twenty* of 'em, man. Hey, was I scared? I was shittin' my pants. 'Cause we—we go, Don White ain't here! He's probably up at that other field, man! We just know him as a—y'know, he's from our town, but he's up at the other field! And they're sayin', *Let's kick the shit outa these guys and show 'em what we're gonna do to Don White!* I said, Wait, wait, wait. What'd we *do,* y'know? We didn't do nothin'. I said—y'know, and I know they're from Marlboro, I see Steve Casares! I played, y'know, Legion baseball with him! And then Steven goes, Hey, Mark, is that you? I go, Yeah! My heart just went, *whoosh!* 'Cause these guys woulda done it, man. They *would* have done it. Y'know? And I'm there, *Whoa.* I just went, *whoosh,* right down, y'know?

    T.   They were pretty big, huh?

    M.   They were big. I mean they were—they were probably nineteen years old. Eighteen. Y'know, here *I* am, sixteen. Y'know? Just got my driver's license, man! Scared shitless! These guys are serious, y'know? They had antenners, they had everything, man. Ready to *kill* y'know? But just because one—a girl—

    T.   What's a tenner?

    M.   An antenna. A *car* antenna, man! They were ready to *beat* on us.

    T.   A cut-off antenna, like a whip?

    M.   Yeah, yeah! That's what that black guy had, who was up on the front of the hood, man! On my friend's car! I was sittin' there—it's gettin' dented, y'know? Here he is, comes over, first time I ever got out partyin' with him really, and he ends up like *this,* man! We thought it was a buncha Indians, man! That's what we—after everything was over, that's what we said. Wow, it looked like fuckin' Indians, didn't it? 'Cause we were scared shitless. And then they went up to the other field. After they let us alone, they told me what Don White did. He, uh, goofed around with a girl, y'know, in Marlboro. And she went back and told her boyfriend. And her boyfriend grabbed all of his friends, y'know? And said, Let's go show Northboro, right?

    T.   So they knew who you were and let you go.

    M.   Oh, yeah, just 'cause I knew that one kid, Casares.

Right? And there was another one, Black—Blackie was there too, another kid I coulda yelled out, y'know, if I had to. I was startin' yellin' to kids I knew from Hudson and stuff, the kids I played baseball with. 'Cause Marlboro and Hudson kinda hung around with each other, y'know? You'd never know what was gonna happen.

T.   What was Hudson?

M.   Hudson was just another town over. See, our Legion team was combined between Hudson and Marlboro. And out in Northboro, right? So I just started namin' guys off on our team that I knew, y'know? And finally I hit him, Steve. And I went, *Whoo,* thank you! But that saved—that *did* save us, man!

T.   That was your passport, huh?

M.   Yeah! That's just what it—that saved us. 'Cause I—you don't know what they woulda done. But they let us go.

Mark here continues the saga of the Northboro-Marlboro feud begun the evening of the quest for Don White (who, by the way, had run all the way home through the woods to avoid capture by Marlboro guys). The following night, the Marlboro guys returned to Northboro's parking field with malicious intent. They cascaded the parked cars with rocks. This time, however, the Northboro forces had convened in strength, such big guys as Dave Pierce and Tom King and Mike St. John having arrived to swell their numbers. After the first rock-slaught, the one-eyed giant, Mike St. John, defeated the "best guy in Marlboro" in hand-to-hand combat; whereupon "everyone started punchin'. . . I mean everyone was just whalin' on each other." Regarding discretion as the better part of valor, Mark hid in the woods until he heard the distressed cries of Tom King, a broken-legged Northboro guy whose cast was not preventing a Marlboro guy from attacking him. While King swung a large stick to defend himself, Mark leaped out of the dark to assist. The stick, vigorously swung by King, struck Mark in the forehead, sending him to the hospital for seven stitches. In the hospital, however, there was the consoling sight of numerous Marlboro men, bruised and bloody; while, aside from his own, Mark's side had not sustained a single serious injury, indicating Northboro to be the clear victors.

It's No High Rich Person

T. I was wondering—what do these kids, what do their folks do for a living? Is there any difference between the kids from Northboro, what their parents do, and the kids from Marlboro?

M. No. No, they all do the same—schoolteacher, or, y'know, they all work around. It's all—it's all the same. It's no high rich person, no big—

T. So there were businesses, or factories, or . . .

M. Yeah, we had some factories, and shit like that. But I didn't—

T. Like what kind?

M. Well, we had a candle factory. But that's no longer in existence. It burnt down. And then we had M and E Company— Machine and Electrification. We had Three-M—

T. What was that, M and E?

M. M & E. It's Machine and Electrification. But that stuff —I didn't really pay any attention, 'cause I wasn't workin' yet. So I really don't know. When it came down to jobs in my town—I worked for the Water Department, and I worked for Pierce Oil and Gas.

2 I Can't See Looking at a Gas Station Job the Rest of My Life

Caddying (I Blow Up on the Seventh Hole)

T. But then when you got in high school, you did summer jobs and stuff?

M. Oh, that's when—when I got in high school, yeah. Well, my first real job, I sold corn. I went around to houses like a paper route—then, that lasted. And then I went into caddyin'. And I used to go over Juniper Hill, Indian Meadows, to caddy. Man, here I am, caddyin' in a guy's tournament. All I have to do is pull his cart. I'm gettin' sick. Don't ask me why I'm gettin' sick. I didn't know. The sweat's pourin' outa my head. Had the diarrhea —ungodly. Had to quit after the seventh hole. Shit in my pants. I'm goin' wild. Had to go in the clubhouse. People went, *Whoa.* I said, Man, I'm a little sick, guys, y'know? Gimme a break! On the seventh hole, holdin'—out on the sixth tee, holdin' y'know, the thing, goin', *Ooohh,* I gotta shit! Man, you can't hold diarrhea in! Here's the guy in the tournament, makin' an important putt. And I'm sittin' there goin', Oh-oh. Y'know, I'm just dyin'. Y'know, tryin' not to disturb the guy. 'Cause he's gonna pay me good, y'know?

T. He's out there trying to get a hole in one?

M. No, here he is just tryin' to putt! Y'know? And I'm sick —and finally I just *blew up,* y'know?

I Go to Work at Uhlman's Shell

T. So what was the gas station job?

M. Then, y'know, when I was fourteen years old, I said, Dad, can you find me—I always wanted to work in a gas station. 'Cause when he used to pull into the gas station that he used to go to, I used to always, y'know, get out—jump out and pump the gas, y'know, and stuff like that. 'Cause I *liked* it. I knew I wanted—

T. You'd probably worked on cars already on your own?

M. No, not really. More of a lawn mower.

T. Yeah. But you were interested in motors. Engines.

M. Yeah, just—more of something like that. Just from readin', or buildin' a model, somethin' like that. My buddy Jeff Berglund, he was into that a lot.

T. So you were kind of young to get that gas station job?

M. Mmm. Oh, fourteen, yeah! Heck, yeah, I wasn't supposed to be workin' then. But yet, see, at a gas station they set a certain limit. Y'know, they say, He can pump gas.

T. But Uhlman had the station, and he was a friend of your dad's anyway.

M. Yeah, he was a friend. So okay, bring him in. So my father came home that night and said, You want a job? Tomorrow mornin' we go over and see Dave. And I go, Oh, he's gonna give me a job! I was excited. That guy made me work one day free. I had to work one day free, man, to get that job.

I Go to Work at Pierce Oil and Gas

T. You were learning something about cars, then.

M. Oh, yeah, I did. Right? I had that job a couple of years. And then I went to work at Pierce Oil and Gas, because Dave Pierce could pay me two twenty-five. And he said I didn't have to get a haircut, where Dave Uhlman told me he couldn't give me two twenty-five *unless* I got a haircut. And Dave and I kinda started hangin' around together. Like he became an older brother to me. I don't know why. But he just, Dave Pierce, he just became —y'know, like I used to go see him, goof around, 'cause he was into that kind of stuff, workin' on cars, workin' on motorcycles. And he had a lot of bikes. Even up till now. He's got a—down in the cellar, he's like a regular bike factory down there, man. Anything you need, he's got it. I mean it's just from collecting—all the years he's been workin' on 'em. And he got into that—and I liked that. I used to like goin' down there and goofin' around, and havin' my couple beers—what I was gonna have outside, I'd have down there. Only I'm workin' on a bike now, instead of just sittin' uptown drinkin' two beers.

T.   So what'd you do with the money you made?

M.   Saved it. And like bought a motorcycle one time. And then I put a car on the road. I'd just got my license and hadda pay car insurance and all that. I just worked enough to keep me goin'.

I Buy a '65 Chevy Bel Air Standard for a Hundred Bucks

T.   By now you had a car of your own?

M.   Oh, when I got to seventeen. Yeah, just about that time.

T.   What was it?

M.   I got a—I bought it off my schoolteacher, man. It was a '65 Chevy Bel Air Standard. Y'know? And the schoolteacher was funny, man. This is a joke. Like we're goin' home, man—this is funny, though. We're comin' home, and like I'm bringin' the teacher home with the car, y'know? He's gonna show my parents. And me and my buddy are in the back, Jerry Milano, right? And Mr. Eaton, one of the teachers. And he's drivin' down there, he's showin' me—he goes, Yeah! 'Cause he's really enthused, he's glad I'm buyin' it. 'Cause all it needed was one little part in it, y'know? I think a little solenoid, it needed. Because sometimes it just wouldn't turn over. And so he goes, Y'see, the radio works good! He goes, The heater works good! The fan! The windows roll up and down! He's showin' me everything—the blinkers both ways work! The lights work! And he goes, pushes in the cigarette—Even the cigarette lighter works for your roaches! I just went *voom*— I just cracked up laughin'. I go, C'mon, Mr. Eaton! I said, I don't do that, y'know? We're just laughin' our heads off! But I got that car for a hundred bucks, right? I had it a week. And it ran great, man! Ohh, I loved it, man! That car was good. And I had it a week. I sold it for a hundred dollars.

Mark then recites the litany of his cars, an American teen epic abbreviated here only because of printers' costs. After just a week, he sold his '65 Bel Air Standard in order to buy a '67 Chevy from another teacher at his father's school. This '67 he drove for two weeks, cracked up, partially repaired, and eventually drove again *on five cylinders until his next purchase. That was a '66 Barracuda, which he got for $1 and drove for two years. In 1975, he drove the Barracuda off an icy ramp in Clinton, Massachusetts, into a field of snow, sustaining damage to its "spider gears" which caused him to unload the car on his gas station buddy, Dave Pierce.*

When I Get on Skis, I'm Crazy

T.   Did you ever go—did you ever ski when you were a kid?

M.   Yeah, oh yeah.

T.   Where, up in Massachusetts?

M.   Yeah. But not in mountains and stuff. Just these—just like this hill, Ward Hill. And I went in '74 I think, or '75—I went with my cousin up to Killington. They got a little cottage up there. Y'know, a chalet? I had—one week there, just him and I. I had a blast. I couldn't believe it. Got drunk, got up in the mornin', went skiin'. Skiied all day. Never got tired, just skiied all day. Came home, hung out, woke up again, went skiin' in the mornin'. *Whoosh*, came home, went out again, skiin'—*voom*, we were home like *that*. It was only a three-hour ride. And we had a blast, y'know? And stayed up there—no one bothered us.

T.   Did you turn into an ace skier?

M.   No! Well, this one kid—here I am, goin' down a hill, and all of a sudden you hit these moguls, man! I mean, you can't go by 'em—it's right across the whole hill. Man-made moguls. And here I don't know how to ski that good—I'm hittin' one, I'm flyin' up in the air. I started rollin' down the hill! I stopped—my cousin's laughin' his head off, right? There's this little kid, goin' by. He's like a small little kid. He yells, Hey, how many snowflakes are on the ground? I look up—You bastard! The kid's just laughin' his head off, y'know? He's with—I think he's with his mother or his sister. I don't know who the hell he was with, some young chick. The kid was young, though. It was weird, man. I just cracked up laughin', at the kid laughin'. I got a good wipeout, man! It was neat. I mean I wiped out, and I thought that was the best thing you could ever do, wipin' out! But then my cousin would go, *Wow*, if you woulda got hurt, man, your mother woulda *killed* me!

**I Go Over to Europe to See the
Tulips, but Get There Ten Months Too Early**

T. So other than a few trips in New England, you didn't travel around much, when you were a kid?

M. Did I? Naw.

T. So baseball's been your travels.

M. Yeah, so far. Well, I went to Europe when I was seventeen. That's the only travelin' I'd ever call travelin'.

T. Tell me about your trip to Europe.

M. I went there for two weeks.

T. In summer?

M. Yeah.

T. How'd that come about?

M. I just saved up five hundred bucks, when I was seventeen, right? That summer. And this kid who was uptown—John Gilmore—I knew him, y'know, I'd goofed around with him. He was twenty-one at the time, right? And he goes—we were havin' a beer, and he was braggin'. He goes, Yeah, I'm goin' to Europe. He goes—y'know, he gets me jokin', he goes, You wanna go? And I said, Sure. He goes, You got five hundred bucks, at least? I said, Yeah. 'Cause, he goes, it's gonna cost you two hundred for the plane ticket, and that'll give you three hundred to spend over there. He goes, We'll go for the whole summer. I said, Fine. Went over. *Voom,* stayed two weeks. Partied. Bought myself a clock. I got a clock at home—I gave it to my mother. I got a clock at home that a guy offered me three hundred bucks for it. I only paid eighty, y'know? I mean—

T. Where'd you buy it?

M. Over in Amsterdam.

T. Is that where your plane landed?

M. It went—we went to, uh, London, and then to Amsterdam. We stopped in at London.

T. What was goin' on over there?

M. Huh? At London?

T. I mean, what'd you do?

M. We just, aw, I just—him and I, you know what we went over for? I'd told people I was goin' over to see the tulips. And they're not open till June! Here I am over there in August! I come, I go to the garden—we went to the big garden that's supposed to be all, y'know, the parade tulips, and shit? We went there. We go, Where're the tulips? Guy looks at me, grounds' guy. And he goes, They ain't even out until June, man! I go, *Wow,* I thought they'd be out all year round! Y'know? And like we were laughin', y'know, John and I, we were just laughin'. We learned a *lot*—I mean, we knew, by the time we left that place we knew Amsterdam almost by the back of our hands! Y'know, that's what's weird about it. We, instead of—like, we used to take trains, and then walk back. But it was weird—*voom, voom, voom,* walkin'. We knew how to go everyplace. It was neat.

T.   What was London like?

M.   Huh? We didn't see much of London. We didn't see hardly—we didn't see any of that, we spent all the time in Amsterdam.

I Spend Sixty Dollars in an
Hour at the Amsterdam Playboy Club

T.   Meet any girls in Amsterdam?

M.   Huh? No, I wasn't—well, I went to a Playboy Club, right? It was—this is hilarious, man. We said, Aw, we gotta do somethin' very—tonight we gotta do somethin' *crazy,* we said. He said, Let's go to a Playboy Club. He goes, You don't have to worry about it, no age over here. I said, Fine, I'll go out with you, y'know? No big deal. We went there. I spent sixty dollars in a matter of an hour! *American* money! But then we—but that was, y'know, I can count back from guilders? Y'know, into American money, how much guilders are worth? And I'm sittin' there—I had enough for mine, right? I had enough for mine. And I said —y'know, I had enough for mine. And John's over at another booth, with some people. And I'm here, y'know, with some chicks. And we—a couple of strippers they had, y'know? Big deal, y'know, you had a chick sittin' beside you, not doin' nothin'. Y'know, sittin' there. Here I am blowin' all this money, man. She goes, That's—You gotta last the night. I'm sittin' there, Holy shit, it's eleven o'clock, I spent sixty dollars! I said, *Whoa,* last the night? I said, How late's the night? She goes, When we close. And

I go, *Whoa.* I said, *No* way I can hack this. I said, Get the hell outa here! I said, I spent sixty bucks already? I said, Hey—I look over at John, I said, Hey, John, you can stay. I'm leavin'. And John goes, Yeah, that's right, too! And we were gonna *book.* 'Cause John ran over his bill. He ran over his bill, right? And I had enough for mine. 'Cause we didn't bring enough. See, we—

    T. You spent sixty bucks?

    M. Yeah—well, *I* spent sixty, *he* spent over sixty!

    T. That really cut into your five hundred dollars.

    M. Oh, yeah! But it was just—it was just one experience. I mean, all the rest of the stuff we knew was gonna be cheap. Y'know? But this party—that was just one day we took out. But it was weird. Like we were thinkin', we were both gonna go to the men's room and *book.* 'Cause we had no jackets or anything like that, we'd just run down the stairs—and all there was was a guy downstairs. 'Cause there was a Playboy Club downstairs, and a Playboy Club upstairs. We were in the elite place, upstairs. We coulda went in the peasant place, y'know? But we took the elite one! And we took the elite dive, y'know? Him and I, we were dead, we was thinkin'—Are you ready, he goes, Let's go! The lady goes, Where are you guys goin'? We said—I said, Where's the men's room? I wanna go to the bathroom, y'know? That champagne— that stinkin' sixty-dollar champagne went right through me, lady! I'm sittin' there, *Whoa,* y'know? She goes, One at a time! And I said, Ah we're stuck, John. And he goes, Yeah, I guess we are. He says, Which one's goin' home? I said, You're the one that ran the bill over! After we told 'em—we go, Well, uh, see, we don't have any, I gotta run home and get some more money. I'll be right back, y'know? That's what we told the lady. Lady says, Okay, this big guy, he stays with us, y'know? And you can go get it. I ran all the way back. And he actually, y'know, sat there and wrote the check out—and we cracked up laughin'.

3 School Wasn't My Bag

I Luck Out of the Vietnam War

T.   Okay, getting back home—you were working summers, and part-time all through school. After Uhlman's, did you work at Pierce's all the way up to the time you went away to baseball?

M.   Yeah, but then took other part-time—

T.   M and E, did you ever work there?

M.   No, I never worked at them. Those places, they—I never got into factory work, man.

T.   Were some of the guys you knew doin' factory work by then?

M.   Oh, my buddies? Oh, yeah. A *lot* of 'em are in factory work.

T.   They're still doing it now?

M.   Oh, yeah.

T.   So are most of your buddies still there? They're still back there, when you go back?

M.   Oh, yeah. But a lot of 'em, most of 'em are at school still. Y'know? A lot of guys—well, probably this is their last year in school.

T.   When did you turn eighteen?

M.   In '73.

T.   After your junior year?

M.   Yeah. '73, yeah, I was eighteen, and then I was nineteen in '74.

T.   So the war would have been still going on, Vietnam, when you turned eighteen. And the draft was still happening, right?

M.   Oh, yeah! It was still *goin'*. Hey, y'know, I never—I was a year late in signin' up.

T. You mean in registering for the draft?

M. Yeah. I . . .

T. You just didn't go down and register?

M. That's right. I didn't.

T. And they never bothered you?

M. No. 'Cause I was still in school. I was still in high school, right? I went—I went down to sign up, right after high school was over. My dad goes, You better go down now, man. I said, Okay. I went down. Went into Worcester. Lady goes, You're a year late! And I go, I ain't late! I said, I just got out of high school. No way you're takin' me out of high school to go over *there,* man! So I had to write a little thing. It's got a paragraph, Why Were You Late? I just wrote, Hey, I was still in high school. That's all I wrote. One line. *I was in high school.*

T. But by that time the war was nearly over.

M. Well, maybe almost. But I coulda gone. And then they flubbed up. They gave me a draft card sayin' I was good. Then a month later they gave me another draft card, sayin' I was no good. And I never went for a physical. Don't ask me what happened. I just lucked out! And I was close enough to go. You know how they had that lottery thing? I was close enough to go. I was, if I wasn't in high school. If I was outa high school, I woulda gone.

I Really Never Got into It

T. You mentioned that a next-door neighbor of yours went over to Vietnam and got killed?

M. Yeah. He was in the Marines.

T. That happened a couple of years earlier?

M. Yeah, this was like—but that guy was—I never hung, really hung around with him. I did a little bit. But he was a neat guy, man. David. He was really—like, I hang around with his brothers now. Paul and Billy, y'know?

T. Did you know his parents?

M. Oh yeah, I know his parents. They're our next-door neighbors, man.

T. Do you know what happened to him?

M. No, I really don't. I was so young when it happened, I didn't even go to his wake, or anything like that. I just heard he got shot. Got killed. And that was it. I didn't hear anything else about it. I didn't hear how. Or why, y'know, or what. I heard it was a closed casket.

T.   Uh-oh.

M.   Whaddaya mean, uh-oh?

T.   A closed casket, that means it was a mess.

M.   Yeah. I guess so. So I really didn't—y'know, I really didn't get into it. It was—y'know, like, I used to just see him like when he used to come home, man. I used to say hi to him then. And all of a sudden now this time he didn't come home. The last time I can remember seein' him, he had a super-butch haircut, and that was it. That's all I remember about him, man. But like, he used to take me different places. Y'know? And goof around with me a little bit here and there. But he was a lot older than me, though. Him and another guy, Ellsworth, got killed. From our town.

One Streetlight in the Center
of Town (What Northboro's Like?)

T.   It's not that big a town?

M.   No, you know everyone. When I was little, I—you know everyone in the town. Just about. Because it was—y'know, it was small. I mean you might just bump into 'em like up at the poolroom, or somethin' like that.

T.   What have they got, a couple of shopping centers and a downtown?

M.   No, they got—we used to have a poolroom. And it just —everyone stopped goin'. When I was a little kid, people *always* used to go to the poolroom. And then everyone stopped goin'.

T.   What's Northboro look like? Has it got a downtown at all?

M.   Yeah, it's got a little one. It's got a—we got a five-and-ten, we got a package store, we got a little variety market like, y'know. And we got two pharmacists, and a hairdresser's, a cleaner's . . .

T.   So it's more of a country town than a suburb?

M.   Oh, yeah! Oh, it's small, man. It's small. We got a bank, a pizza place, one, two, three gas stations, right in the center like. No, more than three. It's got—right in the center it's got one, two, three, four, five gas stations. Right in the center. That's not countin' the one *down* two miles, and another one down two miles *this* way.

T.   So is there a highway that goes through it?

M.   It's right on Route 20, Old Post Road.

T.   And that goes to Boston?

M.   Yeah. That used to be the old road that they used to use, y'know? The Post Road?

T.   So that's where they've got all the gas stations, along that road to catch people passing through?

M.   Yeah.

T.   What is it now, four lane?

M.   No!

T.   So it's just a little road?

M.   It's a two-lane, Route 20, man.

T.   They never changed it from the old road, then?

M.   No. They just—they call it the Old Post Road. Y'know? It's just a small-town-that-never-really-grew-up town. But on the *outskirts,* it grew. Like, I mean it went way out of our town, like a mile—all you can see now is houses and shit!

T.   A couple thousand people in Northboro? Maybe five thousand?

M.   No, they got ten thousand people. But the town is small. If you blink your eyes, you might miss it. It's got one streetlight, in the center of town. That's it, y'know?

T.   Is Algonquin the only high school?

M.   Yeah. But they got elementary schools. One, two, three, four . . . possibly five elementary schools. That's a lot of schools. I went to just about all of 'em.

Nuns Couldn't Have Handled Me

T.   You wear that religious medal—is that a Lady of Mount Carmel medal?

M.   Yeah.

T.   Who gave you that?

M.   Mumsey.

T.   Is that a protection-in-traveling type trip?

M.   I don't know. She gave it to me before I was even in baseball.

T.   Are your family Catholics?

M.   Yeah. Except for my mother, she's Protestant.

T.   But she gave you the medal.

M.   Yeah.

T.   So you never went to a parochial school. I mean, in grade school?

M.   Yeah, I went just to a grade school. Elementary school.

T.   I mean it wasn't nuns, or—

M.   No! No, they couldn't have handled me back then.

T.   So it was just public schools.

M.   *Public* schools could barely handle me! Instead of gettin' checks, my first, like all the way up to maybe fourth grade, I was gettin' minuses. You know how, for your conduct, you get a check it means good? Every time my father was goin' in—What's the minus for? Well, it's like this, Mr. Fidrych—he likes throwin' Chiclets, he likes throwin' raisins, he likes talkin' in class, he likes this. . . . When he gets home he says, They tell me you *like* a *lot*. That's why you get the minuses. I said, Yeah. And then, That's cool. But you know what was weird? Like the teachers—like the first grade teacher, after I finally got outa there, told the second grade teacher. Man, y'know, the teachers knew about me before I even got up into their classes. Y'know? And then they—and once I—for some reason I must have clicked in my mind, right? Because one year I went through the whole year with checks. And the teacher goes, I thought you were supposed to be a wise guy. I said, Maybe I changed a little bit, who knows? It was just—I stopped gettin' minuses, man. It was neat.

T.   So did you go to church when you were a kid?

M.   Yeah. Once in a while.

T.   Somewhere around Northboro?

M.   Yeah, I used to sell papers in front of the church. This kid gave me his paper route. But then he decided he didn't want to quit. So he still let me hang on, y'know? We split fifty-fifty. It was good. It was his paper route, y'know?

T.   So how come you graduated high school at nineteen?

M.   How come? Because I stayed back in first and second grade. I couldn't read. I could do all the other work. But I just, y'know—they said, Your readin's pretty bad. So here's my father, a schoolteacher. Used to have to go to summer school. Y'know, when I was a little kid. Hated it! But all through high school, I never went to summer school. Y'know? Not once! Here, my other friends are goin' through summer school. Shit, I wasn't goin' through summer school. But y'know, school just wasn't my bag, man.

At Worcester Academy You Could Feel Free

T.   So that's just natural, people move on.

M.   Yeah, you scatter. It's like when I went to Worcester Academy for my senior year. That's just what *I* did. I used to hang around in Worcester then. Y'know? Like on the weekends, or Friday or Saturday I'd go over into Worcester. Y'know, if I didn't have a date, I'd go into Worcester. Instead of hangin' out in my town, with my other guys, I'd just go into Worcester.

T.   A lot bigger town, huh?

M.   Oh, Worcester's a city. Y'know? I just found out what the city was.

T.   Was that an expensive school to go to, Worcester Academy?

M.   No, it was only two thousand dollars, I think, at the time. I'm not sure.

T.   But it was smaller—a prep school.

M.   Yeah, it was just—it wasn't nothin' big, there wasn't too many guys there. I'll clue ya, I had more fun there, just goin' to *school* there, than I did at my other school. Because here, you had —I mean, lunchtime, an hour and a half off for lunch. I could go anyplace I wanted. Whereas back at Algonquin, you had to go to this room and sit there and study. Or you'd have to go to the cafeteria. And it's just—you didn't have any freedom there, y'know? I mean, it was like being caged up. And now, here I am a senior, and goin' to *this* school with all guys. And we got like thirteen guys in a classroom.

T.   Were some of them boarding?

M.   Oh, yeah, they boarded there and everything. But now, I mean after class if I had a free period, I could go for an hour, I could go off and *do* something, y'know? I didn't have to just sit there and be locked up in a room. Which was neat, y'know? And that's why I liked that school just a little bit better.

4 I Just Played the Game, I Didn't Pay Much Attention to It

I Just Played the Game

T.   Were you a Red Sox fan when you were a little kid?

M.   No, not really. I went to the Red Sox maybe three times outa my whole life. It was like—we had a Parks Department thing, we used to go with the Parks Department.

T.   So you weren't a fan when you were a kid?

M.   No, I really wasn't into baseball. I was out doin' somethin' else. Because I *played* it—yeah, Little League, pickup scrub teams, y'know, with all the guys that hung around. But I mean, it was just—like if we didn't play baseball, a couple of our buddies might have been in the woods buildin' a tree fort, or goin' out and workin' on a car, just somethin' like that. But then, when I started gettin' into organized baseball—y'know, high school and stuff—I had to take my workin' time, the lady would let me off, or the guy that I was workin' for would let me off to go play baseball, and then come back again. They knew I wanted to play. And it was neat like that. So I really didn't—I just *played* the game, I didn't pay much attention to it.

T.   Did your dad like baseball?

M.   Oh, yeah. He knows more than I do about it, when it comes down to players and that stuff.

T.   Has your dad been a fan for a long time?

M.   Yeah, he's always—y'know, like he gets the *Sports Illustrated.* I never used to just sit down and read it. I was always just too busy to sit down.

I Used to Be a Mental Case (I Learned the Hard Way)

T.   So when you were a kid you played a lot of pickup ball and Little League.

M.   Hey, I'll clue ya, when I was in Little League, I used to —if I didn't win a game, I'd cry. I'd go ape. I'd go crazy. If a guy made a error behind me, on third base, or shortstop, I'd walk up to that guy and say, You're an asshole! I mean, I'd get *on* the S.O.B. Make him feel like *shit*. Because if it'd be a mental mistake, or somethin', I'd get on 'em. And I learned that, over the years —I don't get on 'em, any more. Everyone's out there to do their job. If they don't do their job, fine. You know they're gonna be gone. But if you do your job, you're not gonna be gone. Right? I mean, when I was in Little League—and then, y'know, a little Babe Ruth League—I mean, I was gettin' *on* guys, man! Guy'd make a—an easy double play, he'd just make a mental mistake or something, I'd get *on* him, man! I'd yell at him! I was a mental case. I'd classify myself as a mental case. Now, I don't. But back then I did.

T.   Did you ever get in fights with 'em?

M.   No, not fights. No.

T.   Just ridin' 'em?

M.   Just yellin' at 'em. I mean yellin' at 'em! Like, the short-stop would bobble the ball. It cost me. So I'd go, *You asshole!* Right to his face! Wouldn't let him up for air, right? And now, I look back at that. And go, Wow. And like that kid looks at me now—and he used to play with me. And like they're tellin' me how —God, you used to . . . But, I don't know why. I look back now and I just say, Wow, I can't believe it. Y'know, you used to play with this guy, and you'd call him an asshole. But I still hung around with him, later on. We switched to different teams, but I still hung around with him. But still, it was just—I was crazy, when I was out there. I used to yell at the guys. And then—you learned it. I stopped—I don't yell at 'em any more, now. I just say, Hey!

T.   You're runnin' around *thankin'* 'em now—

M.   I'm out there hopin' that *I* don't screw up! And I'm hopin' that *they* don't screw up. And if they do, all right. I'm just sayin', Hey, that's cool. Don't worry about it! I could see the situation—I learned! I learned the hard way, maybe. But I learned maybe the good way, too.

My Dad Steps In and We Win Three in a Row

T.   You yelled at 'em, but maybe then you couldn't help it.

M.   I could've—not have done it, yelled at those guys, back then and there. And I mean—we had this coach, when I was in Little League. I mean, he was a complete *asshole*. He had three sons. Maybe because he had three sons, and he played them all the time. His sons could not play baseball. And we knew that. And here's a lefthanded kid, pitchin'.

T.   The coach's kid?

M.   Yeah. But yet, he helped us. By taking us out, and sayin', Hey, we'll have practice on Tuesday night. I'll be there, with the bats and balls. And we'll all be there, and play. He was the guy that got us all together. But he *could not* coach. When it got down to games, stats—he didn't know what the hell was goin' on.

T.   So when you pitched a game in Little League, you used to get really excited. Excited about wanting to win the game.

M.   Yeah, oh, yeah. I'd just get bullshit. And I was just usin' him for an excuse. Because, then—actually my *dad* came in. Like he'd—the coach'd go away on vacation for a while. My dad came in, we won three games in a row. Where we hadn't won anything all season, y'know?

T.   Your dad came in and coached?

M.   Yeah. And then we won three games in a row. He was coachin' before—but he wasn't coachin' for *us*. It was just, it was just weird at that situation. Because he—at that point, my dad was just comin' to watch the games.

The Legion Coach Makes Me a Pitcher

T.   Did you want to be a pitcher when you were a little kid?

M.   No!

T.   What position did you play?

M.   I played shortstop, outfield, and pitcher. But if I didn't pitch, I either played shortstop or outfield. I was always in the lineup. I never sat on the bench. Except for when I was in Legion, the guy just made me a pitcher. He knew I was an outfielder, but they had better outfielders than me, they said. Y'know, like I didn't play my whole first season. Not at all. I mean I just sat there. And I went to practice every day, right? And I'm seein' this guy missin' practice, and I go, What the hell, he's no better than me, man! When it comes down to it, he must miss three practices. And all of a sudden we got a game the next day, and he plays. I'd say, What the hell, why shouldn't *I* just take off with my buddies and go someplace? This guy can do it, why can't I? I just said, Ah, no hassle. I just kept on comin', kept on comin'. I never played! You know, it was—Oh, I played one inning. I played one inning, in right field, the whole season.

    T.   This was your first year in Legion ball?

    M.   My first year.

    T.   And you were how old? Legion ball starts when you're fourteen, fifteen?

    M.   No. Like sixteen, seventeen, eighteen, and nineteen.

    T.   So let's see, you were sixteen—that was 1970, you were going to be a freshman in high school?

    M.   Right. And it's just weird. 'Cause you knew you were as good as this other guy. But the coach just didn't feel it. But then every year after *that,* though, I played for the guy. Started pitchin' for him all the time. He just said, You're young, y'know? So I just sat around and felt what everything was all about. But I was the only guy from our home town. Everybody else was from other towns. And it was weird, y'know? The town that was puttin' it on was our town. And I'm the only person that was on it from our town.

    T.   This is the Northboro team?

    M.   Yeah, we're the Northboro Legion. And we're the only one in town.

    T.   And the coach was Rolfe?

    M.   Ted Rolfe.

    T.   You were playing high school ball at the same time though?

    M.   Yeah. No, high school just got over. This is summer league.

    T.   So Legion ball started when high school let out in June?

M.   Yeah, this was—I think I was a freshman in high school.

T.   But then your next year, *after* your freshman year—let's see, '71—you pitched a no-hitter in Legion ball in your first start, right? And then you were 16–3 in Legion over three seasons.

M.   Yeah. I wouldn't know.

Basketball—the Coach Says, I Can't Start You

T.   But in high school, baseball wasn't your only sport, right? You played basketball and football too?

M.   Yeah, I did. I liked it. It kept me, like, in shape. That's why I played those other sports. You could just go play. And it was neat, y'know? All my friends did it—that's why I probably did it.

T.   But you thought of yourself as a baseball player?

M.   No, I took all sports equal when I was goin' through high school. 'Cause all my friends did too.

T.   What about basketball?

M.   Yeah, I used to play. Coach says, I can't start you. He goes, You—if I start you, you foul out, y'know? He goes, I'll throw you in a little bit the first period, a little bit the second period. I played half the game, or three quarters of the game. Ended up with my fifteen points and shit. Had my rebounds and stuff like that. I played good. So he goes and *starts* me, I'm out by the third quarter, y'know?

T.   You'd foul out right away?

M.   Yeah. Y'know, he goes, you just aren't—you're just a sixth man. He goes, I get in trouble with one of the guys, I just pull him out and throw *you* in. And put *him* back when you get in trouble. You're a good filler, he said. You came off the bench cold. When we needed you off the bench, *voom!* Y'know, you could throw up the first basket and it'd give us two points. Or you'd get the tip-in, or something like that. He knew I could just —*voom*—get right in there. Instead of gettin' warmed up, and runnin' around—y'know, breakin' a sweat—I was already *hot* when I got in there.

An Argument with My Baseball Coach About Football

T.   What position did you play in football?

M.   I played defensive end. But then, my sophomore year,

my football coach and I got in an argument. One day we played against Marlboro, right? And I knew some of the guys that I played Legion baseball with. So I went over and *talked* to 'em, right? No big deal. I mean the game was over. But the coach got all over me for it. So I said, Well, this is my last year of football. So all of a sudden he ends up bein' the baseball coach! I said, Aw, I can imagine what my baseball season's gonna be like this year. I said, Hey, it's gonna *suck,* right? Y'know, right after—before I even got out on the field.

He Knew I Knew Baseball, Because He Knew Football

T.   So what happened when baseball season rolled around?

M.   *Voom!* It was a whole different scene, then.

T.   Oh, yeah?

M.   Yeah, it was a whole different scene. He *knew* I knew baseball, 'cause *he* knew football, right? So he could, y'know—tell me football. I knew *baseball.* So I said, Hey, he ain't tellin' me nothin' that I don't already know. He ain't gonna tell me how to bunt, y'know? If you're gonna—y'know, if you're gonna get picky about a bunt.

T.   So he just let you do your thing.

M.   Yeah, he just goes, Fine. Y'know, Do what you want.

T.   So it sounds like he isn't teaching you a whole lot, around this time. I mean in baseball.

M.   No, he just—like, if you were doin' something wrong, he'd tell you. And that's where I'd listen. But if he was yellin' at me for something *other*—like if we played Westboro. If we ever played Westboro, I knew guys that—I used to work over in Westboro, right? I knew people over there. So now, y'know, he didn't say anything. I'd go over there—before the game I'd go over there and talk to the guys, right? And he'd, y'know—ain't no way he could say a thing.

T.   Is he still coaching back there?

M.   Yeah, he came to my banquet. Oh, yeah, he's a good—y'know, then him and I hit eye to eye. Then, y'know. Where he was the dominant guy before. Now we were both equal. And *that's* where we really got along together. That's where we really talked and associated with each other.

T.   This is Jack Wallace.

M. Yeah. That's when we really associated.

Why You Need Coaches, and What's Good About Them

T. So you talked to him just lately?

M. Yeah, he came to my banquet in Northboro, y'know?

T. Oh, in October.

M. Yeah. We talked that thing over again, and we just laughed about it. He helped me. If he didn't take his time out to, y'know, play baseball, to coach us—you gotta have a coach there, a manager, right? So if he didn't take his time out, if he just went home, then we woulda been without a job. That's why everyone that I've been in contact with, or has coached me—I'd have to say they helped me. Just because, it's not every day that a father'll go out and do a coachin' job. 'Cause there's a lot of hassles in it. He's gonna miss supper and stuff. And, y'know, his wife'll give him a hard time. When he comes home—he loses, he's mad. Y'know? Just like I go home, after I lose a game—I'm sore as hell. I don't want to talk to no one. I just want to be able to think things over and, y'know, what happened? I could see his point, but—that's why you need coaches. That's what's good about 'em. They helped me.

My Dad Stuck By Me

T. So who would you say—did Jack Wallace bring you along as a pitcher? Or Ted Rolfe, the Legion coach? Or is there anybody else that—

M. No, I'd have to say my dad did. Y'know, just because he's the one that stuck by me.

T. Did he catch you?

M. Yeah, all the time.

T. From the time you were a kid?

M. Yeah. You'd have to say him, because he'd be at every game. Like now he's never at any games, right? Because, y'know, he's gotta work too.

T. He came to the games you pitched this year in Boston, though?

M. Yeah. But like he used to—

T. So he's busy teaching school?

M. Yeah, he's an assistant principal. But he used to coach me, like after I'd have a bad game—he'd just say somethin'. But he was at every game. And, y'know, knew what I was doin' and stuff. And just, *voom!* He said, Let's take a gamble. I mean I coulda flunked *outa* that school.

T. You mean Worcester Academy.

M. Yeah. Y'know, he said, Let's do it.

A Bad Arm from Hackin' Off Sliders

T. You'd been pitching pretty well in your junior year at Algonquin—you were what, 4–2?

M. Well, we almost made it to the districts—we *made* the districts. We were in the play-offs of the districts to get to the big ones, right? And I couldn't pitch! I had a bad arm. It was funny, man. It wasn't funny, I was mad. This was the first time that that school's ever got that far, right? And now I can't pitch. I went nuts.

T. What happened?

M. I just couldn't throw a baseball. Don't ask me.

T. Strained it or something? You don't know?

M. I don't know. It went until like I was gonna go to Worcester Academy for my senior year. The trainer there heard that I had hurt my arm. So he said, Come up here, I'm gonna work on your arm so you'll be ready for *our* season. Y'know, next year and stuff. So I whirlpooled it for a long time—for about a month. Y'know, I couldn't—well, my junior year baseball was over at Algonquin. And like I still went to all the games and all the practices, right? But I couldn't pitch. I *tried,* but I couldn't pitch. I was pissed.

T. This went on that whole summer?

M. No, no. See, I waited the whole month, right? And then Legion ball started, and he knew I couldn't pitch either—the coach, right? But he just let it go, and I kept on comin' to practice and stuff. And then I said, Okay, I'm ready now.

T. You told the Legion coach?

M. Yeah. I said, I can throw. And then I threw. I threw a good game. And I said, Fine, I'm all set. Y'know, it wasn't hurtin' any more. But I mean I couldn't even throw a ball—if I took one here and threw it back to you, it'd kill me. Ooh! I tore—

T.   In the elbow?

M.   No, it was right in here, like in the shoulder. He just said it was from hackin' off the things, man. I wasn't ready when I hacked 'em off, y'know? Sliders?

T.   You were throwin' sliders back then? That early?

M.   Yeah. So, *voom!* I mean I cured it just like that. I never had that problem again.

T.   Who taught you to throw sliders?

M.   Me.

T.   You learned it by yourself?

M.   Not learned it, but I just, y'know, threw fastballs. And I said, Well, let's just throw a curve. And I throw a curve and they call it a slider. But that's what I always thought was a curve.

5 The Scout That Signed Me Saw Me Throw One Pitch

Changing Schools to Play Ball Was a Gamble We Took

T. So then you went over to Worcester.

M. Yeah, I was gonna be nineteen, so I couldn't go to Algonquin and play baseball. So my dad and I just said, Well—

T. You were ineligible for the public school leagues because you were graduating late?

M. Yeah. 'Cause I was too old. And then when I got to this other school, and you could, we played.

T. Private school league?

M. Yeah, it's Academy. You play the other academies, but then you play the freshman colleges. Y'know, Brown—

T. But they didn't have the eighteen-year-old rule?

M. No, they didn't. They had no rule at all. So I mean you had nothin' to worry about. You could be twenty-one, I think. Eligible till you're twenty-one. Because it's a P.G. school. I mean we were goin' with guys that had already graduated from high school, y'know?

T. Back in your junior year, at Algonquin, you'd been a starter?

M. Yeah, oh, yeah. I was in varsity basketball, baseball. I played regular. But then everything was over—was gonna be over in my life. Y'know? But then I got to play again, over at Worcester Academy. We had a great park.

T. Were you thinking about a career playing ball, at the time?

M. Not really. It was just that I couldn't go—I don't think that I could go through school without, y'know, playin' ball. And he just said, Yeah, *try,* y'know? Go to this school just so you can play. We were shootin' for it, y'know? That's what we were doin'. My dad said, We're gonna take a gamble.

T.   You were going over to Worcester to see what you could make out of baseball?

M.   Yeah. And then if anything happens maybe a school will ask you to play. That's what we were shootin' for. But then no schools asked me to play for 'em.

T.   You mean colleges—baseball scholarships?

M.   Yeah. I said, Shit. I'm done. After the season was over I said, I'm done. And then all of a sudden, *voom!* I got signed just like that.

They Called Me a Thrower and I'm Still One Now

T.   I understand some scouts had seen you pitch in Legion ball and at Algonquin. But over at Worcester were there any scouts around?

M.   There was scouts around. But they only go to certain games that—like, the teams that are hot. They ain't gonna go see no losin' teams. Y'know? They're not gonna go see two losing teams play. Y'know, two teams with the same record? They're always goin' to the games of the teams that are always winnin'.

T.   What kind of records did you have?

M.   My Worcester Academy record, I had a losing season, my senior year. Y'know? But the guy just said like, You throw hard. You throw fastballs.

T.   So you were supposed to be a hard thrower at the time?

M.   Yeah, that's what they called me was a *thrower.* They didn't call me a pitcher, they called me a thrower. And now supposedly they call me a pitcher, but I'm still a thrower.

T.   But were you doing the same things—were you keeping the ball down and throwing a lot of low strikes?

M.   I was just throwin'—well, I haven't changed any pitches. Y'know? Still throw the same pitches.

I Always Did These Things, but Now They're Making Me Notice It

T.   In other words, your pitching style was pretty much the same in high school as it is now.

M. Yeah! Really. It's the exact same thing. The exact same thing. I can't—people ask me, man—

T. Are you any stronger now than you were in high school?

M. No! I don't *feel* any different.

T. Do you weigh any more now than you did then?

M. No, I don't.

T. What do you weigh, about one eighty?

M. One seventy-five, one seventy. It varies, y'know? It jumps up and down like a rabbit.

T. You don't throw any harder than you did in high school?

M. I don't feel I do. I really don't. Because you look back, and people are sayin', y'know—Did you do these antics before? And I look back and go, I don't know! Now you're exploiting them out to where I'm *noticin'* them. Before I didn't notice 'em. I mighta been doin' it. But I wasn't noticin' 'em. Now you're makin' me notice them.

T. It's like if you went to another guy—for instance, Hunter touches his hat between every pitch. If you went up to him and said, Did you always touch your hat? He'd probably say, I just always been pitchin'.

M. Yeah!

T. In other words, I'm sure he doesn't remember the first time he touched his hat, or the second time.

M. No! And now they're hittin' me with it. But then I go home, and people say, Yeah, you did it before. You used to do that.

The Red Sox Talk to Me,
But I Go to the Tigers, Because They Wanted Me

T. So going back to about May or June of your senior year, your baseball draft eligibility comes up about a week after graduation, right?

M. Yeah, I went a week. We went a week, and then they notified the drafts. And like I went to work—here I am, been workin' at a job for a week now, with a couple of my buddies. And the guy goes, Hey, you're drafted. And I go, Yah, get the hell outa here, will ya?

T. You were still doing gas station work?

M. Yeah, this guy—

T. You didn't expect to be drafted?

M. No, I just—hey, no one *talked* to me. *One* guy talked to me. He said, That was it. He said, We'll get back to you if we'll be wantin' you.

T. Who was that?

M. Bill Monbouquette.

T. From Boston?

M. Yeah. We sat down and rapped and talked and stuff, and nothing happened. So I said, Hey, it's not gonna happen.

T. Had he seen you pitch?

M. Yeah, he saw me pitch a whole game. He pulled me aside after the game was over and said, Hey, would you like to play baseball? I said, Fine. I said, I ain't goin' noplace in school. I'll play baseball, y'know? It's a different job and I don't have a job.

T. So the Red Sox let nine rounds of that draft go by and never picked you. Let's see, their first pick that year was Whitey Ford's son. I think he's a shortstop.

M. I wouldn't know. See, I don't follow—I don't follow it, y'know? I just don't follow baseball.

T. So you didn't know Detroit from nothin'?

M. No, I didn't. I said, Well, they're the people that wanted me—I'm gonna go to 'em. I don't care.

T. So you're working in a gas station and all of a sudden they tell you you're drafted.

M. Yeah. All of a sudden it's—y'know? I was workin' at a gas station, and the guy—he had me paintin' a house. He just hired me, and then he goes, Hey, you ain't gonna do this kind of work. You're just gonna paint the house.

T. And as far as you were concerned, you were just gonna do that for a while.

M. Yeah.

T. And then just pick up whatever came along?

M. Whatever. Y'know, if I went to school or something. Because schools rejected me.

**I Find a College That Wants
Me, but My Dad Says, Try Baseball**

T. So then you just gave up on the idea of college?

M. No, I had a—we were hesitant. I said, I wanna go to

New Mexico Highlands University. They said, You can come out. And I was gonna take engineering out there. Two-year course. Y'know? And I just said—y'know, I was so happy to get—

T.   They'd accepted you?

M.   Yeah. But, y'know, it was just neat. 'Cause you don't need a college—you don't need to take that S.A.T. to get in. All you do is write and tell 'em your marks, and they get all the things from the—they go by the school records of what you've done, through school. Then they accept you, instead of takin' that one lousy test that these other schools took. Y'know, what would you get in it, and—No way you can come here, y'know? So the school said, Fine, you can come. So I was gettin' excited about it. I was sayin', Oh, I think I'm gonna *go* here. And then the draft came up. And my father said, Just remember, you can always go back to school, for the two years that you wanted to take. He goes, If you're twenty-six, you can always go back. He says, Try baseball, man. He goes, They're gonna give you the shot now, they aren't gonna give you another shot till you're twenty-one—something might happen to you. So I took it! And that was it. We dropped school, and—Fine, I can go back now.

I Went Through Enough Schooling by *Working*

T.   You could still do that, if you wanted to—go back to school.

M.   Yeah! Hell, yeah, I can go right back to school now. What the heck. But right now I don't have time to. When I want to go back to school, I'm gonna go to school, and I'm gonna stay at school. And I ain't gonna work, and I ain't gonna do *nothin'*. I'm just gonna go to school. 'Cause I went through enough schoolin' by workin', y'know? And it's too—it was too strenuous on me. Maybe I coulda been a better student, if I didn't have to work. Because I hadda work. And I said, God damn, I need— y'know, you need a little time. So I said, Aw, screw that home-work. Y'know, I worked my day! Screw that homework, man! I'll get it tomorrow mornin' or somethin', I'll cram it, I'll do—*copy* it off someone, y'know? To where, if I didn't have to work, I mighta done the schoolin' then, and then still had my other couple times—y'know, an hour. You give a person—y'know, like I couldn't go to the football games now. Because I hadda work. It's just somethin' like that.

The Scout That Signed Me Saw Me Throw One Pitch

T.   When you look through the 1974 major league draft list, it's kind of interesting to see where some of the guys got chosen. Here's Butch Wynegar, the 38th pick. But a lot of these guys that got chosen up at the top didn't do much, and then—well, here's Jerry Augustine, of Milwaukee, the 342nd choice. Kind of interesting to look at these guys and see what happened to 'em. Here's Jim Umbarger from Texas, was the 367th pick. And you were number 232. What *were* these scouts doing?

M.   I don't know. You know the scout that saw me? He saw me throw one pitch.

T.   Oh, yeah? Who was that?

M.   Joe Cusick. He saw me throw one pitch.

T.   He was their New England scout, right? I don't think he works for them any more.

M.   No, he don't. But that was—it was weird. He comes to my house, and he goes, Uh, Mark Fidrych? And I go, Yeah, you're looking at him. I didn't know whether he was really coming.

T.   Was this a high school game he saw you in?

M.   Yeah, I was at Worcester Academy. And then he asked if I wanted to play, and I said, Fine.

T.   You mean they hadn't seen you before that game? You threw *one* pitch?

M.   Yeah, I was in the outfield, playin' the outfield, right? And then—this is what he told me, when he saw me. He goes, You were out in the outfield. . . . I remember the play and everything. The pitcher got wild, and the coach called me in from the outfield. And I had—there was nothin' on the batter, right? I got in there, warmed up, threw one pitch, and the guy swung at it and grounded out to the second baseman. I got the inning over and then went back to the bench. And I went back out to left field, and the other guy went back to pitchin' again. And that's all he saw me throw. And he saw me play the outfield. And he signed me—he signed me as a pitcher.

But he said he heard from other scouts that, y'know, I was a good pitcher.

My Dad Said, Do It, What the Heck

T.   How'd you find out you'd been drafted? Did Detroit call you up?

M.   It was in the paper, and then the scout called up. But I wasn't home. So he just came over.

T.   This was Cusick?

M.   Yeah, he just came over and I signed, right then and there.

T.   Didn't you, like, negotiate about terms or anything?

M.   No, he just said, You want to sign? This is what we're gonna give you. And that's it.

T.   As far as the Tigers were concerned, it was a matter of —you could've always said no, and then waited around to see if you got drafted again sometime, right?

M.   Yeah. I could have said no. But I woulda had to wait till I was twenty-one, right? I said, Hey, no school wants me, take this. Take this job.

T.   It worked out okay, didn't it?

M.   It did.

T.   What kind of money did you get?

M.   I only made five hundred bucks a month.

T.   No bonus? They said it was a ten-thousand-dollar bonus.

M.   The bonus was like three thousand dollars.

T.   Oh, and the rest you got later if you made it—like a contingency thing, if you made it to the majors?

M.   That's right.

T.   But you wanted to play ball. It wasn't the bonus—you wanted to play?

M.   Yeah. It was no big deal. I mean I coulda held out probably. But I didn't know what I was gettin' into. So I just said, Hey, I'll find out when I start doin' it, y'know? And all of a sudden you go down and you find out this person's makin' this, and that person's makin' that. But then you're sittin' there—Well, I'm here. And you say, screw it. If I make it to the majors, *then* I'll make the money.

T.   So you signed up right away.

M.   Yeah, that day. He brought the thing with him.

T.   What'd your dad think?

M.   He's the one that told me. He goes, Do it, what the heck. What else you gonna do? If it don't work out, you can always go back to school, right?

6 My First Time Out in Life (Bristol, 1974)

My First Time Out in Life

T. So when you got out of Worcester and signed with the Tigers, you weren't any kind of sure shot to make it. You still had to break in, when they sent you down to Bristol. And prove yourself.

M. Oh, yeah. I'll never forget my rookie year, man. It was my first time out in life. I'm not gonna be home for two months. Gotta find my own apartment. No car. Y'know, you gotta do this, right? I mean, it'd be neat if they said, Okay, you guys, if you got a car you can take your car with you. Go home, get it. They should do that. Because you know how—here I am, don't know how— I got a suitcase with all my clothes in it. And I'm just sittin' there. And now I go, *Now* what do I do? What am I gonna do, thumb? I said, Come on, I don't even know where I *am.* You know? What's this Route 94, I said, where's that gonna take me? I said, *Whoa,* where do I go?

Pulaski Looks like *Deliverance,*
Covington You Start to Smell Five Miles Out
(Some Little Towns in the Appalachian League)

T. But once you got down there, things went okay?

M. Mm-hmm. I went down there, and had a great time, livin'. It was neat.

T. That's a weird little league Bristol's in, the Appalachian League. All those little towns, and they're all so close together. All in this little corner of Tennessee, Kentucky, West Virginia, and Virginia. Bluefield, West Virginia. And Marion. And what is it, Elizabethton?

M.   Yeah, all those little towns. And Pulaski—Pulaski's the funniest one, man. We're in Pulaski, and—I mean, it looks like *Deliverance.* No shit. It was—but these people were *into* it, though. I mean, these people, they came and paid their thing— they're gettin' cocked. I mean, we looked up behind the dugout and—the coach, Jeff Hogan, just looks at us and goes, Man, this looks like *Deliverance!* They looked exactly like it.

T.   Like idiots?

M.   Yeah! This guy's yellin', *Gimme a bat,* y'know? We said, If we gave you a bat, you'd *kill* us! 'Cause we're beatin' the team as it is. And like he's jokin' around—and I'm sittin' around goofin' with the guy, too. I mean those guys are crazy.

T.   They're little towns, right? Those are all short bus rides.

M.   They were all bus rides. Except when we went to Pulaski. They were Baltimore—the Orioles?

T.   The Pulaski Phillies, I think. The Orioles was Bluefield.

M.   Bloomfield, right. But Pulaski, we'd take that as a road trip. Then we'd stay overnight there.

T.   The other ones you'd come back in the middle of the night?

M.   The other ones were just like, y'know, a half-hour or hour ride. Y'know, no big deal.

T.   Little ballparks? Ramshackle ballparks?

M.   No, there's good ballparks. Some of 'em are good. Well, you might get one or two that were bad. I think the—Hoyt Wilhelm, I think, coached one of the teams.

T.   Yeah, Kingsport.

M.   Kingsport Braves . . .

T.   In Kingsport, Tennessee.

M.   Yeah, that field wasn't too good. And then you come into Covington—I think the Astros? Covington?

T.   Covington, Kentucky, right. The Astros.

M.   Man, *that* town—I mean, that town smelt just like a paper mill. And we had to live in it. Guys that had played in the league would go, Well, we're gettin' close, I can smell it. Y'know? I mean, five miles out you started to smell it. And then when you got right into town you could really smell it bad.

Bob Sykes's Winning Streak and the One That Got Away

T.   Even though it's classified as a rookie league, weren't there some guys on the team at Bristol who'd been two years there?

M.   Yeah, a couple guys.

T.   A few veterans, then.

M.   Oh, yeah. You always need the veteran to help the guys. Like *we* didn't know what we were doin'.

T.   I notice they sent three other pitchers they'd just drafted to Bristol. One of 'em, Bob Sykes, who they drafted on the seventeenth round, went down there and won eleven games in a row. And you only won two, and yet he's still down in the minors.

M.   Yeah.

T.   How come he had such a fantastic year?

M.   How come? You don't know. That's just a freaky thing.

T.   What'd he throw?

M.   Well, he throws a fastball, a curve, and a change-up. It's like, him—he was in my shoes, now. Like, back then. I mean, he could do everything. He was mowin' 'em down. We couldn't believe it. It was great, y'know? We felt great for him. And like, *voom! Now* you look at him. Look where *I* am now, though. And he did *that.*

T.   That's weird. He had an earned run average that must have been brought in on a submarine.

M.   And he did that. That's what I look at. Like Frank MacCormack had a better record than me, in Evansville. And like, I was ahead of him. They put me up here. I look back at those guys, it's neat. I go and see 'em and stuff. Like we went to Evansville this year. And they were all there, all the guys that I'd played with. Y'know? And we were just laughin' and stuff, and goofin' around. And they can't believe I'm up there. And *I* can't believe it. They're still waitin' their turn, just like I waited mine, y'know? It was just I was the right man for the right spot, I guess. I wouldn't know.

T.   Well, it means there's something more to it than what's inside your arm. Or records on paper.

M.   I really don't know what happened. That's why baseball's a funny thing. That year, Bob got everything you could possibly want out of the thing.

T.   He had an incredible season.

M.   He had an ERA of one-five-something.

T.   One point oh seven. Two near no-hitters.

M.   Oh! You want to hear a story? There he is—he's got eight and two thirds innings, he's got a no-hitter goin'. A shutout. It's great. We're all sittin' there goin', Yeah. We're all up cheerin' the mother. He throws the ball. It gets hit to the first baseman. The first baseman thought Bob was gonna cover. And Bob's just standin' on the mound goin', *Wow.*

T.   Thinkin' he's got a no-hitter.

M.   Yeah! And all of a sudden, *sheew,* safe! And the guy goes, Safe! And we're all lookin', goin', Oh, wow. SHIT—we couldn't believe it. I mean everyone just said, Man, you fat fart! Y'know, we just—we go over to my pitchin' coach who was standin' there. We go, Grod! Shouldn't Curtis have been over there? And Grod goes, Hell, no! He goes, What'd we teach ya? So we go, Whaddaya mean what'd we—it was his *area.* And he goes, Dontcha always go over to first when it gets hit to the first baseman? We looked at the guy—Yeah. He goes, See, he didn't get his fat ass over there! He lost a no-hitter. And he goes, *Ha-ha-ha,* he'll learn now. He'll be over there every day and tomorrow.

John Grodzicki Tells You Straight

T.   This was your pitching coach, John Grodzicki?

M.   John Grodzicki. He was an old-timer.

T.   I looked him up. He got into twenty-four games for the Cardinals in the forties. He won two of 'em.

M.   I wouldn't know. But I'll clue ya, he tells you straight. I mean, you start mouthin' off to the guy and sayin' I can't do it —he goes, Screw you, siddown, I don't want to listen to you, man. If you think you're doin' better than me, go sit down. Y'know, get the hell outa here. He used to come over to our house—like he used to come over to the apartments, different apartments. He'd cook his golapkis, right? And like we'd give him beers, y'know? And we'd have a good time.

T.   He'd cook his what?

M. Golapkis. He'd come over, he'd figure ballplayers have it hard—he went through it too, so he knows. I mean, you don't eat that good. Like the trainer in Bristol, he'd cook spaghetti or chili. Grod cooked golapkis.

T. What are they?

M. It's stuffed cabbage. It's hamburger, rice, and eggs, and salt and pepper, and whatever you want. And you roll it up.

T. So that was his idea of nutrition for you guys?

M. No, not nutrition. No, no. It was just, he'd come over, and he'd tell us stories. It was more like he was bein' a teacher, y'know? But he'd come by and have a few beers with you and tell you, y'know, where you stand and what you're doin'.

Going Nuts in a Four-Man Trailer in Bristol, Tennessee

T. Did you have an apartment in Bristol?

M. Oh, no, we had a trailer. We had a trailer with four people in it, man. You can't live with four people in a trailer.

T. What kind of a town was Bristol?

M. It was—oh, it was small. We were in a trailer court, man.

T. What goes on in Bristol, Tennessee?

M. I didn't know anything. I just used to go back to the trailer and drink.

T. But what do people work at in that town? Have they got a factory? A coal mine?

M. I don't know. I never went into town, really, because I had no vehicle. After the game was over, we'd go right back to the trailer and just sit there and drink. And have a few beers. And during the day it was Nodsville. I mean, you didn't do *nothin'*. I had no radio, I had nothin'—I used to just go nuts.

Deep in the Appalachian League I Get a Dear John Letter

T. Were there any girls? Anything going on?

M. Nothing, man. It was *dead*. I mean the chicks that were around, they didn't like me because I was too open. Probably. And I just—nothing. Y'know? Chicks ain't no better than me, there. I never dressed up to go out, y'know, to any of the places. Hey, come on, I said. Ah, what the heck? Those chicks, they—the ones I met were neat chicks, y'know? But I just—you just met 'em, and you never goofed around with 'em, that year. Because I was involved with a chick at home. So I didn't goof around, that's why.

T.   You had a girlfriend since high school, you mean?

M.   Yeah. Y'know? I was still goin' with her. And I had in my mind, I said, I ain't goin' out with no chick. But then—at the end, y'know, I said, All right. I just left it. I really didn't care.

T.   In a town like that, what could you do?

M.   Oh, you could do a lot, if you wanted. I mean, a lot of guys were datin' chicks. I mean they had a whore down in Bristol. The coach said if we ever got caught with her it was gonna cost us a hundred dollars. Her and her mother would take you on. Right? I mean, I forget the name that they had on it. There was a name—it was like The Three Sisters, right? I mean the three sisters and their mother. I mean their mother would go to bed with you.

T.   That's a little heavy.

M.   Yeah, it's a little heavy for a guy who's just comin' along. But I never really—I talked to chicks, I never really goofed around with 'em. I just cracked up laughin'. I said, I don't need a chick like that. I don't want to catch nothin', y'know? But then, that's just 'cause I was thinkin' of my chick back home.

T.   What did she think about you bein' a ballplayer, at the time?

M.   She thought—she gave me a Dear John letter. And just said, Hey, y'know—you must be foolin' around. And here I *wasn't* foolin' around. Y'know, that's what blew my mind, I wasn't. If I was, I woulda just smiled like an asshole and said, Hell, I don't need her. Y'know? But I wasn't foolin' around at the time, y'know? That's what pissed me off. So she gave me that. I have to admit, the last two weeks—this is like the last two weeks of the season she hit me with that, right? And I said, Screw it, man.

T.   You were just about ready to come home, when you hear that.

M.   Yeah, yeah. And I just said, Forget it. I said, The hell with it. And then I went and found myself a chick just like that —that night. Y'know, I said—*voom!*

T.   You mean down there in Bristol?

M.   Yeah, I was sore. And this chick came back from, uh,

Texas, that the kid I was livin' with now would, uh—he was datin' *another* chick, and *that* chick moved in with him. So, y'know, we just goofed around.

Trouble at Jim Dandy's Trailer Camp

T.   You stayed in the trailer all summer?

M.   Yeah, oh, yeah. We had three trailers. Man, we had— and one night . . .

T.   A trailer camp, you mean?

M.   Yeah, Jim Dandy's. Jim Dandy's Trailer Camp. And there's a record, *Jim Dandy to the Rescue?* Right? And it was like —once in a while you'd hear it. You'd be goin' home to your trailer court, and you'd be bummed out, sayin', God, I gotta go home to this thing that's, y'know, four by four by about ten feet long. And you'd be bummin' out, goin', *God damn.* Y'know, gettin' drunk. And then we got there, and we, like—when we were at the trailer courts the people didn't like us that much. We'd come home at eleven o'clock. We didn't have to go to work till five, right? At night. So we'd come home at eleven. And we'd have a few beers. Y'know, and like the guy had his radio there. We'd play it loud—whatever trailer had a stereo. We had *three* trailers —*bing, bing, bing.* All down in the bottom, right? And so one night the people in the trailer court messed with us. We came home from a road trip, right, and like all our trailers were broken into. But they didn't—they didn't *take* nothin'. They didn't take a thing. They just showed us—If you don't stop doin' what you're doin', we're gonna take everything you got. Y'know? They egged the place, too. We had eggs all over.

T.   These were just the local tough guys?

M.   Yeah.

T.   Punks?

M.   You know what they were? They were hippies. Druggies. Y'know, that were in the place. I mean, they were just—when the weekend came, man, there was parties up there. All the way up, I mean left and right.

T.   What's that country like down there? Smoky Mountains?

M.   Appalachians, I think it is. But I mean it's just weird.

The trailer court that we lived in—it was funny, y'know? People used to come back and do that. So then a lot of guys started movin' out. We got *scared,* man. And they moved out.

T.   On account of this hassle situation?

M.   Yeah. So it ended up bein' me and Bob Sykes. The two guys—and Kevin Slattery had his own trailer. Us two. And we're sittin' there goin', What are you guys leavin' for? They're just tellin' us to stop foolin' around, so we'll stop foolin' around.

T.   Sykes had another trailer?

M.   Sykes was in a trailer, and I was in a trailer. And my guy got moved up to A ball. That's why—and Bob's guys, that were in his trailer, moved out. So him and I moved in together.

T.   What'd the other guys do, get a motel or something? Where'd they go to?

M.   Apartment complexes. Like a couple other guys might've moved out, y'know—they just doubled up. But it *was* gettin' scary, though, it really was. I mean it—like, it *was.* 'Cause you knew the trailers weren't really that *safe.* It was just gettin' scary. But I said, Hell, there ain't no one's gettin' *me* outa here. What do I care what goes on? Y'know, I met—I *knew* the people. 'Cause I met 'em different than the other guys did, on the team. Like, 'cause I walked and thumbed a lot of places with a lot of 'em. They picked me up, 'cause I had to thumb, and they knew where I lived. And they lived two trailers up. I never hung around with any of the people up there, though, y'know? And when Bob and I moved together, it was neat. We had a good time, and no one else hassled us after everyone else moved out. That's because we were quiet. And we just went along with what we did. Just went to the ballpark, came back, and that was it. No big deal, y'know? And it quieted down. But before, it *was* hectic. Hectic as hell.

Mark goes on to relate the events of his twentieth birthday, August 14, 1974, on which occasion a surprise birthday party was held in his honor at the Jim Dandy Trailer Camp. Deep in the festivities, a noise complaint brought Joe Lewis, the Bristol manager, onto the scene. Lewis inquired first at Mark's trailer, only to interrupt another Bristol player in the midst of a heterosexual encounter. This player, says Mark, "was so scared he put his under-

pants on inside out *and* backwards" *when he came to answer
Lewis's knock on the door; his girlfriend hid in the closet. Mark was
at the time happily partying with friends, two trailers up the line.
Lewis summoned him; it was now 1:30* A.M. *Mark, assisted by a
teammate, returned to his own trailer to face the music.*

Joe Flips Out and I Donate
Twenty-five Bucks to the Team Party

T.   And it's dark?

M.   Yeah. And I go to get into the trailer. I went like this to
grab on, and I missed and fell back. And I grabbed it again and
came in—pulled myself in. And Joe goes, Look at you! And I'm
just frozen now. I said, Joe, you gave me two days off, like,
y'know? 'Cause I was tired, and it's my birthday, and they bought
me a case of Heineken, Joe, and I got drunk. And he goes, You're
goin' home now—tomorrow! You get your plane ticket home!

T.   And you believed him? You thought he was sending you
home?

M.   I was scared, man. He flipped me out. Really flipped me
out. He goes, I know all *about* you. And I said, Whaddaya mean?
He goes, I know everything you've done, and don't think you're
foolin' me, man. I said, I'm not thinkin' I'm foolin' you but you
gave me two days off—that's the only reason you see me like this.
And I was scared shitless. He goes, I don't give a shit—you got
me up this late, you're goin' home. You don't want baseball.

T.   How did he—the landlord of the trailer camp called
him?

M.   Yeah. And so then Jeff Hogan, our coach—his wife
was—

T.   Do you think Lewis was shittin' you? Do you think
he—

M.   No, he was. He was throwin' it all—at the time, he was
throwin' it into my mind, right? And, like—I *was* scared. Because
I, y'know—in his mind he knew there was no way he was gonna
send me home. There was no way he had that authority. But I
didn't know that myself. I mean he was—man, he sat there and
yelled. He goes, My wife just got in. Both Hogan's wife and
Lewis's wife just got in, right? I mean, they haven't seen their

wives in a long time. I can *imagine* how they're feelin', right? And he goes, I'm watchin' a movie with my wife. And you took me up —I hadda drive all the way down here, and now I gotta drive all the way back. Like he might be a half hour away, y'know, forty-five minutes away—I don't know where he lives, right? And he's screamin' at me and shit. And Hogan goes, Yeah, I'm just ready to do up my wife, and all of a sudden the *phone* rings! I just cracked up laughin', man, when he told me that. His wife, y'know —I just cracked up laughin'.

T.   What are these guys like, Hogan and Lewis?

M.   Hogan's young. Lewis is, well, he's—

T.   Is he an old ballplayer?

M.   Yeah, he's an old—he's a ballplayer. But he's not—I wouldn't call him an *old* ballplayer. He mighta been forty-some-thin'. But they're all guys that have gone through it, y'know? They know what I'm goin' through.

T.   And Hogan's like in his thirties?

M.   Yeah. I mean, no, no. He was probably in his twenties.

T.   And what's he, like an infield coach?

M.   He was just a coach. And then you have the manager, y'know? Jeff coached first, and Joe coached third. But, y'know, it was just weird at the time. Because I was scared shitless.

T.   So then what happens?

M.   So then he goes, You're fined twenty-five dollars. It was my first time I'd ever been fined. I said, Wow, twenty-five dollars.

T.   Just you got fined?

M.   Yeah, just me. Oh, he fined Bob. But then when Bob got to the ballpark, Joe said, I can't fine you because you were home. He goes, I can only fine Mark. So he fined *me.* And like, after he ended up leavin', it kinda ended up we both were laughin'. Y'know? Like one time he said—he brought a beer with him when he came up to the trailer. He actually brought a beer with him, at the time, right? He goes, Jeff, go out in the car and get two more beers for us. I go, Don't worry about it! Don't worry, I got some Heineken right here! He looks at me, he goes, *Sit your ass down!* He goes, When I wanna hear somethin' outa you, I'll ask.

T.   This is the same night?

M.   Yeah, this is all that same time, right? But it was just—

y'know, I thought, Well, I'll offer him a beer. Maybe he'll like me. But I'm still goin' home, now, tomorrow. But I'm still tryin' to say, Please, let me stay. I can't go home and say, Hey, the only reason I'm comin' home is I—

T.   Meanwhile, you're tanked, and you don't know what—

M.   Yeah, I'm scared shitless! And I can't go home and say, Yeah, I got super drunk, the coach kicked me off the team! I said, It'll really look good goin' home—Hey Dad, they kicked me off 'cause I was drinkin'.

T.   What a birthday present!

M.   Y'know? That's gonna really look good. And Joe says, No, sit your ass down. But then after he left, we were—all of us were in a laughin' mood, like. 'Cause the movie that we were watchin'—Bob was watchin' it. I said, Aw, that's no big deal, I saw it before. You didn't miss nothin'. He goes, Yeah, but I missed what was in my *bed!* Y'know? And we just started laughin', like. And they just left. And I was fined twenty-five bucks. And I get to the ballpark the next day, right? No big deal. Everything carried on. Joe cracked up—he comes in. Y'know, he didn't know all the other guys were at the party, right? He comes in—he goes, Ah, I caught Mark yesterday, he donated twenty-five dollars for our party. Y'know? Because at the end of the year, all the fine money you got, we had a big party. All the beer you could drink. And we went to Bonanza and ate steak. And we had a separate room, and we just drank our beers. And what was left over we all brought with us. It was such a good party. I mean, if these guys are donatin' twenty-five here, and ten there—*voom!* You were on.

A Card Game in Covington
(Joe Was a Hard Ass, but a Good Hard Ass)

T.   So he wasn't a bad guy, Lewis, after all.

M.   No, he was not. He was a *hard* ass. But it was a *good* hard ass, because, y'know, you—

T.   You gotta ride guys.

M.   That's right. I needed it, too. Like, if he gave you an inch, and you took a mile, he told you about it. He said, What the hell's comin' off here? I'm gonna start makin' bed checks! Y'know? I mean, we had a great time. You think of like kid stuff, man. We were throwin' water on—y'know, like comin' home with a date. So you're a couple floors up, and this guy's walkin' with his chick or something. You dump a bucket of water on the mother. And you sit there goin', *ha-ha-ha!* And then that guy gets a pay-back on you.

T.   Most of you guys, this is the first summer you've been away from home?

M.   Yeah, we were all—most of us were just out of high school. Some of us were in college, but the guys that were in college, they did different things.

T.   Were any of 'em married?

M.   A couple of 'em were. Those guys that were married, they'd go home and do *their* thing. But like we had card games and shit. One time, it was maybe two thirty in the mornin', there was a card game goin' on. I wasn't in it—I really never played cards, 'cause I couldn't see losin' the money that those guys were losin'. I mean they weren't bettin' like fifty cent, nickel. They were in the *dollars,* y'know? I mean, I could—I just sat back. I said, Wow, I lose five bucks in a card game and I'm *out.* I don't give a shit what you say, y'know? I got enough to last me maybe one hand, but then I'm out. But like, they were playin' late at night. We'd have maybe two, three guys in a room, right? So it was in our—my room, right? All of a sudden we hear this, y'know, *knock knock,* on the door. And the trainer goes, Who is it? All of a sudden you hear, *boom, boom!* A *foot* tryin' to kick it in! I knew right away who it was. I mean, no one just goes and answers the goddam door. I rolled over in my bed. And he just started *yellin'* at those guys, *I don't give a shit who the hell you guys think you are!* And I'm over there, y'know, sleepin'. He's not yellin' at me —he didn't *see* me. I'm hidin'. They had guys run out—we had balconies right next to each other. All you did was hop over. So then you jumped, you jumped through—it was like runnin' from this window here, and steppin' on a balcony outside, and goin' over to *your* room. That's what they were all doin'—they were all goin' outside, after that.

T.   Where was this?

M.   We were in Covington, then.

T.   In a hotel, you mean?

M.   Yeah, a hotel. And like, it was only the two guys that

were roomin' together that got caught. But there was three of us *in* the room, y'know? I was there too, but I was sleepin'. He didn't see me. He was just yellin' at those two. 'Cause everyone else was gone, right? It was just those two guys playin'.

T.   Who's this that comes in? Is this Lewis that comes in?

M.   Yeah, Lewis came in. The trainer opens the door—and he's yellin' at the trainer all the way down the hall and screamin' at him. And like all the guys came back and had—we were all laughin' our fool heads off. But the next day it was no big deal.

T.   So Lewis, your manager—he's like the police department, too.

M.   Yeah, oh, yeah, he watched us, and stuff. But, y'know, he was good. He was a neat guy. Like we'd win games, and he'd have beer on the bus. I mean he'd go out—he'd tell the bus driver to pull over at a supermarket, and he'd go in and buy two cases and say, Good game, you guys. Y'know? This is your reward. And it was neat. Other than that, we'd never bring beer on the bus or anything like that. Something like that, and then you feel more— he's kinda tryin' to treat you like a man. But yet he's not givin' you that *full man* that you should have. Like havin' the curfews. Y'know, they call you up on the phone and shit, in the minors. But you *do* need it, y'know?

They Make Me a Reliefer at Bristol

T.   You worked all your games in relief at Bristol. Were the Tigers thinking about making a relief pitcher out of you when they signed you?

M.   I don't know. I really don't know.

T.   The funny thing is that at Bristol you worked in relief, and then at Lakeland you started, and then at Montgomery you worked in relief, and then at Evansville again you started.

M.   That was what was weird about it.

T.   Who was calling the shots? Was it Jim Campbell, or the minor league director, Evers? Or somebody else?

M.   No, I don't know who does that. But like I just went down to spring training, right?

T.   You mean in June—you reported to the Bristol team in Florida?

M.   Yeah, for like a week down. They asked me to go down,

right? So I went down there, and we worked out. And they said, All right, now, the startin' pitchers are gonna be these guys. But like we went through the whole week, and when we got to Bristol they said, These are gonna be the startin' pitchers. You're just a reliefer. I said, Wow, shit, what's that? Y'know, I never reliefed. I mean, maybe once in a great while.

T.   So you'd always started?

M.   Always, I always—that's all that was in my mind, y'know, was a starter.

T.   Maybe they had you figured for relief on account of you kept the ball low and threw a lot of strikes?

M.   I don't know. No, they—everyone that went down there, you'd talk to all the pitchers, they'd say, Yeah, I started, I started. So it was like, y'know, *now* they start makin' 'em pitchers. Pitchers, y'know? Like they brought us in—I said, Fine, I've got a job. That's all I said to myself. I said, Hey, they want me to relief, I'll try reliefin'. I never, y'know, I've never really gotten serious in relief, but I'm gonna try.

T.   So they didn't make you a reliever until you got back up to Bristol?

M.   Yeah, this was at Bristol. And that was like long relief. And I didn't throw that much, but then the short-relief guy that they made, like he kinda ran outa gas or something, y'know?

T.   Who was that?

M.   Ah, it was like Alex Johnson, or Alley Cat, we called him. Allen Johnson, somethin' like that. He was from North Dakota. Or South Carolina, somewhere like that. And he just ran out of gas, so they made *him* a long reliefer, and they made *me* a short one. And I just got in the groove and I started pitchin' and doin' all right. I had twenty-three games there, and I was doin' fine. Y'know, I ended up on the all-star team. It was neat reliefin', but yet I'd always ask for a start. I said, C'mon, Grod, when are you gonna give me a start? He said, Stay at what you're doin', you're doin' all right. And I said, That's true. And I was doin' good. And then one time I wasn't doin' so hot, wasn't strikin' guys out, right? And I just said, I'm—I didn't say nothin' to 'em, I just said, Hey, well, maybe they know my stuff. All I'm doin' is throwin' a fastball and a slider, y'know—they know what's comin', fastball and slider. And then the pitching coach just came back,

Grodzicki. And he says, Hey, you haven't been strikin' out too many guys any more. And I said, Grod, I'm up every day, what can I do? Y'know? And he goes, You're tired. And I said, Yeah, I'm tired. I mean every game I'm up, y'know, throwin'. I haven't had a day off, man. And Joe Lewis comes over and goes, Why didn't you tell me that? And I said, Hey, I'm new, I don't know what's goin' on! I'm just tryin' to win that job upstairs! I mean this minor leagues is nothin', y'know, compared with—it's like, now that I've got it, I know how to appreciate the minors, because I've had it.

Joe Lewis Told 'Em to Leave Me at Bristol

T.   Seeing as how you were pitching so well, how come the Tigers left you at Bristol all season instead of moving you up to A ball—to Clinton, say, or Lakeland? Joe Lewis couldn't have needed you that bad at Bristol. He had the pennant clinched with a month to go.

M.   Well, once when we were playin', Joe pulled me over—after we, uh, won the thing—and he goes, They wanted you to go to Clinton, but I told 'em to leave you here. He told me that at the end of the season. He goes, You coulda gone up to Clinton, but I wanted you here. Because, y'know, Clinton, it wouldn't have meant nothin' to go up there. Y'know, it just wouldn't have. He goes, Here was better, Mark. Y'know, you respect a guy for that.

I Didn't Know Who Butch
Wynegar Was, I Just Went Out and Played

T.   What about the hitters in the Appalachian League—do you remember any of the good hitters?

M.   No.

T.   How about Butch Wynegar, do you remember him?

M.   No.

T.   He was with Elizabethton. It's weird that you finished one-two for the Rookie of the Year up in the majors, after both coming out of the same draft and the same rookie league.

M.   I don't even know if I played against him. Did I?

T.   Yeah, he was with Elizabethton. He hit about .360 and led the league.

M.   Yeah?

T.   Elizabethton, they were a Twins farm.

M.   Yeah. Well, I didn't follow it. Like I told you, I don't—I didn't follow anyone, because it wasn't my bag. I just went out and played. And like, y'know, Bob would say to me, How can you drink a six-pack every night? 'Cause every night I'd come home and drink a six-pack of beer or more.

T.   Bob Sykes didn't drink?

M.   He never drank, hardly, at all. And like, he'd go, How can you do this? And I'd say, Bob, I'm just bored, y'know? *I'm bored,* man. If I had a chick I wouldn't be—y'know, gettin' half as cocked as I am, while *you're* up there sittin' home!

Coming Down That Hill
in Pulaski, I Thought We Were Goners

T.   You hadn't seen much of the country before you went into organized baseball. Did you find out a lot about America from traveling around those backwater leagues?

M.   Well, travelin'-wise, we were takin' bus rides. I mean, that's not—*that's* travelin'. You're seein' more, that way, than you are flyin', right? But then if you're gonna ride a good Greyhound, you don't mind it—when you can at least kick back. But when you're ridin' one that—the windows are cracked in it, y'know? And the *exhaust* fumes in the back, you gotta open the windows just to get the shit out!

T.   I take it the ones you had at Bristol weren't all good Greyhounds?

M.   I mean the buses are gonna *make* it, yeah.

T.   But just barely, right?

M.   Yeah! And like, one time, here we are, we're goin'—we're takin' a bus up to Pulaski, from Bristol. Over—Overstreet, I think the bus driver's name was. And he—we're goin' down a hill. And we were talkin' about it, y'know? Because all it is is down—all the way *down* down, y'know?

T.   Wondering if Overstreet had any brakes, eh?

M.   We're sayin', Can you imagine if the brakes ever went? He goes, Yeah, I could. He goes, Don't worry, I just hit the emergency brake. No big deal. We got into town and here's a *stone wall,* y'know? And he has to make a right. He's goin' down—he goes, You know how we were talkin' before? He goes, You wouldn't believe it, but I just blew an air bag. I mean, *Whoa!*

T.   Shake you up a little?

M.   He *told* all of us too, he yelled out, *You guys hold on!* That's all he said was, *Hold on, you guys!* He goes, We don't have any brakes! He literally right out an' told us. All it was was just a little hill, too, right? And there's a red light and a green light there. And we're goin', *Wow!* He's honkin' his horn, pulls up on the emergency brake. He goes, The emergency brake don't work! We're goin', *Whoa!* He's got it in first, he's lettin' the clutch in and out like a *mother,* just tryin' to brake it. He's hittin' *poles,* right? But there was no telephone poles to hit, or he woulda *hit* one.

T.   This was during the middle of the night?

M.   No, no, this was durin' the day! This was during the *day,* about uh, three o'clock, four o'clock, maybe. When there's just ungodly traffic! And he's tootin' the horn, and people are goin' to both sides, and he's scarin' the *shit* outa people! But we're *in* the bus, goin', You got a *stone wall* here, man! It's either we go into the stone wall, or he makes the turn—and hope the people down there hear him! Right? So we lucked out. The person actually stopped his car, 'cause he saw us comin'—'cause Overstreet was beepin' his horn, he saw us comin'. And we got around the corner, and like we smacked up into a bigger pole. But he was knockin' —like knockin' the signs down? Little signs—a signal here, and like, little blinker lights, and a little tree here—he knocked them things down, man! And like—

T.   Coulda killed everybody—

M.   Not killed everyone—people coulda got hurt. But we all got out of it safe. And then the coach just looks at us and goes, *Whew.* He goes, All right, you guys, I don't know what to say. He goes, Come back in an hour! Go around, mess around, and come back in an hour. He goes, Hey, you guys, come back in two hours. Y'know? It was just weird.

T.   This was in Pulaski?

M.   Yeah. We were just—y'know, we were commutin' to go there. We were *all* talkin' about it. And if you saw the bus—one side was all smashed up. And Overstreet, this guy—his shirt was

soaked in a matter of seconds there, he was so scared. He said,
Man, I'm happy. He said, Man, we could've—Oh! *Whew.* He
couldn't do anything either—he was still in shock. Man, just
comin' down that hill—I thought we were goners, everyone did.
I mean, *everyone* was a little sca—everyone shut up, y'know? No
one said a word. We just listened to him. That's how it was. I'll
never forget that scene, man. Y'know?

I Lose My White Spikes and
Spag Special, and Pick Up the Name Bird

T.   The coach at Bristol, Jeff Hogan, was he the first person
who called you Bird?

M.   Yeah. Yeah, that was the first day.

T.   The first day you were there?

M.   No, the first day down in spring training, down in Lakeland, Florida. Like, we went there for a week, then we split for
Bristol. I just ran out on the field—I got my uniform on, I had
my white shoes on, and I had my Spag Special glove, y'know? And
all these other guys, they had these other things. And I just—I just
didn't *buy* equipment, man! I didn't know what kind of equipment
to have.

T.   *What* kind of glove did you have?

M.   Just a Spag Special glove. Spalding, y'know? It was just
—I just came with what I had. What I was playin' with before.
And like, they said, Hey, you can't have white spikes. You can get
new ones now. I said, What the hell, where am I gonna get the
money? They said, Spend some of the bonus we hit you with! I go,
How can I spend that bonus, you didn't *give* me anything. They
hit me with that, y'know? I go, Holy shit, y'know? I had to pay
for my *schoolin',* y'know. I mean, Worcester Academy was two
thousand bucks. So I gave my dad half of it. And then I got a
thousand of it—I bought a stereo system. I had nothin' else left,
and I had *other* bills to pay. *Spend* that bonus, they're tryin' to
hit me with! Shit! Give me forty grand, and I mighta spent my
bonus. And I mighta came here with a new glove and all that shit.
Right?

T.   Did you get new equipment somehow?

M.   I lucked out. The week we were there, some little kids

broke into the locker room. They stole the equipment! They stole my glove and spikes! So I got new ones—I lucked out.

T. You got 'em replaced.

M. Yeah—I actually lucked out. So it was neat, y'know?

T. So how come Jeff calls you—

M. I just run out on the field and he goes, Bird. And I just turn around. And he goes, That's your nickname I gave you. And you know, he told me—he goes, If you stick in baseball, that name's gonna stick with you. And you watch what that name's gonna be. And it was weird. And I said, What did you call me that for? And he said, You look like that goofy bird on *Sesame Street.* And I said, Whaddaya mean? He goes, Hey you just look like the bird on *Sesame Street.* So that's your nickname. I can't—Fidrych is too hard to, y'know, *say.*

They Called Me Bird in the Minors and It Was No Big Deal, but Then a Page Turned and Everything Took Off

T. Had you ever seen *Sesame Street?*

M. Huh? Yeah, when I was a kid. My little sister used to watch it once in a while. But it was weird. Like, no one even thought about it, all through the minors. They didn't even talk about it. They just called me Bird, they didn't think anything of it. And you go, *voom!* You hit the majors, man, it's a whole different page. The page just folded right over. The minor leagues is gone, and now—this is what happens.

T. And all of a sudden that name comes back, right?

M. Yeah.

T. That *is* weird.

M. I mean, y'know, everyone knew me through the ball team as Bird. But *they*—they didn't think it was no big deal.

On Five Hundred a Month I Had My Fun and I Was Happy

T. They didn't think it was a big deal then, because *you* weren't a big deal. Things are different now.

M. But I'll clue ya, I don't goof around half as much as I used to.

T. You mean in the minors?

M. Yeah. I used to goof around more than I do in the

majors. But goofin' around in the majors is different.

T.   Probably more fun.

M.   Yeah. It's more fun in the majors.

T.   You don't sound too convinced!

M.   I mean, but—in the minors, I mean, like goofin' around in this hotel room. Like when I threw that water out. Someone mighta been *down* there, y'know?

T.   Oh, when you threw that ice water out?

M.   Yeah.

T.   What's down there, anyway? Just more Hilton?

M.   Nothin', but just—but a ceiling. But that don't mean—but that's what *we* woulda done, y'know? Or you destroy a guy's room, and you just walk out and laugh your head off. There's just weird things like that. You did more—well, what they'd call, what they'd classify as *immature* things, right? But really they're not immature things, 'cause they *teach* you, y'know?

T.   Well, that's also called havin' a good time.

M.   Yeah. Here you are, makin' five hundred bucks a month —gettin' this paycheck that you never even *thought* of seein', and livin' for a hundred and fifty bucks a month, because this place only cost you a hundred that you're stayin' at. I mean, y'know, and you just—it was *neat.* I had all the beer money I wanted, and I had all my food money. And I was happy, y'know?

T.   Were any of those guys making big money down at Bristol? The guys who got big bonuses?

M.   Oh, you don't! Minor league guys, your first year you all make the same. Five hundred bucks a month. And that's it, y'know? No big deal.

7 I Made Them Drop Me Off at the End of My Street (Lakeland, 1975)

What's Spring Training For?

T.   So after the season ended at Bristol, you felt pretty good.

M.   Yeah, I did. I felt confident. And then I come to spring training, right? What's spring training for? Spring training is for, what do they classify it as—for workin' out, right? Getting in shape? Doin' this and doin' that, right? Hoot Evers pulls me over and goes, Mark, what is *wrong* with you? And I go in his office. He goes, Hey—you were gettin' 'em *out* in *Bristol*. Can't you get 'em out any more? I said, Hoot, this is spring training, I'm just down here gettin' in shape, gettin' my fastball ready. I said, I'll be ready when the season starts. If you put me in A ball, I'll be ready. If you put me in Double-A, I'll be ready. I'm just workin' out, y'know? And he goes, You better not be talkin' out your ass. Now get outa here.

T.   Hoot Evers is the minor league guy, the director of player development?

M.   Yeah. But it was just weird. Like he was comin' at me to see where my head was at. And I just *told* him. I said, Hey, I ain't down here to *blow heat* right now. You want me to blow heat? I said, I'll go out there and blow heat. But where do you want me to do the job? Here? Or in A ball? Or wherever you want it.

After Bristol I Go to Winter Ball with the Guys They Have High Hopes In

T.   What had you been doin' all winter, after you came back from Bristol?

M. Just running.

T. You ran at home?

M. No, I took—I went to winter ball.

T. Oh, the Florida Instructional League?

M. Yeah. After Bristol, this was neat. I went down to Clearwater. Played in Dunedin. Went down to Clearwater for two months, lived with Bob Sykes. We had a great time, y'know?

T. You played in Dunedin, but you were staying over in Clearwater.

M. Yeah. I had a great time. Came home for Thanksgiving. And then I took time off all the way up until New Year's Eve.

T. Did you start down there?

M. No, I reliefed.

T. Sykes was pitching down there too?

M. Oh, Bob. Yeah, he was a starter.

T. How'd he do?

M. Oh, he did all right. Yeah. He did pretty good. *I* even did all right, y'know?

T. Who do they put down there? They put guys from Clinton and Bristol?

M. No, all different teams. Like, from Detroit—we had a few *major* league guys down there. Like Tom Veryzer was down there when I was there for my first year.

T. So the guys they wanted to bring along were all down there?

M. Yeah. The guys that they had high hopes in, right? So down there we were all goofin' around, havin' a *great* time. And then you came home. And I just ran, like in January. After New Year's Eve. I said, Okay, it's all over now, now I'll go start runnin' every day. And I used to go runnin' with my dogs, y'know? I just had a good time.

A Run-in with Frank
MacCormack in the Spring, When I'm Keyed Up

T. When we were talking before, you said you had some kind of a run-in with Frank MacCormack down at Tigertown that spring?

M. Well, it was before I *knew* Mac, right? One time we were

in Fetzer Hall. And like, one time at night, when we came home
—I was pretty well smashed, right?—he was givin' me some shit.
Like sayin', You're dumb. Y'know? Little League shit, he gave
me. And I said, Frank, I said, shove it. I don't need it, y'know?
I mean, I don't know you. I don't know who the hell you are. And
you're givin' me shit. You ain't goin' that good to be givin' me shit.
Because *I'm* in the same place you're at.

T. This was during spring training of '75, before either of
you'd been assigned to a team?

M. Yeah. Before I even *knew* the guy, right? And I said,
You're givin' me shit. And I don't even know you. And one day
when we were playin'—I was playin' pool and he was playin'
Ping-Pong—he got on me for some more shit. All right? And I
said, *Whoa.* I dropped my pool stick, and I said, Come on, if
you're gonna get on me *now,* let's fight for equal rights, then. I go,
You're just gettin' on me to where—just because you can talk
louder than I can. Let's get down to it, y'know? You're gettin'
down on *talkin'.* I ain't good with the mouth, maybe you're good
with the mouth. Let's see if you're good with the *body,* y'know?
That's it. *Voom!* It stopped. He went back and played Ping-Pong.
I went back and played pool. It stopped. And all of a sudden, now,
I lived with the guy. Right? The next year—I mean, that year,
spring training, he went up to Double-A, I was in A ball. But then
I got moved up to Double-A. And like, we got to start playin' with
each other.

T. He went up first to Montgomery?

M. Yeah, he went up before me, when it came to Double-A.
And like, I never played with the guy. So I didn't really know what
it was. Everyone told me, He's just *like* that. He's just cocky. And
I said, Fine. I didn't know the guy. But we had—we had said to
each other's *minds* what was goin' on between each other's *heads.*
Because I just figured, Hey, ain't no way I'm gonna get kicked
down by *this* guy. If he was a little higher, I would've. Y'know?
But he ain't no nothin', to me. So then, we just built up. And then
I lived with the guy in Evansville and found out really what he
was like. And actually was. And, y'know, he'd say somethin' to
you, and if you'd say somethin' right back to him, then it's equal,
y'know? No big deal. We just—we still goof around together.

That's why, when I was up in the major leagues, and then he came up, I said, Screw it. I'll let him live with me. Because I told him in the beginning when he first came up—I said, Mac, find your own place. I said, I want to, y'know, just live.

T.   He came up to Detroit around May, June of this year?

M.   Yeah, y'know, when he came up. I said, Frank, I'm just livin' by myself, and I want to. Because my family comes in. And, y'know, I want 'em to come in and be comfortable. I don't want, y'know . . .

T.   He didn't know anybody else, in other words?

M.   No. Well, then he goes, I'm gonna live with Jason Thompson. Well, that's neat. Because he played with Jason, right? But then Jason's lady came down. So Jason said, No, you can't live with me now. 'Cause my girl's comin' down, she's gonna live with me permanently. So Frank goes, I can't live with *myself* up here. And I said, Frank, all right, okay, live with me now. And I said, I'll try it. I said, I don't give a damn, y'know? And now, I knew the guy a little bit. I said, Screw it. But we got to where —it got to a point where now I knew the guy. Where before, I just didn't even really know him, that much. But yet, we didn't hit off on terms. But then later, we *did* hit on terms. Because I knew him, and he kinda knew me. And he wasn't about to say shit. He wasn't about to be cocky again, y'know? Because I knew him. And after that, fine.

T.   It must have been tough on him when you guys got up together at Detroit, and you're out there doin' the job, and he sees that. And he's goin' out and lasting two, three innings.

M.   I wouldn't know. To that point, I wouldn't know. But still, to where I *used* to know Frank, and to what we ended up to bein' *like*—that's two different things, y'know? One minute I was ready to smack the shit out of him. I was ready to, y'know, punch him. But he didn't swing first, so I said, Fine, I won't. He wanted to just see it. If all it took was a push, then I woulda proceeded. Because I was in such a mood of bein' keyed up, at that time. And now, I look at him, and say, Hey, Frank—I went to, I actually drove five hours to get to his party. Y'know, 'cause that's—I said, Hey. I knew the kid now. I started *knowin'* the kid now. And I knew what he was like. And I said, Fine. I drove five hours to his party. And drove five hours home, after that. Just 'cause I wanted to go to his party 'cause I knew him. Other than that, y'know, what have you got?

Stubby Overmire Says,
Just Keep on Doing What You're Doing

T. So you were keyed up that spring. Hoot said you weren't throwing good, and the Tigers left you down at Lakeland. Overmire was your manager there?

M. Yeah, Stubby Overmire.

T. What was he like? He used to pitch for the Tigers when I was a kid.

M. He was a good guy. See, he helped me out a lot too. Y'know, y'see—you're gonna take the team that we played with in A ball, they were all a bunch of guys who'd played at Bristol together. A lot of the guys—and here we were, a winning team. And now we *aren't,* any more. I mean we tore the league *up* in Bristol. And now we're not even doin' anything here. And like Stubby's sayin', Hey, keep on throwin' the way you are. He was drivin' it through my mind—You're doin' okay. You're completin' your games, it's just that they're not gettin' runs for you. But I'm flippin'. I'm just, y'know, you're losin'—and I'm not thinkin' that way. I'm not *thinkin'* it.

T. But you weren't getting knocked out or anything? You pitched pretty well?

M. I was completin' my games, but I was gettin' knocked out once in a while.

T. You were only 5–10, but you completed ten out of sixteen starts. That ain't bad.

M. Yeah, I completed ten out of sixteen. But that's the only thing I had goin' for me. You gotta look at it *mind-wise,* though. I mean I wasn't lookin' at it, ten complete games. I was sayin', *Big* deal. Ten complete games, what have I got to show for it? Nothin'! But yet that's all they wanted, y'know?

T. So the ball club was losing too, right? They came in fourteen games under .500.

M. Yeah, we were all—I mean, the team was—

T. You said a lot of your low pitches were going to the

backstop. Maybe you could have used a more experienced catcher.

M.   No, we just weren't playin' together. Y'know? We were just doin' different things.

T.   Was Stubby helpin' you out?

M.   Yeah. Now, he was the one—he keeps your mind in control. Him and Mike Dwyer. Here I am, losin', I go, *Mike*—

T.   What's Dwyer's job? He was a coach down there?

M.   He was the pitching coach. I'd go over to Stubby, or Mike, and say, *What's wrong?* What am I doin' wrong? Am I throwin', y'know—tippin' 'em off? And they'd go, Just keep on throwin'.

T.   Were you walkin' guys or anything?

M.   No! They said, Just keep on doin' what you're doin'. Just keep on pitchin', don't worry about it. They said, They're not gettin' enough runs for you. I'd lose 2–1, 3–0, stuff like that.

T.   But it gets to your head anyway, losing all those games.

M.   I mean—you get beat 10–0, and it's the same thing as gettin' beat 2–1. Or 1–0. Because it's just—you *know,* in your *mind,* you want that *W.* Not *L.* Y'know? And it's just *voom, voom.* But then I got the second life at Montgomery.

**I Live by Myself in a
Hot Dog Stand in the Florida State League**

T.   So what was it like in Lakeland? Say, compared to Bristol, what was the life like down there?

M.   Lakeland and Bristol? It was a whole different thing. Lakeland, It was like, bigger.

T.   Longer bus rides?

M.   Yeah, longer bus rides. An hour, y'know? Or, you had that Fort Lauderdale and Miami and Key West and one other one, those were really super-long.

T.   West Palm Beach.

M.   Yeah, West Palm Beach.

T.   Some nice towns.

M.   Yeah, that's what's neat about that.

T.   Stay in big hotels?

M.   Well, you'd stay in a better room than *this.* Except for in Key West, we stayed in one that was just like this.

T. Considering this is the Hilton, that's not too bad—even if this *is* a small room! And then did you have an apartment back in Lakeland?

M. Yeah, I had a little—they called it, guys on the team that used to come over and goof around, they told me it was a hot dog stand. 'Cause it was a little—I had a little trailer. Like, the trailer part had my kitchen and my bathroom, but that's it. And then they built on to it. It was an old, old one, man. It was *neat,* though. I just saw it, I said—

T. Did you like Florida?

M. Yeah, I loved Florida. I just, at that point—I was happy at where I was stayin'. I had a good time, and a couple of guys were right down the road, and that's how I got to the ballpark. 'Cause Pat Murphy had a van, y'know? He used to bring us to the ballpark and stuff. And other than that I used to just thumb around and get picked up by faggots, man. I mean, that was—here I am—

I Made Them Drop Me Off at the End of My Street

T. Ah, Florida. Is that what it's like down there?

M. I mean, here I am goin' home from a baseball game. Wantin' to go home and cook somethin' to eat. Y'know, I get home, and then I want to go out again. So I get to the bar, and it's like one o'clock at night. Y'know? Or maybe a little earlier. I'm thumbin' home, and then *voom!* You get picked up by these faggots. And the guy—and you're just sittin' there goin', Wow, y'know? Here I am, I could get *killed,* now, man. Just 'cause, y'know, this guy . . . and the guy, it was a taxi—I used to call it a taxi ride. I mean, you could—I could tell a faggot the minute he picked me up. Just by that first word he said. And it'd be an instant ride to where you wanted. And then they'd *hit* you with it, y'know? They were so stupid, they wouldn't hit you in the beginning.

T. Taxi drivers?

M. No, I'd call 'em taxi, y'know, a taxi ride, because it'd get me right where I wanted to go. And you shut the car door and say, Thanks a lot buddy, see ya later.

T. You mean these guys are cruising the ballpark?

M.　Not cruisin' the ballpark, just cruisin' *Lakeland*. Just ridin'—y'know, all night, just ridin' around. I mean I had a guy that could've been my grandfather, man. Picked me up—weird.

T.　You mean, a retirement type?

M.　Yeah. I just look at him, man, and I said, Uh, how much? And he goes, Seven dollars. And I said, I make more playin' baseball. See ya later.

T.　Out to lunch, eh?

M.　But yet, the guy drops me off right at my street. I never brought—I never brought 'em to my place where I lived.

T.　That's a weird amount of money, though, ain't it?

M.　What?

T.　It's sort of arbitrary—seven dollars. It's like a motel rate.

M.　I don't know. See, 'cause it was like gettin' to a point—I was sayin', Hey, what the hell is this? Y'know, every night! I'd be thumbin' home at night and get hit by one. And I'd always have 'em drop me off at the end of the street, and then I'd walk in.

I Get Down at Lakeland, but They Move Me Up

T.　So in between these other little episodes you're a starting pitcher now, at Lakeland.

M.　Yeah.

T.　Do you remember anybody coming down from the farm system—Hoot Evers or anybody, coming down to see you pitch?

M.　Oh, yeah, they all go through the system. Like, they came to Bristol for maybe a week or two, and they came to Lakeland. And, y'know, they see you pitch.

T.　Is it any tenser for you when those guys are watching?

M.　You wanna do—you wanna impress them. But you know what's funny? They're not there, and look how good you're doin'. And then all of a sudden you try to impress them, and you don't do as good. Y'know? Like, there was one time at Bristol I came into a situation—I could have normally just got *out* of it. But I didn't, because I wanted to do so *super,* y'know, that I just didn't do it. But they knew—they know the talent that you have. That's the one thing that they drive through your mind. Don't try to overimpress someone. Just go out there and play the game. Y'know? And I found that out, it's all the same game. And I moved up from like rookie ball, all right, then I go to A ball. All right, I started out in A ball, I won three games in a row. I was sittin' there, holy shit, I'm gonna hopefully get moved *up!* I ended up havin' a five and ten record in A ball, right? So I'm sittin' there, at Lakeland, y'know—see, my mind is flippin' now. I said, Oh, this is it, baseball's *over* now. Five and ten record, ten complete games I'm doin' horseshit!

T.   And all of a sudden—

M.   All of a sudden, next day I come in—and Stubby Overmire goes, Hey, give your uniform to Bronson. And I said, *What?* And I said, Oh, shit, I'm *gone.* And he goes, You're goin' up to Double-A, to Montgomery. And I just—I just sat down. I said, *Whoa.* You gotta be shittin' me—five-and-ten record and I'm goin' up to Double-A?

8 A Whole Other Relief in Your Life (Montgomery/Evansville, 1975)

Two Weeks at Montgomery and a Les Moss Haircut

M. So then I moved up. And when I went up to Montgomery, I said, Wow—it was like a whole other relief in your life. I mean, Wow, they gave me a second chance. To go up to a better club—they were winnin' now, up there, right? And then they stuck me back at reliefin'. There it was again! They stuck me back at reliefin'!

T. Maybe that was some kind of front office move—maybe they just needed a reliever.

M. Y'know? I mean, I'm sittin' there—'cause I walked in to the guy. He goes, You gotta get a haircut! The minute I walked in.

T. This is when you just joined Montgomery?

M. Yeah. My hair mighta been this long.

T. That would've been Les Moss?

M. Yeah, Les Moss.

T. He caught for the White Sox when I was a kid. He always *looked* like kind of a hard guy.

M. Les Moss, he just likes—he likes a short-haired ballplayer. All right, fine. I said, Fine, I'll go get my hair cut. I went and got it cut. I came back, and he goes—I thought I told ya to go get your hair cut! And I said, I did, I did! And he goes, Yeah, I know. Only next time I tell ya to get a haircut, go get a good one. And I said, What am I gonna be doin', startin' for you? And he goes, No, you're reliefin'.

T. Maybe he got his orders from elsewhere.

M. Yeah. And I said, *What?* And then I said, Fine, that's

cool—I don't mind! He goes, you're gonna relief tonight, you're gonna relief for the rest of the season probably. I said, That's good. I got in there, I won I think three games, or two games—I don't know, I forget what I won. But like I didn't lose any games. And I was there two weeks. And I did good. And I was feelin' *so good,* 'cause they were makin' the double play. And they were really havin' a good time.

T.   They won the Southern League easy, maybe that's why they were having such a good time.

M.   Yeah!

I Get an Apartment on One Day's Notice, Pay a Month's Rent, Get Moved Up and Never Come Back (Montgomery)

T.   You were saying you had to find an apartment there in one night?

M.   Yeah, oh—

T.   Most people think the ball club takes care of a lot more stuff—

M.   Than they *do!* Oh, they *don't!* When you're in the minors, man—*ooohh!* It's like, *whew.* They pull this deal, y'know—like I get sent up to Montgomery, right? And here they are—I drive all the way, eight hours, with my pitching coach, right? We get there, in Montgomery. They give me *one night.* Next day I gotta find an apartment and all that junk, right? They gave me one night. I got in there Friday, so that gave me till Saturday, right? They're tryin' to tell me that the next night I have to pay! I'm sittin' there, Wait, wait! I said, How can—I can't even get an apartment, man, on Sunday! No electricity, nothin'—I said, What do you, what's this shit? The guy goes—it was like, y'know, he squeaked it out of his ass and said, Okay, I'll give you another day. Y'know, just 'cause—but I had to bitch about it. Somethin' like that—you don't have to! The guy can't realize it's Sunday? The next day? I mean, and I was gonna have to pay fourteen dollars outa my own *pocket!* Just 'cause I—and I'd lost—I'd just *paid* a month's rent back there in Lakeland.

T.   And you weren't making a hell of a lot of money.

M.   Right. But then, it's like when I got sent up to *Triple-A,* right? Here I am, got sent up to Triple-A. When I got sent up, I'd

just paid a month's rent, up to August first, right? I'd paid it before
we left on a road trip. 'Cause August first, or whatever, we woulda
been on the road trip, and I couldn't have paid it. 'Cause we were
goin' away for fifteen days. It was fifteen, or maybe, y'know,
thirteen, somethin' like that. But I got sent up.

T.   You were making what, about six hundred a month at
the time?

M.   Eight hundred. I made eight hundred when I was in
Triple-A. And then I got there. So I'd paid a whole month's rent
in Montgomery. And now I got to Evansville, I gotta get another
apartment now! So I lost that *whole* month's rent—a hundred and
a quarter, I lose.

T.   And the club doesn't compensate you for that?

M.   No, they compensate you for seventy-five dollars.

T.   So in other words, coming up through the minors is a
double test for a kid. He's got to pitch and manage his life too—
and have them change it around from on top, every once in a
while. And yet, you've got to land on your feet every place you
go, or it's back down the ladder.

M.   Yeah!

T.   Like, not take two weeks to adjust. Or make a lot of
excuses, but just do it, now!

M.   Yeah. But like, if they'd just give the guy three days, or
four days in a hotel . . .

T.   So really what's happening in the minor leagues is a
growing-up process of having to go through those experiences as
well as what you're doing out there pitching, right?

M.   Yeah! Oh, yeah! But lookit—so then you got to look at
it this way. All right, they move you up to Triple-A now. Right?
You're supposed to be happy, right? Even though they're only
gonna give you seventy-five dollars outa the hundred and twenty-
five you just lost—*plus* the fifty-dollar deposit that you had—so
you're losin' seventy-five automatically yourself.

T.   What happened to your apartment in Montgomery when
you left? You just left it empty?

M.   Yeah! I just said, See ya later. I broke my lease, y'know?
Bye, now! And then—y'know, and then, Oh, the deposits for
electricity that I hadda make. And this and that, y'know? All that

shit. No big deal. That was that. So now you get up to Triple-A
—but then they give you a raise.

T.   To what, a thousand a month?

M.   No, I made twelve hundred. But the point is, when I
went up from A ball, that's when I lost money. And they
didn't give me that much to compensate for it, you know what
I mean? But then in Triple-A, when they give you twelve hundred a month, that's kinda makin' up for it. But still, not
really. Y'know, they're askin' you to move. But in the big
leagues, I heard it's a lot different. There's no questions about
it. You just send them—you just show them the bill, and
that's it. And that's—I really don't know about the big
leagues. But like I heard that if you get moved or traded you
don't lose a penny.

In the Minors You Just Worry About Yourself

T.   So when they moved you up from Double-A to Triple-A,
were you aware that there was a vacancy situation up on top with
the Tigers? I mean, it was a real opportunity time for all of you
down in Evansville and Montgomery—were you thinking about
any of that? Or was just moving enough of a problem?

M.   At the time I was just worryin' about movin'. Because
like that's—y'see, that's the whole thing. When you're in the
minors, you don't give a shit what the major league is doin'.
You're worried about *yourself.* Sayin', I want to make that *team,*
right? Because you knew that it was across—way over the river,
man. But you didn't give a damn what that team did. They coulda
won—they coulda lost nineteen in a row, you'd be sittin' there
laughin'. 'Cause *I'm* winnin'—'cause *we're* winnin' what *we're*
gonna do. And we're doin' what we're gonna do, down in the
minors. We don't give a damn about them up there.

T.   And vice versa, now?

M.   Yeah. It's just like, when you get up here, you say, We
don't give a damn about you down there.

T.   But at the time you were too busy anyway—

M.   I didn't even have my *clothes* in Evansville! I had one
shirt, one pair of pants, that I flew to the place in.

The Jump to Triple-A (Ten Dollars Got You a Good Meal)

T. It must've been kind of hard to keep your mind on pitching when you had survival-type stuff to take care of.

M. Yeah, it *was* weird. It was—in that situation, it was weird.

T. Was Triple-A a big jump, baseball-wise? Did it feel like a big jump, or was it just more baseball?

M. It was more baseball. But the jump was, you're *flyin'* now. That was the only jump. And you're playin'—you started playin' with, like, say you got one more .300 hitter. Y'know? Everyone's on the—everyone's on equal stuff, y'know? They might pull off a little bit better double play, than just a double play, you know what I mean?

T. A little better infield?

M. Yeah, a little tighter one. Y'know? *That's* what it all falls to, somethin' like that. But, y'know, the *jump* that you're talkin' about—the only jump is just the jump *flyin',* now. Dressin' up, stayin' at better hotels, gettin' more meal money. Things like that. You get better pay. *That's* the jump.

T. What's the meal money in Triple-A?

M. Ten dollars a day. It might be eleven dollars a day, now.

T. So that makes it a better class of place you can go into now.

M. Yeah!

T. 'Cause what're you eating on the road when—say when you're in Montgomery, what're you getting a day for meals?

M. Five bucks.

T. What about before that?

M. Before that, when I was in A ball, you got three fifty.

T. Didn't go very far, right?

M. No. Ten dollars got you a good meal.

T. You get twenty-four fifty now?

M. Yeah. See, that's the jump to the big leagues.

T. They give you that in cash?

M. Yeah.

T. Every day?

M. Yeah, every day when you're on the road. Just when

you're on the road, though. That's—they're payin' you, to either eat or keep the money. Y'know?

In Triple-A, the Double Play Takes a Lot off Your Mind

T.   A couple of days before you went up to Evansville, Jim Campbell came down to Montgomery and saw you and Bob Sykes and Frank MacCormack pitch.

M.   Yeah, he was down there when we played.

T.   He came down on the second of August, and on the ninth you were called up to Evansville.

M.   Yeah. Maybe they timed it that way. But I wasn't lookin' at it that way. I was just lookin' at bein' brought up. But then when I was playin' with these guys in Evansville, they were makin' plays that I never even *saw* in A ball!

T.   Better catching, too?

M.   Yeah, they were blockin' 'em. I was just goin' wild! I mean I could throw my slider now, in the dirt!

T.   So then there *was* a big improvement in the class of ball up there, over Lakeland and Montgomery.

M.   Yeah, it was gettin' so much better. And the players were gettin' even *more* better. Y'know? And like, you were just throwin'. And I was just out there, I threw the ball and just said, Screw it, they're gonna make the plays. Y'know, they're gonna hit it to this guy. Bases loaded, one out, and they're goin' for a double play now. Ain't goin' home—they're goin' for a double play. And you're goin', *Wow! They* get you out of it. Just like that! I've had, many times, bases loaded, with one out, and —*voom,* just get out of it. You know how much that takes off your mind, when you go back in the dugout? You're startin' all over again, when you go back out.

The Quarterback Can Only Throw the Ball (You Need Those Guys Behind You to Make You Look Good)

T.   Well, knowing that the other guys can make the plays behind you has got to give you confidence. It's like in that football game we were watching on TV today—you were talking about that touchdown pass Chandler caught on an overthrown ball. You said he was protecting the quarterback, Chandler was making the

Buffalo quarterback look good. Is that how you feel about the way your teammates support you when you're pitching, that they make you look good, the way Chandler made that quarterback look good?

M. Yeah! Yeah, they threw the ball, right? And that guy made up for the quarterback's mistake of overthrowin' it. But then it made *that* guy look good. But it also made the quarterback look good. And yet they say, Look, the quarterback did it. Forget the quarterback! That quarterback can't do shit but throw the ball. Right?

T. It's like, where would you be without your infielders, for instance.

M. That's right!

T. When you're a pitcher, how you do is so much a matter of context—like on a rookie-league infield, or if you were playing with high school infielders, you're a different pitcher.

M. That's like I told Lance Parrish when we were with him yesterday, remember? Lance says, What's the difference? Remember?

T. Oh, yeah—he meant the difference between the minors and the majors?

M. Yeah. And I said, Lookit, Lance, remember what we had in A ball? I said, Look what I have now, y'know? And I was just tellin' Lance what it was like. A ball was A ball, right? We had a winning team in Bristol. Yet you took that winning team in Bristol, put 'em in A ball, and we were horseshit.

T. The competition was just getting a little steeper.

M. Yeah, we were horseshit. The guys that they had there, that they thought—y'know, the same guys. We came into A ball, and *voom, voom, voom*—you move up. Just like Lance is learnin' now. He moves up. He's seein' better ball. You *are*—you're just seein' better baseball. And if you're not the better baseball player, you're just gonna be gone. You're gonna stay down there.

The Guys at Evansville Never Got on Me
(They're Going Crazy Their *Own* Way, They Have Wives)

T. So you just sailed right in and did your thing in Triple-A?

M. Yeah! And like, those guys never really—y'know, they

didn't get *on* me, for what I did. They just said, Keep on doin' it, man, you're doin' good. I mean they knew you're goin' a little crazy? Yeah, fine. Big deal. Everyone is! Y'know, in their own way. But like these guys, they didn't care what I did. And like, when we'd go on the road trips, man, that's—I mean, here you are gettin' moved up, and you'd see an older ballplayer, you're seein' guys twenty-seven years old. And they're fooling around just as much as you are. And that's why you're havin' such a good time, y'know? Because, y'know, they're gettin' away from their wives, and like—this is what we used for a thing. It's like, ballplayers are all smiles—like, in the minor leagues? They're all smiles, when they leave their wives. Right? They come back, they're just—*back to the old babe again.* It was just—y'know, that was a saying that the guys who were *not* married had, right? 'Cause it was weird, you'd see all the wives goin' nuts, man. You'd be sittin' on the bus yellin' at a guy, *C'mon.* Y'know—Okay, tell your wife to buzz off! C'mon, get on the bus, we gotta get outa here! Y'know? And all of the wives are goin', Aw. . . . It's neat, 'cause the wives are neat, too. They're all there at the end of the game. They always say Hi to you.

T.   A lot of the guys were married in Triple-A?

M.   Yeah, oh, yeah. I found that out, a lot of 'em. Just like in the majors now, a lot of 'em are married. Y'know? And it's weird. 'Cause you just don't hang around—you just can't hang around with 'em now. You *can*—you can up to a point. But like I'd say, Hey, let's go to a bar. You know you're just gonna go to that bar. If you're married, you're not gonna—like some snizz comes up to you, like a *lady.* You just—y'know, it's weird.

We Were All One Family
(Living in Evansville with Four Other Pitchers)

T.   When you guys were at Evansville—you and Frank MacCormack and Mark Lemongello . . .

M.   Yeah, Lem, and Eddie Glynn—

T.   It looked at the time like all of you had an equal shot. I mean, to make it with Detroit. Because they needed pitching, and *all* you guys were doing well at Evansville.

M.   We were all together. We were all one family, like.

Y'know what I mean? That's just what it was.

T.   When you guys got to Evansville, it turned the team around. That's what Fred Hatfield said, These new pitchers picked us up and turned us around.

M.   That's just what it was, it was just a family, man. Right then and there. We were all just a family.

T.   So you and those other pitchers hung around together in Evansville?

M.   Yeah, we hung out. Me, Eddie, Lem, and Mac hung out. We all—and Dennis DeBarr. But Dennis didn't hang out. Dennis would just go home and sit in the apartment, y'know? He didn't go out, like when we went out at night. We could all just go out and jump in the car and take off.

T.   So you guys had an apartment together?

M.   Yeah, we all lived together, too. Y'know, there was five of us livin' together.

T.   Some of the other guys had the apartment before you came up?

M.   Yeah, they had it. Lemongello and—Lem and Dennis DeBarr had the place when we got up there. But it was weird. We *did* all hang around in a family, like. And that's why each of us kept us goin'. Y'know? And that's why I'll never forget it. Like, and then *I* made it. And now Frank comin' up—I'm gonna *help* him. 'Cause I knew, when I came up—I knew what it was like. But it could have been the reverse. Say, Frank came up, and then I came up, right? Would he have treated me the same way? Hopefully, he would've—because of what I went through in the beginning, to find out what it was like. That's like in the beginning, my first day in the major leagues, some veterans took me out to eat. And they said, Hey, remember, we've been around, right? And now we're helpin' you. When someone else comes up, help them. Because you *do* need it! You've gotta get your feet, *voom,* to the ground up here. Just because of what's goin' on. I mean you're gonna see things thrown around—and you're goin', I can't *believe* this is happenin' right here. Y'know? You just get that. Where, now that you know what's gonna happen, you just let it blow. And it just blows by, like somethin' normal in *your* day would just blow by. Y'know?

T. Take it as it comes?

M. Not take it easy as it comes, but I mean things that you'd be fascinated with before ain't fascinating any more. Because you know what's gonna happen. It just blows by. You see, instead of say a dollar, now ten dollars gets blown by. But it's equal to a dollar. It's, y'know—that's the only way to classify it as.

T. Inflation!

M. Yeah. That's just the only way. Y'know? One minute you're livin' down *here,* the next minute you're livin' up *here.* That's all. It just blows by.

You Got to Fly in Evansville, Which Was a Whole New Atmosphere

T. But back in Evansville you still had a lot of time to kill.

M. Yeah, not a lot—well, we went around. And just goofed around together. Just, during the day there you didn't do nothin'. And up here, during the day you might have this to do and that to do. But still, like I didn't have a *car* in Evansville. So Lem had the car, and Mac had the car. And Eddie. So, y'know, we just all goofed around.

T. Was that a better deal than Double-A? Bigger towns?

M. Evansville? Well, you got paid more meal money, right? But yet you still got the same hassles. But you got to *fly* in Evansville. And you took the bus in Double-A. Double-A, you take an eight-hour bus ride. Now you take a—say, an hour plane ride, and then a two-hour bus ride. Instead of takin' the whole bus ride. Y'know, you get to fly.

T. The guys we were out with yesterday, Lance Parrish and Dave Rozema, they haven't even been to—they were in Montgomery last year, so they haven't been to Evansville yet?

M. No! They're still on the bus rides, y'know? They still haven't hit—they still haven't even hit half the things they're gonna hit.

T. They might both be at Evansville this year?

M. Evansville! All right, so they go to Evansville. Now they're gonna be *flyin'.* Y'see? You get more of a taste. You do. You get more of a taste.

T. So you get used to it bit by bit?

M. Yeah. You get more of a taste.

T. It's like learning how to swim? A little bit at a time?

M. Yeah. That's just what it is. And like—see, now, they've taken eight-hour bus rides. Ten-hour bus rides—it might've broken down here and taken thirteen hours. And here's, say, Rosey. I mean, not as much for Lance. But say Rosey's gotta pitch tomorrow. He's on an eight-hour bus ride, all of a sudden he gets *delayed.* He wants to get back to his place and just sleep, y'know? 'Cause you just—in a bus, you can sleep just so much, y'know? And if you're exhausted, you're gonna definitely conk out. But he's probably thinkin' about tomorrow's game. Somethin' like that. That's just—in my situation.

T. But for Lance—

M. But the guy who plays every day, that isn't in his mind. He's just goin' back 'cause he knows he's gonna play tomorrow, he knows he's gonna play the next day, he knows he's gonna play the *next* day. That's just a different atmosphere. Like compared —to like those, y'know, plane to bus. It's too hard. . . . But *now,* in Triple-A, you just fly in a plane, y'know? You fly in a plane instead of drive in a bus. That's the deal now. You're walkin' through an airport. You're walkin' through as a team, though, y'know? And like they're lettin' you on. They're lettin' you on the airplane as a *team.* Y'know, like—they say, All right, no one can board, but the Evansville Triplets can board now. So we board, and then the other people board. Y'know? That's what it is. You just—instead of havin' to go through the hassle of bumpin' into people and that, you all board as a team. And, *voom,* sit down. And then, *voom,* the rest of the guys board. That's what's good about it, y'know? That's—the whole trip about that was, when I was hittin' *that.*

T. So flying at Evansville looked pretty good from the perspective of the bus rides at Montgomery—but could you go down there again? What if they sent you to Evansville tomorrow?

M. I could! I could go down there tomorrow! Just like that! If I did bad and they said, Go down and learn, y'know? That's what's gonna happen. And I won't quit. I'll go back down there. I'll go down and play in Evansville a year. But I won't quit. I just won't quit until they say, Hey, you're done. That's when I'll quit. Just because I don't know anything better.

9 Throw a Guy into a Winning Atmosphere, He's Gonna Win

You're Gettin' Your Teachers, but It's What You Want to Absorb in Your Mind

T. So it sounds like what's happening, instead of them teaching you stuff, as you come up through the leagues—it sounds like the real education of the minors is you getting used to stuff. Getting used to the different levels of ball as you move up.

M. You get—you learn! You're *learnin'*.

T. And so the guys you're playing with are pulling you up, more than anybody teaching you?

M. Yeah.

T. I mean, you're learning from each other, too, so that it's more of a growth and experience thing than a school situation?

M. No, I wouldn't classify it as—you're gettin' the teachers. You're gettin' your teachers, but it's what you want to absorb in your mind.

Fred Gladding and the Mind of a Coach

T. Fred Gladding, the Tiger pitching coach—he was your pitching coach at Evansville too?

M. Yeah, he was in Evansville. He didn't—Hey! When I came up to Evansville, he just told me, Hey, I can't teach you anything. He goes, You *know* it, right? It's just, I'm gonna *tell* you, once you're goin' wrong. Y'know, he's like—it's like, instead of goin' to a psychiatrist, you go to *him*. Why waste your money on a psychiatrist? You just go to this guy—and he'll say, Hey, what's happenin'? 'Cause he's been through the whole scene himself. So he knows, right?

T. So he—so they made you a starter right away, once you got to Evansville?

M. Yeah. So you just hit *that* atmosphere, right?

T.   And then this year, when you moved up to Detroit, so did Gladding.

M. And then, *voom,* you come back to it now. 'Cause this year he said to me, Hey, *I* ain't gonna take any of your glory. You're the one that made it. I'm just standin' beside you. Just sayin', if you need help, you can come talk to me. And that's it. And you go talk to the guy. In Evansville, when I first came up, y'know, he—I was just throwin'. He goes—he just told me right off the bat, he goes, I'm just gonna stand here beside you. You just throw. I said, Fine. He said, You just go out and throw. And you lose a game, and then you talk to him. And it's weird. Like, you're tellin' him how funny you felt during that game. And he'll tell you how—he'll go, Yeah, I could tell how you felt. I could tell where you were goin' wrong, and what was goin' on. And during the game he'll talk to you if you need help and stuff, too. You use this stuff. Y'know, never think that you're better than no one else. Like sayin', Hey—he's your pitching coach. Hey, *I'm* pitchin', you're just the coach. And sayin', Get the hell outa here. You don't *do* that. 'Cause you're gonna need him. You need his help, y'know? I mean, you might get a—you might be ten years, you might have *ten years* in the big leagues, right? And all of a sudden you see this pitching coach that just comes up—and he runs you, and does all this. And you won't give him the courtesy to talk to him? That's horseshit. You're no bigger than him, y'know? But yet, you've had ten years in the big leagues. Maybe he might have had five years. But they just want him to hang around as a coach. So in other words he's got the mind of a coach. Y'know? I just—y'know? How can you classify a coach?

I Don't Have the Mind of a Coach

T.   Could you see yourself as a coach?

M. I couldn't see myself goin' back to high school and coachin', now. Where, I have the ability. Supposedly, I have the ability to go back where I could be a coach in high school. Right? Wouldn't you classify me—

T.   Sure.

M. You would! If a high school came up to me—even a college. Y'know?

T.   You could do that right now.

M.   Yeah! I'd go to a college right now, if they wanted me as a coach. Right? I could literally say, I'm *better* than that guy. Because I've played the game, where that guy hasn't played the game. Right? But yet, I feel that I don't have the ability to do that. Because I don't have the mind to do that. And I don't feel that those guys would listen to me. And if they ain't gonna listen, I don't—y'know, I don't want to coach 'em. That's why I wouldn't go back—to Little League, or high school.

Rome Wasn't Built in a Day, Said Grod

T.   You were saying your pitching coach from the early days at Bristol helped you out a lot—that he said something to you about bouncing back when you'd had a bad game?

M.   Yeah, that's right, John Grodzicki. He told me, Rome wasn't built in a day, and it surely didn't get destroyed in a day. He said, Keep that in mind, while you're goin' through the leagues. And like, I *have* stayed with that subject. I don't know why I stayed with that subject. But I said, That's *right,* y'know? I said, *voom!* You could have it today, right? But then it might take ten more years to get it again, as same as today.

T.   This was down in Florida he told you this, your first week in organized ball?

M.   Yeah! The first—I mean, when I stepped on the mound, and like, I threw horseshit. And I said, Wow, what the fuck's wrong with me? And he goes, Just remember, buddy—before he even knew me, before I even went out and had a beer with the guy. I mean, when you get to know a guy you go out and have a *beer* with him. And, y'know, you *know* him. Before I even had a beer with him he just said, Hey, buddy, look at me, I come through it. He says, Hey, Rome wasn't built in a day. He goes, you don't have it today, you might have it tomorrow. You might have it the next day too, and the day after that. The next day you might not have it again. 'Cause here—you'd be pitchin' *so* good, right? And all of a sudden you'd hit this bad streak. You'd go two games and get —and you'd go, John, what's wrong? Y'know? And he'd go— Fuck, you put your uniform on. That's just what it was—his famous saying, any time I got in trouble, any time I got knocked out. I'd go up to this guy and go, What did I do wrong? And he goes, *You put your uniform on today.* Drop it. And I'd go, Well, I wanna *talk* about it! He goes, Fine, let's talk. He goes, What do *you* think you did wrong? I go, Well, I was throwin' the ball high. He goes, You weren't throwin' the same game. That's it, y'know? But talkin' to him was neat. But he'd just really say, Hey, Rome wasn't built in a day. And *voom,* that was it. And it was neat, because you *got* to it. Y'know, I understood what he meant.

Grod Tells Me to Throw Out My Knuckleball
Because This New Atmosphere of Baseball Is Like War

T.   Did Grodzicki help you with your pitches or your delivery or anything?

M.   Like I had a knuckleball, when I first came in? The first day I saw the guy. First day—he goes, All right, I want all the pitchers over here. I want to see how they pitch. So I throw, and he goes, Let me see all your pitches. And he goes, When you're warmed up, call me over and I'll watch you. And then he walked away. I called him over, I threw my pitches—I was warm enough, I felt good. I was ready to *go.* Y'know, in a game, I was ready to go. Threw my knuckleball. He goes, That's out. I said, Whaddaya mean that's out? It *got* me here! How can you say it's *out?* And he goes, They're gonna kill it. He goes, Take my word for it. It don't *do* nothin'. Back there it did somethin', because those guys don't know how to hit the ball.

T.   How long had you been throwing that knuckleball?

M.   All through—ever since I been *pitchin'!* Y'know?

T.   Did you think it was a good pitch, at the time?

M.   Hell, yeah! And I'm sittin' there, *Whoa.*

T.   He said drop it?

M.   Drop it. To literally *drop* it. He said, Throw a change-up. And then he said—he showed me different ways. I mean, through the years he's showed me different ways to hold the change-up, right? But since then I haven't thrown a knuckleball.

T.   And that happened when you were with Bristol.

M.   Yeah, before Bristol even started. This is when I first got down there.

T.   Your first spring.

M.   First *day* that I ever threw in front of the guy that I was supposed to throw in front of, right? He tells me to drop a pitch. And now, you know how much your—you know how much your pride goes down? Drop a *what*? That was like, Quit the game.

T.   That was losing part of your strength, right?

M.   That was like, Quit the game, to me!

T.   You threw it a lot?

M.   *Whoa!* Three and two, I'd throw it!

T.   No kidding?

M.   I mean, I would throw it for a pitch where I wanted to strike a guy out, or I thought I had him fooled because he didn't know what was comin'—he thought my fastball was comin'. It was like a change-up to me. But Grod said, *Here,* it don't move enough. Down *there,* it moved enough. He goes, You're playin' a different atmosphere of baseball now. You're playin' a more— it's like war. Y'know?

Grod Fascinates Me in Pitching

M.   And like, the only reason he ended up bein' the way he is now is because war hit him. Like he had—he made his peak, right? He was playin' professional—and all of a sudden war took him away. He went away, he was a paratrooper, right? And then —he came back to baseball, but it was never the same him, y'know? So it was like war. That's why I—in his mind, the way he talked about it, y'know—he was a paratrooper, he hurt his leg jumpin' out of a plane, bein' in the entire World War. . . .

T.   The Second World War?

M.   I don't know what war it was, but he just jumped out and hurt his leg and he was never the same pitcher, man. But right now he could throw pitches to major league guys that would get them out. But yet, they could key on his pitches. But yet, you get him —he fascinates me. Oh, he fascinates me in pitchin'. And like, guys like—batters in the minor leagues? They'll say, C'mon, Grod, throw that change-up. *Throw* that to us. Like he'll throw it—and those guys'll look *so* sick that it's ungodly! You'd say, This guy can still pitch. I mean, you gotta meet—

T.   He's still coaching in the minors for Detroit?

M.   Yeah. He won't take a big-league job. I said, Grod, how come you're not up in the big leagues?

T.   Where's he now, Montgomery?

M.   No, he travels. He just travels in A ball, Double-A, and Triple-A. Hey, you go on down to the minors—they all know Grod. I mean this guy—he's a pitchin' coach. And we just got this new guy, Fred Martin. I don't know, I don't really—I know it's Martin, but I really don't know him. But he was good, education-wise. Him and Grod I would say are the same kind of guy. But yet I didn't see *him* that much. But I saw Grod to where, y'know, I *know* Grod. Y'know? And it's like, you'd call him, by now you'd go—he'd be kind of your idol, but just because he was straight to you, man. I mean, if you told—if you even mouthed off to him, he'd just say, Do it your own way. He'd say, You don't want my help, then forget it. Y'know? I won't give you my advice. But he goes, I'm givin' it to you straight.

T.   So then, other than the knuckleball, they never changed you around too much as a pitcher? From the beginning, in other words.

M.   No! The only thing he said—Drop the knuckler.

T.   Other than that one pitch, did you work the same way when you first came in? Did you work fast, and dig in front of the mound, and all that stuff?

M.   Yeah! And he said, Do it! Y'know? But he just said, Your knuckleball isn't gonna make it. He literally told me, right from the first go. He said, Your knuckleball ain't gonna do it. And he said, If you don't want to drop it, don't drop it. Take it your own way. So I just said, All right and threw it out. I literally just said, All right—I mean, back then, my father, everyone would always say, Hey, you don't listen, you don't do this, you don't do that. Right? So I literally said, All right—I'm gonna *listen* to this man. I *did.* I listened to him. And it got me here. Y'know? I don't know why. I said, It got me here.

T.   Have you talked to him since your big year in the majors?

M.   When I made it, he came up to me. Like he just, y'know —you gotta meet the man. You just gotta *meet* the guy, to really know what he is. Y'know? You just gotta meet him. And like, he just smiled. And he said, Remember, I didn't do it for you. You did it yourself. And it's just, I don't know—maybe it's just 'cause he was around. But it's all the other coaches, too.

Les Moss Charged You for Everything, But I Had the Value for It the Minute I Stepped Out on the Field

T. So, Grodzicki helped you. And from what you've said, so did most of your managers along the way.

M. It's just like Joe Lewis, when he straightened me out that day I got fined. And the other days, y'know? You just said—*voom,* he just cut it right then and there, and just *told* you. Just like Les Moss. You come up—I got to Double-A. This Les Moss guy, man. He tells you to get a haircut right off the bat, right? Tells me to do this, tells me to do that. I mean, the way he ran his team, he ran it to—like, I got there? Like, if you weren't on the field, right? Like if you had to have a pitcher hittin' to the left side of the infield, and you had a pitcher hittin' to the right side of the infield? All through battin' practice, right? And then infield practice— y'know, you had to have guys out, pitchers out to hit to the outfielders, right? The startin' pitchers, right? And relief pitchers, hittin' to the other ones, right? But all the pitchers had to be doin' somethin'. And at one time and spot, if he had to designate—say, y'know, there had to be three hittin' *this,* and there had to be two hittin' *that.* But if a guy had to take a shit, he told you, and you went and filled his job. Just because, if you didn't go and fill his job, and there wasn't someone—if Les came out, and he checked all the positions, and if there wasn't someone at that position, he'd charge you ten dollars. But not just the person that was missin', the whole pitchin' staff! Just because that was their job. They had to go and do it. So we got charged ten dollars for it. So you ain't gonna back up for no guy? For ten dollars? If a guy has to—I can see it, he has to go. But if he just, y'know, has to rap to someone and says, Take my job—you go, Screw you, buddy, you get out there and do it. Y'know? I mean, we *did.* That's what it got down to. You *did* say it. Like if a guy was rappin' to someone, sayin', Here, take my job—you said, Hey, you, get out and do it. It's your job. I already did my job, right? It's time to work and it's time to work, y'know? It was ten dollars. I mean, he caught the whole pitchin' staff—it was ninety dollars, right there. One guy was missin'. It was ninety bucks. So you gotta back up.

T. What do you suppose Les did with all that cash?

M. Oh! But then, he made it fun, too. Because every two weeks you get paid, right? You get paid at the end of two weeks. He took the pool that he had for that two weeks and split it up into numbers. And then, you drew a number. And said, Hey, this is the guy that wins. So some guy on the team won the money *back,* right? You split it three ways. Y'know, three guys won. It might go fifty, forty-five, thirty. It might go like that. But you all won it—y'know, you had a chance to win your money back. And it was just—that was neat, y'know? Because a ballplayer would come in. Like, one of the ballplayers, he got picked off from first base, it cost him five bucks. 'Cause he wasn't heads up. Y'know, he just got caught *dazin'.* I mean, if it was heads up he would— I mean he had it, literally, where he *knew* if you were dazin'. Y'know? I mean if you got caught and you weren't dazin', it was fine. It was neat, y'know? It was just—if they had a play on, or if you were just tryin' to get more.

T. You mean, if you were hustling, he didn't fine you?

M. Yeah. And then you got—missin' a signal and not buntin' a guy over. He'd charge you five dollars for it. I mean—but yet, he gave me a chance. He said, uh—it might have been 2 and 1, and he said, All right, now you gotta bunt the guy. Right? And you don't bunt the guy over. So now it's 2 and 2. He gave you a chance. Now—but all you had to do was get that guy to second base. If that guy stole second base for you, he saved five dollars for you, right? He *saved* five dollars for you. But yet if you got the guy—hit him over, or sacrificed him, or flew out, and he got to second base—you saved your five. But if that guy didn't get to second base, it cost you five bucks. He was playin' a smart game, though. He had a winning season, right? Everyone was happy, y'know? If you wanted to lose money out of your pocket, you're gonna lose it. But if you thought money was comin' right out of your pocket—then you had the value for it.

T. You were only there a few weeks in Montgomery?

M. I was there two weeks. But I had the value the minute I stepped on the field. 'Cause everyone came up and told me. They said, You don't do this, you don't do that. They said, Hey, it's gonna cost us all. It don't just cost *you,* it costs *everyone.* When it costs everyone on the team, then everyone's gonna be normal to each other.

Stubby Overmire Treated You like a Man and Took the Pain with the Glory, Even Though There Wasn't Any Glory

T.   Overmire didn't do anything like that?

M.   No. Stubby—Stubby was more of a . . . he was a coach that helped you. I mean, you could go ask him. He'd help you, right? That's what he waited for. He treated you as a man, right? That's the way I classify him—Stubby treated you as a man. Y'know, he's more of a, like—you take a major league coach. That's the way—at the end of, after I went through the whole system, right? And then I looked back, right, when I went to Triple-A? I looked back at Stubby, and I looked back at Les, and I looked back at Hatfield—after the whole, after the end of the year. And you could see the difference. Y'know, Stubby is like a major league coach, y'know, or just a manager. Because if you needed help, he was there. Like when I needed help, I'd go talk to him. And he was there, and he always talked. But yet he treated you like a man. He said, Hey, I'm not gonna make you work if you don't want to work. But if you want to work, I'm willing to, y'know, be there, every time you want to work. Any time I wanted balls hit back to me, *voom!* He was there, or Mike Dwyer was there. But he said, Hey, you're a man now. He said, If you're gonna foul your life up, you're gonna foul it up. I mean, I got no say over it. I don't even know you, right? I'm just sayin', Hey—I gotta manage you. If you want to make me look good, you're gonna make me look good. If you're not, you're not.

T.   And at Lakeland in '75, no one was making Stubby look too good.

M.   Y'know? And that's one thing a manager's gotta take. That's bad, y'know? People say, You gotta fire this guy, this guy's no good of a manager! Whaddaya *mean* he's no good of a manager, man? He's a guy that's gonna take the pain with the glory, y'know? He's sayin', I don't even know *who* the hell these guys are. But yet I'm gonna get into 'em, and get involved into 'em, and talk to 'em. That's the whole thing, you're playin' for him because he's out for just as much as you are out for, y'know? For life. I mean, what the heck. It's just—that's where it gets down to weird things.

Fred Hatfield Was Out to Win

T.   And then at Evansville—what was Fred Hatfield like? I remember him as a player in the fifties—skinny guy, a third baseman.

M.   Hatfield? He was out to win.

T.   When you pitched that game for Evansville to clinch the pennant, he's supposed to have said that if you hadn't won he'd have broken the bottles of champagne over your head. Or that he'd have thrown all the champagne away if you didn't win. That was the game against Omaha, August 27. Fortunately, you won it.

M.   Yeah. I mean that was—he was just gettin' cocky there, at that point, y'know? It was just—I don't know. He maybe—he might have thought more of me than what *I* thought, y'know? He might have said—I didn't know he said that. I really didn't. But like, he would've. He's *sick* enough, he *would've* smashed every one of those bottles, man! That's how I can classify that guy. He would have done it. Just because he would have been so mad if we really messed up, y'know? But if we—he would have kept us still together, you know what I mean? But yet he would've, if he quoted that to someone and they put it in—he would have smashed the bottles. Because he said what he meant, that's one thing about that guy. But like, maybe he knew somethin' that I could do, that I didn't know I could do. Y'know? 'Cause it's like that other game, first inning, guy got a home run off me, man.

T.   You're talking about the championship game against Denver in the American Association play-offs? Final game, you were behind 3–0, pitched seven shutout innings, and won it in what, twelve?

M.   Yeah! I went the rest of the game and they didn't even touch me.

T.   A twelve-inning game, right?

M.   Yeah. They didn't even touch me, man. The guy that hit the home run didn't get another hit the whole game. I just, y'know, *that* was just, that game there—and Gladding said, That's the best game I ever seen you pitch. Since you been up.

Throw a Guy into a Winning Atmosphere, He's Gonna Win

T.   Those games you pitched at Evansville were *all* good games. You had nine starts, including the play-offs, and you only lost two games. And even those were 2–1 and 1–0! Jim Campbell and all those guys must have been getting an idea or two.

M.   Yeah. Throw him on a winning team, he can win. But you throw *any* guy on a winning team, he's gonna win. I don't give a damn what you say. Look, you could—I could take *you*. And you could be 0 and 10. And throw you on a winning team—you're gonna win. Just because you're playing with a winning team, and you're gonna have it in your mind, a winning team, y'know? You're just gonna have to—it's just instinct, I take it as. I mean, lookit—at Lakeland, a five and ten record! I got a losin' atmosphere now. I mean, some kinda losin' atmosphere. And all of a sudden you hit a winning atmosphere? You know how much that brings you up? It brings you right to a winning atmosphere. And then you take their losses—their little losses that they're gonna have. You're gonna have one two-game streak of losin'. But then you're gonna have a four- or five-game winning streak. So you're just takin' all that. It's just percentages.

T.   You're talking about confidence, really.

M.   That's right! That's what it is, right there. I mean, you hit a losing, you hit a winning, and you hit a winning, and you hit a winning—that's it, you're gonna *stay* a winner. Like I say, I played on a winning team in Bristol. I got a bat for it, for the championship. Right? In Triple-A, I got a *ring* for it. For the championship. What do I got for the major leagues? I didn't win no pennant. I didn't win nothin'. But yet I got Rookie of the Year.

T.   You got an All-Star ring.

M.   All-Star ring. And I got most complete games. Best ERA. But yet, I don't have a World Series. So what the heck am I? Y'know? If you get down to that. But yet, I did have a winning season. I did have a good year. Where, y'know, I shouldn't have had a year.

T.   When you say that when you went up to Montgomery and Evansville, and you were around a winning atmosphere—do you think that difference explains the fact that when you moved up your control got better? I don't know if you know it, but you walked a lot less guys in Double-A and Triple-A than you did at Lakeland and Bristol.

M. I didn't notice that.

T. You struck out less guys, and walked less guys, and threw fewer pitches. Right around that time—starting then, July, August of '75, when you hit Double-A ball, that was where the change was.

M. Yeah, but I don't look at that.

T. But maybe that change happened because of confidence, if confidence is what makes you throw strikes. I mean makes you go right at 'em, and not walk people, because now you've got confidence that the guys behind you can make the plays.

M. Yeah! They're gonna hit it to guys, and they start makin' the double plays, and—

T. Right, that's what I'm trying to say. Letting them do it for you.

M. And, y'know, makin' those plays that they made . . .

T. That's like your idea for the title of this book—"How They Made Me." I mean, your feeling of how much you've depended on the people around you, and the people behind you, all along.

M. That's right. Y'know, they did it.

Vern Ruhle Said, There's Eight Other Guys Out There

T. Because if you try to strike everybody out—

M. Vern Ruhle told me that! See, he—like, when I was in Bristol, I was a strikeout pitcher.

T. Yeah, you struck out and walked more guys.

M. I was a strikeout pitcher. And that's what they thought I was gonna be, is a strikeout pitcher, I think. Then I went to winter ball that year, right? After Bristol? And I'm down there throwin' hard! And gettin' zip. I ain't *strikin'* no one out! Y'know, they're groundin' out. *I ain't strikin' 'em out!* And I'm just gettin' mad in the showers. And—I didn't even *know* Vern Ruhle, y'know?

T. Right, he'd been up with the Tigers already. They sent him down to pitch winter ball? You met him down in Florida?

M. Yeah! And Vern goes, Mark, you ain't a strikeout pitcher. He goes, Realize that. He goes, You attack the batters good, but you just ain't a strikeout pitcher. There *are* strikeout pitchers. But yet, you're a pitcher that's a ground-out pitcher. Next game you pitch at, just take it at that. Then you'll get your strikeouts. He said, Think about gettin' the ground-outs before you think about gettin' the strikeouts. Because I had my mind on —if I don't strike the guy out, I'm hurtin', right? That's what I had my mind on. Then he changed it. He said, Just say, Hey, get the fella *out.* And that's it. If you strike him out, *voom,* that's a strikeout. It's neat. But if you get him out, he's out. He goes, Remember, there's eight other guys out there, bustin' *their* ass, too. Not just you. I said, *Whoa,* that's true, too.

T.   So you really listened to that.

M.   Yeah. I mean, after I—you find out! I was wonderin'— I'm not strikin' anyone out.

T.   You started striking out less guys, but you also stopped giving up so many walks. In Bristol and Lakeland, you were walking one guy about every two and a half innings. And at Montgomery and at Evansville, and at Detroit, you're walking one guy about every *five* innings.

M.   Well, see, now you're gettin' down to stats. I don't get down to that. I really don't notice that. The only time—

T.   But what those stats mean is that guys are hittin' the ball.

M.   Yeah. But the only time that a walk is costly to you is when you already got a guy on base. Whereas if you walk him on base, and then it *burns* you—I mean you could walk two guys on, right? And you get outa that inning with no runs, right? Those two walks don't hurt you at all!

T.   Except in one way—that if you let guys hit the ball, you're throwin' less pitches and you've got more strength, start to finish. Stamina, endurance, whatever you call the thing, that keeps you strong at the end, sometimes even stronger than you started.

M.   Yeah, you could look at it that way, too.

T.   Look at all those games you won in the late innings because you were still strong, because you weren't throwin' very many pitches. Because you weren't walkin' around between pitches. You were just goin' right at 'em.

M. Not walkin' around between pitches. You just throw the pitch. You could walk around ten minutes, throw one pitch for a strike, and the guy hits it, *voom*—that's only one pitch. Where you could walk around and throw two pitches, or three pitches. But if you just walk around and throw *one* pitch, then you're all set. You can walk around, hey! Everyone does it their own style. That's the whole thing. Everyone has their own style.

T. But whatever your style is, the fewer pitches you have to throw, the better.

M. Yeah, that's right.

My First Year in Winter Ball I Bust My Ass, My
Second Year I Eat Sno-Cones and Learn to Throw a Change-up

T. So that Vern Ruhle scene happened in winter ball in '74 —and then you went back down to winter ball again the next year, after Evansville?

M. Yeah.

T. You'd been really hot at the end of the year at Evansville. Did you stay that hot down in Florida in the Instructional League?

M. No! Hell, no, I went down there—I went down there with a different *head* that year. Like, my first year, comin' out of Bristol, when I went to winter ball it was a big thing for me. I thought it was still all the same game, man. You go there and bust ass, y'know? You're out to *win.* So my second year—I'm goin' to the Instructional League this year, I said, *Whoa,* wait a minute! I said, I ain't goin' down—I said, I've proved myself.

T. Did you get any time to go home between Evansville and Florida?

M. Yeah, five days.

T. Where'd you finish up the season, at Evansville or on the road?

M. I think I finished up at Evansville. I'm not sure. I'm really not sure. We mighta finished up in—

T. Virginia? Evansville won that Junior World Series thing, maybe the game was back in Virginia.

M. Yeah, I think we finished up in Virginia. I'm almost positive.

T.   At Tidewater.

M.   Yeah. I think we were. 'Cause we came back early, and I got super-drunk, y'know? No—no, we finished up in Evansville! Yeah, 'cause we had a big smash there, I remember that. All champagne and like that, throwin' it around. But—after that I went to Florida, my second time. When I got to Florida, I said, All right. I said, I ain't goin' down here to bust ass. Grod said, You're only gonna pitch five innings a week at the most—no more than that. He goes, Just go out there and play. I said, Okay. I went out there, I wasn't the same person. I wasn't the same pitcher. I went out there and took my change-up. I said, I ain't out here to win, I'll throw it five times in a row. I said, I'm down here for a vacation, but I'm gonna learn how to throw a change-up. That's just what I said to myself before I went down, y'know? I said, that's what I want. I said, It ain't gonna be like the other year, where I worked out. Oh, sure, I'll run every day, like I'm supposed to. Stay in shape. But I want to learn how to throw my change-up. And I ain't—y'know, instead of sittin' on the bench yellin' and screamin', I was, like, doin' something' else. I mighta been workin' on a change-up—or eatin' a Sno-Cone. Or down in right field shaggin' balls. It wasn't the same. I wasn't as hyped to play it, and stuff. I came to the park—but still, I got just as much out of it my second year as I did my first year. Because I came out of it with a change-up. Where my first year, I went down there to work on a change-up, too—and I didn't come out with one. Because I spent more time playin' the *game* than sittin' on the sidelines workin' with it and goofin' with it. 'Cause I was—when I was in there I was just throwin', y'know, fastball, slider, and once in a while a change-up. I wasn't *throwin'* like three change-ups to a batter, or say ten a game. I was still only throwin' one a game, if I threw any. So that's why I say the second time was just as educational as the first time. I threw more change-ups. I said, Okay, they beat me. It wasn't like I was gonna lose my job.

T.   The change-up's the pitch Grod wanted you to develop to replace your knuckler, right?

M.   Yeah!

T.   Did you throw that change-up a lot more this year than you did in '75?

M. Oh, yeah. Yeah, I did.

T. So that work you did down there paid off.

M. Yeah. Well, see, it wasn't like I was gonna lose my job if I just worked on it. I said, Wow, I played at Evansville. I said, Whatever I do in winter ball, they ain't gonna—they're just not gonna say, Hey, release him. Y'know? But yet, in Bristol—the year before, when I'd just come out of Bristol, I said, Yeah, I've played only two months, now it's gonna be four months. That year I said, I've got to establish myself.

T. You felt like you had to *show* something, after '74?

M. Yeah! Y'know? So *now,* I already showed something, in Evansville and Montgomery.

My Letter Gives Hoot Evers Second Thoughts

T. So you had two and a half months off after winter ball, and then it's time to go south again for '76 spring training. You've had two whole seasons in the Detroit organization now, and you're still not on the major league roster, but you're a hot prospect.

M. All right. So then, spring training, when I had to come back, I like wrote to Hoot Evers. I just said, Hey, I need a car for this spring training. This spring training here. 'Cause I went through it all now, I went through Triple-A and all that stuff. And I write to Hoot. And I say, Hoot, I'd like to be able to *drive* down to Florida. And he goes, Hey, read your contract. What does it say? You split with the team, right? I said, Yeah, I know that. But other guys drive down. And he goes, Yeah, but they're from California, they're from here, they're married and all that. And I said, Yeah, okay, that's neat. I said, Hey—I wrote it right in quotes. I said, Just think, someday you're gonna be minus one ballplayer. And it'll be *me.* And I put it back in quotes—*Because of faggots.* Y'know? And I just rested my case right then and there. I sent him that letter. And after that, he said, No. Y'know, when I was in winter ball? And then right before—I was just, I'd got my—I was goin' down with my buddy, right? I was gonna— he drives down, right? And I'd pay for all the gas down. And a couple buddies go—it gives 'em free gas down, and it's neat, y'know? Then they can spend it all down there, right? And like they'd drive me down. They drove me down before, right?

T.   A buddy of yours from back home in Massachusetts?

M.   Right. And so he was gonna do it again this year. And then the last week, when we were gettin' ready to go, Hoot called me up and said, You can drive your car down. I said, *Whoa!*

T.   Maybe he'd read your letter over again, eh?

M.   Yeah. I mean, I—it was just, I just felt *good.* Maybe he gave me a second thought. But I just got in my car, and I said— oh, I was happy as a pig in shit. I get to have my car down there now. I don't have to—y'know, I have to be in bed by eleven thirty, right? So I had to leave the bar at ten thirty, to make sure I got home. Because Zimmerman's Bar was at least a half hour away, now. I mean, thumbin', it was even longer, because people didn't even pick you up, there, a lot of times. This was *late* at night, that they'd pick you up. And, then—now, I can just quit at eleven and *zoom* in.

T.   So this year's spring training, you didn't have the problems you had at Lakeland the year before.

M.   Yeah, I could quit at eleven and zoom in for eleven thirty. No hassles, no nothin'! And just go to bed. Where, before —I mean, they lock the *doors* on you, man! And you just—

T.   Who locked 'em?

M.   *They* did.

Playing Cops and Robbers in Tigertown with Hoot

T.   You mean they locked you in at Tigertown, the minor league thing down at Lakeland? It's a dormitory thing?

M.   Yeah! A dormitory where you have to be in at eleven thirty or they write your name in, right?

T.   Meanwhile the big-league guys are livin' in apartments and stuff?

M.   Yeah. Oh, yeah, they go up—they're big league, y'know? They're first class. I mean, we looked at those guys. And say, Wow, eleven thirty, here they are—get to stay out. . . . *You* get fines, if you get caught later. I mean, if you asked, they didn't mind. They gave you permission if you asked. But if you didn't ask—but you might *ask* now, and that night might not be that good. So you'd come home early, right? 'Cause it's no good. And then you get a night where—you got a snizz with you now, a lady, right? And all of a sudden, *voom!* You gotta—Hey, see you later, I gotta be home at eleven thirty! Wow! Whaddaya *mean,* eleven thirty? And here I am. And this guy's twenty-five. I'm roomin' with this guy Ike Brookens, right?

T.   A relief pitcher—he'd been at Evansville?

M.   Yeah. He's twenty-five, twenty-six years old. They go, *You* gotta be in at eleven thirty! He's *married,* got a *kid.* Him and I used to laugh our heads off. I go, Ike, I can't believe it. I can see 'em doin' it to me, but *you,* I—

T.   His wife's back home?

M.   Yeah, his wife's back home. But he's down here, and him and I are roomin' together. And it was neat, man. And like I broke curfew for my first time, this year. I just stayed out—I was feelin' good. I came in through my window. The *windows* are even bolted down, man. They got screws—

T.   What floor were you on?

M.   First floor! They got me on the first floor. *That* was a mistake, y'know? Third floor, there was no way you could get up there. Unless you had a—you knew how to rope the window, or tie something to it. But they had screws, right in the aluminum, so you *could not* lift the windows open.

T.   Aluminum sash windows?

M.   Yeah. You push 'em down. But they screwed 'em in. And like, if you got caught with the screws out, you got screwed. Right? But, like, I knew I was gonna be stayin' out that night. So I said, Hell. I unscrewed the screw. And I closed it, and then put the screw back in. I bent it down, so it looked normal.

T.   What would they do if they caught you?

M.   They'd fine you.

They Said, You've Got to Have a Suit.
I Said, What Am I Going to Buy It With, My Looks?

M.   Then they get on you for your dress. Y'know?

T.   What, this year, in the spring?

M.   Just, y'know, in the minors—I'd go to the ballpark like *this:* cut-offs, a T-shirt, right? In Detroit I can't go there like this. They just say, No way.

T. You had to look like a big leaguer now.

M. Y'know? But still, I could *see* that. I could see goin' to work like that, puttin' on a long pair of pants. But you could wear a *T-shirt* to Detroit, y'know? This is funny. I could wear this T-shirt right here to the ballpark. I just couldn't wear cut-offs, I had to wear long pants. I mean, what's the difference? If I've got a T-shirt on, man? But it had to have a *print* on it. The T-shirt couldn't be a plain one—it had to have a print on it.

T. Some clubs—like the Reds and some of these clubs, have incredible rules.

M. Yeah, dress code.

T. Ties, and all that kind of stuff.

M. Yeah. I couldn't see wearin' a tie. Well, look at it this way. I didn't have any suits. They said I'm goin' north with 'em, right? And they said, You gotta have a *suit*. All right. And so Jim Campbell goes, All right. He goes, All right, now you go down to this clothes store here and tell 'em who you are. And tell 'em I sent you there. And, y'know, they'll give you a good rate on clothes. I walked in there—and I walked out the minute I walked in. I mean I just looked at clothes—I said, There's nothin' in here that I want. Pick up a suit coat—a hundred and something dollars. I said, Forget this! Hey, what am I gonna buy it with—my looks? And then—I said, What's the cheapest you got? The guy shows me this outfit for seventy-five dollars. I said, Oh, God *damn!* I just walked out—I said I'd come back. And then Campbell saw me cuttin' through the parking lot. And he calls me up. He goes, Hey, did you go there? I said, Yeah, I went there. I said, I came back empty-handed. Because I ain't gonna buy anything outa that store, it's too expensive for me. I said, You gotta be kiddin' me —me blowin' that money there! I said, I can go out and buy a hundred pairs of dungarees and get more satisfaction out of doin' *that.*

T. For what a couple of classy leisure suits would set you back.

M. Yeah! 'Cause when I went in there, I went in there with my T-shirt on. I mean I was a super-grub when I went in there. These guys were laughin' at me. And then Campbell took me back. And he said, Let this be a little *bonus* to you.

T. Not bad. But I mean—fair enough. You made the team, so the general manager of the Tigers took you in and bought you a new suit. That's fair enough, if they want to have that rule.

M. I mean, that was a good perk. Here, I was gonna buy a K-Mart special for twenty dollars and throw it on my back. And I'll put a tie on, I mean, and I'm all set. But then, you know what it is—like, it *was* a pay-back. See, I didn't get a bonus in the beginning, right? So now, *here's* the bonus. He did that, y'know? He knows—he knows just what I got. He goes, We know you weren't a high draft choice and all that. All right, now *here's* your bonus because you're doin' so well. And that's what you need, I mean you can strive for something like that, because they give you a bonus. Y'know? I mean, I got this bonus here. And I got *this*. It was just neat. And now I look back at all the bonuses I been gettin'. Even though I wasn't, like, a hundred-thousand-dollar kid that signed, y'know? But he's not up there yet, and I'm up here now, and I'm makin' my bonus.

Mark Fidrych in his office, 1976. "I'm out there workin', *now."*

Jim Campbell   Ralph Houk   Walter A. (Hoot) Evers

Fred Gladding   John Grodzicki   Stubby Overmire

Joe Lewis   Les Moss   Fred Hatfield

Dave Rozema

Lance Parrish

Bruce Kimm

Frank MacCormack

Tom Veryzer

Alex Johnson

Vern Ruhle

Ron LeFlore

Joe Coleman

Rusty Staub

Dave Roberts

Mickey Stanley

CRAIG PORTER, DETROIT FREE PRESS

Landscaping on the pitchers' mound. "My dad always said, Keep it level, and dig your own little hole."

In the Tiger dugout. "I might run into the clubhouse and get somethin' to eat, somethin' to break the monotony. Because I can't just sit there and sit on the bench."

SUSAN SHEINER, DETROIT FREE PRESS

"When the people called me out, it was a great welcoming."

On Mark's birthday, 1976. "Some autographs for kids around the neighborhood."

The Pied Piper of Southgate. "This year I was the magnet."

Before the game, opposing All-Star starters Mark Fidrych and Randy Jones display a full spectrum of baseball sartorial elegance.

Mark and John "The Count" Montefusco in the Bellevue-Stratford, All-Star time, 1976. "Montefusco goes, Man, how come you don't pop off? . . . Best pitcher in the league, and you're not even poppin' off!"

"Mike Love asked me if I drank carrot juice."

The highlight of Mark's birthday party, an 18-foot hero sandwich towed in by helicopter. "That fat man all in white made the great sandwich. We all ate it fresh."

RONALD UNTERNAHRER, OAKLAND (MICH.) PRESS

Mark meets Old Blue Eyes at the N.A.P.B.L. banquet, December 7, 1976. "And Frank Sinatra! My mother woulda been goin' nuts!"

Mark's parents and two of his sisters. Left to right: Virginia, Carol Ann, Laurie, and Paul Fidrych.

TWO: THIS YEAR I WAS THE MAGNET

10 How Many Games Will They Give Me?

This Year I Was the Magnet

T. We were out this afternoon with a couple of guys you played with in the minors, Dave Rozema and Lance Parrish. They're coming up for their shot next spring, like you did this spring. They're trying to do what you did. Weren't you thinking about—I mean, being around those guys, it might have made you think back to when you were in their shoes. Like with Rosey, they're already calling him *another Bird*.

M. Yeah, oh, yeah! I mean, Rosey right now is in the exact same spot as I was in when *I* came up. It'll be great for him. Because you know what? Ten to one they'll forget about me. They'll jump right to him. *He's* the magnet, now. I mean I'll be able—it's like a lot of ballplayers go, Hey, you wanna get out of the locker room easy? All you do is walk out with Mark. A lot of my friends that were playin' baseball, they said, Hey, let's leave early. We'll just walk with Mark. That was a joke, y'know? Because if they'd walk with me, no one else'd bother 'em. They just got to split. It was the same as a magnet, man. Right there.

T. Yeah, that's insane. A month after your first start you were gettin' more attention than anybody else on the club!

M. They put a telephone up? One time I come back from a road trip, I come back to my locker, and they got a private phone, man. It wasn't hitched up to anything. They just had an old phone that they cut. They put it up on a little chair, like. They put a private phone there, y'know—for my calls. It was just a joke, man, but it was a good joke. And I'm sayin', Get the—get this thing outa there! And everyone's laughin' their heads off, goin', *ha-ha-*

ha, y'know? But it was a good atmosphere joke. That's what I liked about it. It was good.

T.   You really think that could happen again to somebody else?

M.   But still, Rosey is the same kind of thing. If he came up and did the exact same thing—*Voom!* They'd drop me and go, *voom,* to him. A magnet. Just like that. I know it. That's it—that's what everyone said. Like Ron LeFlore said in the beginning of this year—like when he joined, last year, or the year before, right? He said, I just wish everyone left me alone. He said that in one column that I read. And it was weird. Like no one really—they didn't exploit him like they did before. Like they're doin' to me now. And he told me, too. Y'know, he said, Hey—

T.   You mean the writers were all over *him,* before *you* made it big? On account of he'd been in prison and all?

M.   Yeah! He said, Hey, don't let everyone burn *you* out, too. He said, they burnt *me* out, a little bit. But he said, Don't let everyone burn you out. But it's weird—'cause, y'know, he'd come up and tell you that. 'Cause he went through it. But then like he —it was a little calmer for him. Maybe that's why he *did* better, y'know? Because no one really exploited him that much. Once in a while, when he was in his thirty-game hittin' streak, fine. But until he hit that thirty-game hittin' streak, he was gettin' very little. But before, he was gettin' a *lot.* Just like *I* was, he was sayin'. Y'know? Gettin' this, gettin' that. And then he said finally, Now they got a new magnet to go on. Me. Y'know? And so it's true. They get a different magnet, they go to that. They just let you play your game, then.

I Don't Need Any More Glory

T.   It might be a good thing if that happened. Then you could just go ahead and pitch and be yourself.

M.   Yeah. Oh, I'd love to see Rosey come up. Just 'cause I've had a year in the major leagues, right? I know I can pitch in the major leagues. Rosey ain't gonna take my job, right? Just because—

T.   Luckily, there's a few jobs open.

M.   Yeah. I'm just sayin' that I know I can pitch there. If I couldn't do my job, then, fine, I could see him takin' my job. But he's got no job to take from me, right now. Right? And like, if he makes it at his job, fine. If he does it better than me, fine. It's great, y'know? It's great for him. I've already *got* the glory, man. I don't need any more glory.

T. Right. In fact, you might enjoy it if you got left to just go straight ahead and be a ballplayer.

M. Yeah, you could be a player. But you could get—you'd still get your awards. But you still ain't gettin'—what? Like it's —you're not gettin' really *pushed.* Like if he comes up—and he'll get pushed. Another non-roster man, makin' it. They thrive on that. It *is* good material, though—that they dig that deep in, y'know? They really get down to diggin' that deep, and sayin', Wow, no one's done *this* since back in 1909. Y'know? And now you're lookin' back, goin', Wow, that was—what, sixty-seven years ago? And you go, Wow, that's true, y'know? No one's done it since then. All right. But Rosey, it's just—*voom!* If he makes it, *voom,* it's different. It ain't me.

It's Like Anything in Life,
If You're Hot They're Gonna Keep You Going

T. Okay, so when the club came north this spring, even though you'd just done so-so in your spring-training games, they brought you along. Ralph Houk said he had you in mind as a starter all along, but you didn't get a start the first five weeks of the season. They used you twice in relief. It sounds like they didn't know *what* to do with you.

M. Probably. Y'know?

T. They were playing it by ear, I guess, seeing how you worked out—

M. And seein', y'know, what happened all year, with the trades and all that shit.

T. Yeah, they'd traded Mickey Lolich, and then they traded Joe Coleman in May.

M. I just lucked out, man. They said, Let's try him. They tried me, y'know? That's all it is. They give you a shot, and if you do good the first day, you're gonna be playin' again the next day. If you do good again, then you keep on playin'; if you do lousy, they're gonna get someone else who can get in there and do it *now.* But if you're hot, they're gonna keep you goin'. It's just like anything, y'know? Anything in *life.* People are gonna keep you goin' if you're hot.

You Wonder, How Many Games Are They Going to Give Me?

T.   So you've just got to wait for that first shot and make the most of it.

M.   Yeah! But when I was in the minors, y'know, seriously, when I was—I played Triple-A, right? Went to winter ball, Rosey was 15 and somethin'?

T.   In '75? He was 14–5 at Clinton.

M.   All right, so I said, Oh, does this kid have a *record!* And then they tell you this—y'know, You better watch out! And I just said, *Whoa*—I mean, I'm in Triple-A, he's only in A-ball. When he starts pitchin' next to me in the rotation, *that's* when I'll start thinkin' about him. But till then . . . y'see? All right, then he came into Double-A. Like I'm in the majors now. This year. Just before I got pitchin', right? I came up to Jim Campbell's office one day. And Jim goes, You better watch it, Rosey's gonna be takin' your place. He won another game, a two-hitter or something like that. Jim hit me with that, y'know? I just looked at him. I said, Wait a minute, I haven't even *pitched* yet. I said, Whaddaya mean tellin' me he's doin' better than me? I haven't even pitched yet! I been up here three weeks now, and you're tellin' me I'm already goin' down! And I haven't even thrown a game yet! How come you're tellin' me that stuff? But then, it keeps you—in my *mind,* I'm sittin' there goin', Oh, God damn! That's true too! This is a guy that can, y'know—*voom,* you're down and another guy's up. They just go, This guy's gone, we got another guy to replace him. We ain't foolin' around, y'know? That's probably what he's tryin' to throw through my mind, he's just tellin' me, Hey, Rosey just threw a two-hitter. Or Rosey just, y'know, won this. Or this other pitcher. And you're thinkin' in your mind, I haven't started pitchin' yet. How many games are they gonna *give* me, now? When they give me the chance to start, how many games are they gonna *give* me?

T.   So Rosey's down there at Montgomery, burning up the

Southern League, and they're using him to scare you?

M.   But still, like I said, they handled it like they wanted to. And it ended up like this, so everyone's happy. But say it ended up the other way?

T.   Say you came down with a cold the morning of your first start. Or you just pitched a lousy game—

M.   Yeah! Or if the second game, same thing happened. You just don't know what's gonna happen to you in your life.

T.   Well, it's always a gamble—when you're starting out in anything.

M.   Like now, when people go, Oh, how many games are you gonna win, when they hit me with *that*—how can you predict the future? I haven't even played a season yet, how can I have a goal, right? So now, next year I'll have a goal. I gotta at least win just as much as nineteen, if not more. Right? *That's* a goal you can have, right? That's the only goal I got. In the major leagues, everything stops. You can't go any higher.

T.   The first day that you go out there, though, your goal's gonna have to be to get *one*.

M.   Yeah! And the next time it's gonna be *two,* and the next time it's gonna be *three!*

My First Big-League Start Was the
Reward for What I Went Through in the Minors

T.   Like the day you went out to pitch that May 15 game in Cleveland, your first start, if you were thinkin' about winning nineteen . . .

M.   I woulda probably *lost* that game!

T.   You probably would have lost it. Instead of going out and winning it and pitching a two-hitter like you did.

M.   I was just thinkin' about that game right *there.* The game you're playin' is the only game that counts!

T.   But from the way you went at that one—you were so up for it, Rico Carty of the Indians said he thought you were trying to hypnotize them! I mean at the time that must have been the biggest game ever, as far as you were concerned.

M.   Really! Oh, yeah. I mean, it was—you know what it was? It was like, when I was in the minors—when they pitched me against the Red Sox, in the minors, my home town got to see it, right?

T.   You mean in March—that exhibition game was telecast back to Boston, when the Red Sox pounded you?

M.   Yeah. 'Cause we were in spring training. They got to see it—they showed me gettin' my *ass* kicked. But then, that Cleveland game—that first start. That was the reward for what I went through in the minors, right? I got up in the majors, pitchin' my first major league game. I said, *That* is what I went through it in the minors for. It took me goin' through the minors just to get up to—just to get that one game. Spring training, it's different. You get the game, it's playin' major league *ball,* yeah—but it ain't major league. It's when, *voom,* you're gettin' that major league *salary.* And *voom,* you're gettin' that major league *start. That's* what you worked for—the first major league start. Because that first one's gonna decide whether there's any more—if you're gonna start a second one, and a third one, and a fourth one. Y'know? And keep on goin', hopefully. But that's when it stops, y'know? That's when you go back down. Then you're back down in the minors. You ain't no major-leaguer any more. You're a minor-leaguer again. Oh, you can act like a major-leaguer—Ah, I've already been up there, and you're down in the minors. This minor-leaguer's gonna say, *Pfft,* big deal! You been up there? You ain't up there *now!* You ain't nothin' to me, buddy! Y'know?

If I Had to Go Back Down and Start Over (It's All in Your Mind)

T.   What if for some reason you had to go back down and start over?

M.   If I went down? You can't *blasé*-around if you're a major-leaguer. You're gettin' minor league pay. You're gettin' this—it just wouldn't be the same.

T.   You know, there was—did you ever hear of this guy Steve Blass? He pitched for the Pirates?

M.   No.

T.   In 1971 he won eighteen, nineteen games, and even won two in the World Series. He was a big star. And then something happened to him. He just lost it, couldn't get anybody out, walked everybody. All of a sudden, he just couldn't do it. For about two years, he was just screwed up. And he never got it back. He had to go down and—first they sent him to Charleston, Triple-A.

M.   Mmm.

T.   And he still couldn't make it. And he had to go down to —like he finally went down to Class-A ball. Thetford Mines, can you dig it? And finally retired from the game, at about age thirty.

M.   Yeah. But they kept him around, because they knew that he'd had it. But yet, he just couldn't get it *back*.

T.   His arm was all right, and everything.

M.   He was *there*, though. Y'know? He was there. He knew what it was like. But yet, y'know, he went through—he went back to the minors. He didn't quit. Until they said he *had* to quit, really.

T.   Even Jim Bouton. Like, did you know what Bouton did? He went out and tried out for the Class-A Portland Mavericks. Last year, in August—pitched about four games. Even though he —he quit his job working on television sportscasting, and he went out to the Northwest League. Class A, it's an independent team. And he pitched four, five games in September, trying to make a comeback.

M.   Hey, if he does that, he does it. He could make it, you never know. Anyone can, if they—it's just sayin', Oh, *wow*, I screwed up back there. Or I screwed up this much. Why can't I go back? You can. It's all in your mind, y'know?

This Game Is Youth

T.   Well, maybe *almost* all.

M.   But I mean if you get *too* old you can't go back. That's true. This game is youth. Y'know? I mean, it *is*. That's one thing that's wrong with it. Because you do get that guy that—y'know, say the guy that's twenty-five. And you take the guy that's, y'know, forty. The guy that's twenty-five is more than likely gonna do better. But if the guy that's twenty-five *doesn't* do better, the guy that's forty's just got a better sense of baseball than the other guy. He can make up for his mistakes, where this twenty-five-year-old don't make up for the mistakes he makes. That's the only thing you see in that. Other than that a twenty-five-year-old should be able to run fast—to do *anything* faster than that forty-year-old guy. There's a big difference there—twenty years, almost. Fifteen, when you get down to it. That's just like, I'm sayin' that I should be able to run faster than like a thirty-four-year-old guy. Y'know? But if you get a thirty-four-year-old guy that's runnin' faster than me, that's just showin' that he's still in the game. Y'know, he ain't ready to *go!* But you get a guy that I'm faster than him—look at Rusty. I'm faster than him. I bet you could run *backwards* and go faster. But yet, now he can—he capitalizes on his speed, now. He can play the outfield. But he makes up for his speed. He *knows* he's slow—so then, *voom,* he makes up for it. By his eyes, fielding, and stuff like that. And his bat, things like that.

The Veteran Can Make Up for It (Rusty Staub)

T.   He knows how to play, in other words. He's been around ten years.

M.   Yeah! So he knows—he knows his percentage in what he's gotta do, and stuff. He knows it.

T.   But that's one thing you *get* with age, y'know?

M.   Yeah! That's what I'm sayin'. He's making up for the speed that he lost, y'know? I'm just usin' him for an example. I'll take him as an outfielder any day. Y'know? I mean, how many times is a ball gonna be hit out to right field? How many times is a ball gonna be hit to left field or center field? Right? You just hope the guy is gonna make up for it. And you just do that, and fine. It's *there,* y'know? I mean, you know how many games he's *won?* Because of his *bat?* That's why when these people get on me, sayin', Ooh, hey, if Rusty'd made that catch out in right field in the All-Star game, you mighta been doin' better—I look at 'em. How the hell can you *say* that, man?

T.   And how about all the games during the regular season—

M.   Listen, man, he *got* me to the All-Star game! Y'know? How about the games that he got me there? Now—one game, I'm sayin' the guy's no good? *He's* there! If he wasn't no good he wouldn't *be* there! And people come and say, Oh, if he wasn't so slow—

T.   A reporter wanted you to put him down for making one bad play?

M. Yeah! I mean literally! You just—God! I mean, how could a person come and *say* somethin' like that? I don't know. That's just—that's just what you call *baseball,* I guess. That's what they told me.

Ten-Year Veterans Told Me, We've Never Seen Anything Like It

T.   The ballplayers told you you've got to expect that?

M.   Mmm. Like, a lot of the ballplayers—you take a ballplayer that's played ten years, man. And, y'know, like, I'll say, What's happenin' to me? He'll go, Hey, I been playin' ten years, nothin' like this has ever happened to me.

T.   Yeah, that's just what Rusty Staub said. He said, I played with the Mets in the year we won, and nobody could believe it. And I've seen Tom Seaver in his greatest day. And I've been to the top. And he said, I never saw anything like *this.* He said, Total electricity! And he said, I don't know what's goin' on. I don't know what this is. He said—I mean, here's a guy that's in his thirties, he's been all around, and said something like that. That must have made you feel good.

M.   Other guys told me the same. Y'know, been ten years in the big leagues. Sayin', y'know—but they helped me, though! See, those guys said, Hey—they said, *We* haven't seen it. And *you're* seein' it now. Hey, we're gonna educate you, buddy! Y'know? And they did, y'know? They literally did. And if I quit tomorrow, I don't think they'd be burned. It's just, when your fun's over, your fun's over. But there ain't no fun to this game. This is my *life,* right here. And if I don't do it, I don't know *what* I'm gonna do in life.

I Don't Know What I'd Do If There Was No Baseball

T.   What if you couldn't play baseball any more?

M.   If I go back—like if I got hurt, if my arm got cut off right now, and if I had my contract that I got right now, I would sit in my house and I'd go nuts. 'Cause I wouldn't know what I'm gonna do. Where do I go look for a job? But then, if I was gonna go look for a job, I'd put my arm back on. And so, I have two arms now. But I still say, I just wouldn't know what to do. Y'know? Do I go back and work gas station work?

T. You could probably pick up something.

M. Yeah, or whatever happened. But still, it'd just be—it'd be goin' back to my normal life. That's what it'd be doin'! I'd be goin' back workin' for the Water Department, workin' for R and T Furniture, workin' for Uhlman's Shell. Workin' for, y'know, Pierce Oil and Gas. Y'know? All the jobs I *had*—that's just what I'd be doin'. I'd be goin' all the way back to that again.

T. Back to pumping gas and changing tires?

M. Gas station work, *that*'s what I'd be goin' back to. But yet, I would be workin' there, and still kinda have—y'know, my thing to work with, though.

T. It might be kind of fun.

M. I don't know if it'd be fun.

T. It might not be bad if you were in a place where nobody knew you.

M. Y'know, it'd be just the same, man. It'd be goin' back to that. It's either that or I'd have to find something different. My life, to people, has been exploited to baseball. And when they see I've failed baseball, they're gonna be sayin', Aw, this guy messed up this, screwed up that. Y'know, look at this—they'll go, Lookit, he had the chance of a lifetime. Mark Fidrych had the chance of a major league baseball player. And look what he did with it. He blew it out in five years! I might blow it out in five years. But that's five years I'll never forget in my life. I might have blown it out in a year.

I Look into the Future and See a Gas Station

T. But look at it this way, too. You're only going to be able to play baseball for a certain length of time, and then you're going to have to do something else. And so far it doesn't look like you'll want to go into doing whatever it is those people down in the lobby are doing. I mean, a "career" in baseball. You're not the type to stand around in a suit and discuss things. So what you're going to be doing is probably something pretty far different from what you're doing now. In, say, fifteen years. By the time you're thirty-five you might still be pitching or you might not. You might be doing something different, and right now you don't know what it's gonna be. What I mean is you might not stay in baseball—there might be something else.

M. I don't think I will.

T. Because when you're not playing—

M. If they ask me to be a coach, or something like that, I really— right now I feel that I could not be a coach. I just feel I couldn't. And so I just, y'know, say to myself—I play baseball, and that's as far as it's gonna go. I ain't gonna push it.

T. Suppose you only play ten years.

M. Yeah.

T. It might start being like—

M. I could retire then!

T. And get about six, seven thousand dollars a month for the rest of your life, or something?

M. Yeah, retire—but then do part-time work. Work here, work there. But yet—all right. I like to work on cars, right? So I like to work on cars now. So my future—I got enough money right now where I could stop this game and own my own gas station. Own my own workshop, if I wanted to. And say, Hey, people, come to me, I got the name! Right? If I want to work on cars, I got the name. And I'll tune your car up. And I'll give you —like, say, Midas gives you *this.* I'll give you *that,* too. Y'know? Do the same trick Midas is doin'. 'Cause I can do that now. So you start out like Midas, or something like that. Where, all right, say I play ten years, and get more. I can start after that—like at thirty-five, start becoming a mechanic *then,* too. Y'know? A mechanic is always gonna be there.

My First Day in the Big Leagues, I Strike It Rich Education-Wise

T. We were talking about veterans a few minutes ago. I understand that when you first came up to Detroit, you had a veteran pitcher for a roommate, Joe Coleman. Maybe they put you with Coleman because they figured you were—

M. Education-wise, y'know? To help me out. And, y'know, it was weird. Like these guys, they—the first day of the season we got into Cleveland, right? We just broke camp, we got to Cleveland. And like they took me out to eat, John Hiller and Rusty Staub and Dave Roberts and Joe Coleman. We all went out to eat together, right? And we were just sittin' there eatin'. And they didn't let me pay for the bill. Y'know, I ordered what I could pay for. And they said, No. Dave Roberts picked up the tab for that. So then we went to the local bar, right? In the hotel. And sat there and drank. And they wouldn't let me buy a round! Right? And then they all just looked at me and said, Hey—remember, you're a rookie. We're veterans. We've been around a lot, right? Just treat a rookie the way we treated you just now. When *he* comes up. Because we know what you're goin' through, 'cause we've already gone through it. And right then and there you just go, *Wow.* Y'know? It's like they accepted you for what you *were.* And they're just—you're showin' your appreciation.

T.   It sounds like you came up to a good ball club—you came to the right place.

M.   Heck, yeah! Like, you'd be sittin' there eatin'—you'd go out to eat, right? You'd be goin' through the lobby, and one of the veteran ballplayers would say, Hey, have you eaten yet, Mark? I'd say, No. They'd say, Well, I'm goin' out now, you wanna eat? Fine. You'd go eat with the guy, and he'd pick up the tab. Y'know? You'd *try* to pick up the tab. You'd try to pay for your meal, and he just wouldn't let you.

T.   That helps a lot, when you're trying to find your feet on the ground.

M.   Yeah, that's what I needed, to get my feet on the ground. And they—oh, they helped me out *so* much. When it came down to real necessity in life. To learnin', y'know? It's just—y'know, you could just *talk* to 'em. That's what was so good about it. Maybe that's why I ended up the way I was, y'know?

Reporters Say This and That, But I Look at Alex Johnson as an Intelligent Man

T.   And Willie Horton, you were saying he was good to you when you first came up?

M.   Yeah. Oh, you could talk to him. You could talk to anyone, really. Y'know? I mean, like you goof around with each player differently. Like, this guy you might goof around with at night. Or this guy you goof around with, you get in the locker room and goof around, or you get on the field and goof around. That's like Alex Johnson, right? Everyone would come down hard —reporters and all—on the guy, right? That he was this way and that way. And now I look at him as a baseball player, and I say, Hey—I look at the reporters and the umpires that used to go at him. I'd say, Why don't you just leave the guy *alone,* man? Y'know? 'Cause he helped me out, that's why. I mean, I used to come out every day. I'd say, Hey, Alex, let's go out and do b.p. And I'd like throw balls at him, and he'd hit pepper back to me. I mean he'd be hittin' 'em hard. And like I'd take two balls and try to get 'em *by* him. And he'd hit 'em back. And we were gettin' into it. And that helped me in the fielding.

T.   Somebody must have helped, because you didn't make an error all season!

M.   Y'know? So I mean he helped me. And people are callin' him *bad?* I just say, Hey—y'know?

T.   Yeah, he's bounced around a lot. People called him a troublemaker. Reporters, mostly. But not to his face too much, I bet.

M.   Y'know, I just can't see them doin' that to some guy like that. I say, Hey, he's helped *me.* I mean, screw those other people. I don't care what *they* think. I think he's a good guy. And then, like I needed tools to work on my car? I said to Alex, I want a tool to work on my car. You got any tools? He said, Fine, here. Handed me the tools—he brought 'em in. He goes, When you're done, give 'em back to me. I gave 'em back to him. Y'know, I said, What is this—now this is just the *opposite.* And like then I read one article, from a reporter, sayin', Hey, Alex Johnson. . . . If you really sit down with Alex Johnson, Alex is an intelligent man. Y'know? If he wants to be intelligent, and if, like, the reporter let's him be intelligent, he's probably more intelligent than the *reporter* is!

T.   What some writers have done to a guy like that, they've taken money out of his pocket.

M.   That's right.

T.   Because after all those bad raps, the next year he gets released or something, from two or three ball clubs. And yet he can *hit.*

M.   Yeah—no one wants to pick him up, he might be a bad ballplayer. But he *ain't* a bad ballplayer at all. That's what's weird. Y'know, he hits, when he wants to. And *gets* 'em.

My Introduction to the Majors, and a Downfall

T.   Your big-league debut was that game in Oakland when Baylor got that hit off you in the ninth. That was, let's see, April 20. You came in, threw your first big-league pitch, threw another one—and Baylor hit it into left and the game was over.

M.   Yeah, y'know, that was—hey, that was a situation I *wanted* to be in, y'know? I'd been a relief pitcher now. I said, Hey, they don't want me to start, maybe I can make it as a reliefer. I said, I did it before, why can't I do it now? I came in the situations before, when I was in the minors. Like, y'know, guys'd be on, the tying run. I come in, just, *voom*—just throw normal, just say, Hey, ground ball, high fly, you'll take all that, just don't let 'em get a hit. Make 'em hit what you want, y'know? And I got in there and I just hung a slider and he just went *tcchht,* thank you. That was it. And it was over.

T.   You weren't nervous, then?

M.   I had *wanted* to be there. When I was runnin' through there, I said, I'm lovin' it! I was lovin' it, I was thrivin' on it. And *voom,* it was a downfall. I go, Now I know what the major leagues is like.

T.   It was over fast, wasn't it?

M.   Two pitches! I said Wow, this is what the major leagues is like. And I walked in, and all the guys go, Hey, don't worry about it. You only threw two pitches, man. We'll give you a chance *someday,* y'know?

T.   Well, they could hardly send you back to Evansville off the evidence of just two pitches!

M.   But that was good. I mean, that's when you really found out what the majors was like. Y'know, the guy just got, *tcchht,* that little thing there, and *voom*—there's a fast guy on third, and it was gone. It was good night. And I'm goin' home and drinkin' —and that's where it's at.

No One Knows What's Going Through Your Mind

T.   Well, the main thing is, you got in there, and it didn't scare you off. You had the wherewithal to come back, when they gave you a start, and not let that first game bother you.

M. No! It's like—a person goes, Were you *scared* when you went out in front of the people? And I go, I'm just playin' the *game*. I was tight. But once the first inning was over, and I got through the first inning, I was fine, y'know? I was relaxed. I was just pitchin' the game. Whatever happened, happened. And they go, You mean you weren't really that scared? Well, you just can't answer the guy when he asks you a question like that. Because you're the only one that knows what's goin' through your *mind*. Right? I could have a wicked hangover. No one knows I've got a wicked hangover, right? I'll throw a *beautiful* game.

Don't Think About the Game (Just Go Through It)

T. That's what's called being a professional, isn't it? You just go out and do your job whether you're scared or not. And then after a while you stop being scared.

M. That's like when I first came in as a ballplayer, when I was in the big leagues, right, the first day I was gonna pitch, a ballplayer comes up to me and goes, Hey, what'd you do last night?

T. This is before your first—the Cleveland game, in May?

M. Yeah. And I said, Well, I got drunk, goofed around and stuff. He says, Do the exact same thing you did last night. He says, Don't even think of going home and trying to sleep, to get your eight hours' sleep. Have your beers so you can relax—just go out and do *that*. I saw what he meant. In other words he was sayin', Just don't get too scared—don't think about the game. Y'know, Do what you were doin' before. And then I just kept on doin' the same routine. So then when I get in a losin'—y'know, later, I lost three or four in a row—I'm sittin' there, *Wow*. But then they say, Remember, it's just what a batter goes through when he goes, y'know, 0 for 4. Don't worry. You're gonna get back on the winning scale. Don't worry. Just go through it, y'know?

11 A Town Reunion in the Men's Room at Fenway Park

Living in a Dream, but Wishing the Fun Was Over

T.   Making it to the majors, though, less than two years after high school—that must have seemed like a dream, at first?

M.   Y'know, it's funny, though, not thinkin'—like when I was a little kid. Wow, I'm pitchin' against Carl Yastrzemski now. But when I was a little kid you wouldn't even think of it. I didn't. You'd see the game on TV, and you'd just go, Wow, I can't even *picture* playin' there. Now that you're there you just—it's fun, but now, the fun's not really over, but you feel that you wish it *was* kind of over. Just so I could just play baseball now, and just relax. And be able to walk the streets without I have to do this and have to do that.

T.   It could get back to that. Or something like that.

M.   Yeah, but I think if I get 'em all, then someday I'll have —y'know, *that's* the only thing I can hope for. I mean, it got to where I'd be at Tiger Stadium and the guys'd finally have to tell me, Get outa here, will ya! You're drawin' a crowd! I mean, We just can't handle it! And then you're leavin' and some little kid'll call you a nerd, y'know? And you go, *Wow,* that little kid's givin' me a bad mouth. Y'know, you get this all in the back of your mind because you don't want 'em to think that you're stuck-up. And you're *not* stuck-up, but yet you want to have a little time. Like I'm flyin' over in the airplane here. If I didn't fall asleep, I'd have been signin' autographs for everyone on the airplane.

T.   You were flying out from Detroit?

M.   Yeah, it came from Detroit, flyin' out. A lot of people from Detroit, and they saw me. And like I woke up, and the stewardess told me, You should see the line of people here wantin' to get your autograph. I said, *Whoa.* I said, Well, there's only an hour left in the flight, it can't be *that* bad. So they came up, and one lady was takin' pictures. It was neat. When I woke up, y'know, I was feelin' good, and I didn't care. It didn't bother me. But it was just *work,* y'know? That's why I want to fly first class.

I Get George Scott's Bat

T.   You ever do that when you were a kid, get any ballplayers' autographs?

M.   No, I never did. I never took an autograph from any sport player, in my life.

T.   Not even this year, when you were meeting all the famous ones?

M.   Well, y'know, this year I got George Scott's bat. Y'know, I wanted his bat, and like during the game—

T.   One of those black ones he uses?

M.   No, no, it was a white one. And I just yelled over to him, y'know? I told Bill Freehan to ask George if I could have a bat. I said, if he wants—if he's gonna give me a bat, tell him to tip his hat, and look over at our bench. So Bill told him. He looked over, tipped his hat, and the next thing I knew I had a bat sent over.

T.   I guess he liked you. Y'know, he said after the first time he faced you that people called you flaky and loony, but he liked what you were up to. That's *confidence,* he said.

M.   It was neat, y'know? 'Cause I have that bat downstairs in my house—I redid this house down in the cellar, so it's on the bar now.

T.   Back home?

M.   Yeah, back home in Mass.

I Get Hank Aaron's Bat

T.   Did you get any other bats besides George Scott's?

M.   I got his, and I tried to get Hank Aaron's, but I couldn't. But I got it today, I mean the other day, in Fort Lauderdale.

T.   When you were doing the Aqua Velva ad?

M.   Yeah. Someone brought a bat and it had Hank Aaron on it, so I took it. I just said, This looks normal. This'll do it. I knew

Hank, y'know? I mean I pitched against him, so this is why I just wanted it, I just wanted something like that.

I Strike Aaron Out the First Time
I Face Him, but He Takes Mac Deep

T.   How'd Aaron do against you, do you remember? Let's see, May 21—

M.   Oh, he got a couple. He got maybe a hit or two.

T.   Here it is—he went one for four.

M.   But the first time I faced him, he had—they had men on first and second, two outs, right? And I struck him out. That was the first time I ever faced him. I struck him out with a fastball on the inside. I mean he—y'know, I couldn't believe it. He missed it by that much. By half a foot! He just *swung,* and I don't know what—it might have done somethin', but he missed it by that much. I mean he had no help for him. I threw it, I was in shock. Got back to the dugout, I said, *Whoa.* I struck out Hank Aaron! And then my buddy comes up to the major leagues, Frank Mac-Cormack, right?

T.   This is later—in June?

M.   Yeah, when he came up. And Mac goes, *Wow,* today I'm gonna be pitchin' against Hank Aaron. I said, It's neat, Mac, I got him out the first time. Struck him out. But *Mac*—Aaron went *deep* into left on Mac, y'know? And I was just crackin' up.

Pitcher Against Hitter Is Just Battle Against Battle

T.   Okay, Hank Aaron, he's a guy you're going to be aware of. The top hitters, sure. But normally, you don't think too much about who's up there, do you?

M.   No! It's just battle against battle. Who's gonna get the hit, or who's gonna get 'em out. That's all it is, is a battle.

T.   I mean, it's a distraction, isn't it, to even think about who's up there?

M.   Yeah, I just throw.

T.   So you were talking about Aaron, and how he hit that home run off Frank MacCormack. Do you suppose MacCormack might have been thinking, *Wow, Hank Aaron,* instead of, *Get him out?*

M.   Yeah. It's just like, my first time I ever faced Hank

Aaron, guys on second and third, I struck him out. And that was just weird. At the point where—here he is, I mean, a *superstar,* right? And here I am, a little guy, pitchin' to *him.* And knowin' he's a superstar. All of a sudden you get him out, that one time. It makes you feel good. Right? But yet, the next time up, he gets a hit. It's just—you lucked out, at the time! You literally threw the pitch—but yet, he was lookin' for some other pitch. Or, he was still lookin' for that pitch, but you just snuck it by him. You lucked out. You snuck it by the guy. Because he's a superstar— you gotta know it. And in back of your mind, you're sayin', *Wow,* this is Hank Aaron! You are! When I was on that mound, I'm sittin' there goin', Wow, this is Hank Aaron! Just like when I saw George Scott. I said, *Whoa,* this is George Scott. Just like when I saw Carl Yastrzemski, I said, *Whoa,* this is Carl Yastrzemski. And you're just sittin' there lookin' at these guys. And you *know* it's them. But you're sayin', Hey, they ain't no better than you! But yet, they're gonna try to beat you just as bad as you're gonna try to beat them. Y'know? That's the whole thing it is.

A Town Reunion in the Men's Room at Fenway Park

T.   Well, you had a good short course in hitters in those first three starts. You saw Carty, against Cleveland, and that same month against Milwaukee you saw Scott and Aaron . . . and then your second start, the game in Fenway, Yastrzemski beat you with a home run. That game in Fenway—your first game in Fenway, that must have been a trip.

M.   Yeah! I didn't find out until . . . now I'm in front of—

T.   Where your buddies there?

M.   Yeah. Now I'm in front of people that know me, from my town. I mean my friends were tellin' me that they'd go in the men's room, and they're seein' people that they haven't seen in a long time in Northboro. At this park, y'know?

T.   It was like a party, eh?

M.   That's just what it was! It was like a family get-together, where they knew me, and they knew each other, but they hadn't *seen* each other in, y'know, a while. Right? So you're gettin' this —you're gettin' this *feeling* there, right? See, I'm sittin' here, *pitchin'* the game now—

T.   Were they all sittin' together?

M. Not sittin' together. I mean, *this* person mighta been up in *this* big section, and this person—it depends on who could buy the best ticket. Let's put it that way, y'know? And it was like this person could afford a box seat, but yet this person wanted to sit out—way out in center field. *Voom,* they went to the bathroom together. They went to the bathroom at the same time. Y'know? They just bumped into each other. That was the whole big deal about that.

I'd Rather Have Won It 10–9 Than Lost It 2–0

T. When Yaz hit that home run off you, how'd you feel?

M. It blew my mind. It blew *my* goddam mind. Just because . . . hey, the only reason it blew my mind was because, here I am, goin', I'm in front of my—Fenway Park, I want to *win!* I ain't even thinkin' about losin'. I mean if I win—I might win, 10 to 9! I'm gonna be *so* happy, walkin' outa that park. 'Cause if I finish the game—or even if I didn't finish the game and won 10 to 9, right? I'm gonna be *so* happy that it's gonna be ungodly.

T. You had reason to be happy about that game, anyway. You pitched a good game, even if you lost.

M. Yeah, you pitched a damn good game and you can still be happy about it. But I wasn't as happy as when I won, 6 to 3. I wasn't even *near* as happy. . . . I lost 2–0. And here when I won 6–3, I was so happy I walked back to my town. I said, *Whoa.* Y'know, I was *happy.*

T. You mean when you pitched in Fenway again in September and beat them—let's see, it was 8 to 3.

M. Yeah. But 2 to 0, I was—I didn't want to—

T. Who won that 2–0 game, Tiant?

M. Yeah. I didn't even want to talk about it. I went back to my buddies then. But like, other than that, I didn't, y'know?

T. Well, only your second start, that was a tough way to lose, on one long ball.

M. Yeah, yeah. I just didn't even want to, y'know—

T. But then the other time, in September—

M. Yeah! Comin' to Fenway the next time, I'm pitchin'—I said, *Whoa!*

In the Bull Pen at Fenway
My Whole Life Flashes Before My Eyes

T.   Was Fenway the only place you'd ever seen a big-league game before this year?

M.   Oh, yeah. I never went to a big-league game before, other than that. And here, I mean, my friends—when I was warmin' up in the bull pen, right? Even the people in the Red Sox bull pen—like they're next door to each other, right? And like, they're lookin' at me, and I'm warmin' up. And *their* pitcher's warmin' up, but the other guys—I mean, I had people, I mean buddies, just people I went to school with, from my home town. I mean, they were—it was like they lined the whole fence, goin', *C'mon, you, fucker! GET the mothers!* Even though they're from Boston, they're goin', y'know, *Come on! Let's see what you can do, Mark!* And I looked around, and—

T.   Could you hear 'em?

M.   *Hear* 'em? It was like, here I am warmin' up here, and they're right there. Against that wall. That's how close they are. And like, I'm seein' all of 'em. And I *know* all of 'em, too. Just about.

T.   Your whole life's flashing before your eyes, huh?

M.   Right! That's just what it was doin'. It was! And like I turned to these two ladies—

T.   You go, Am I dreaming? Or is this me?

M.   That's just what it was! And like, I'm lookin' at—y'know, I look at these two ladies that I knew, that I went to school with. And I said, Hey, Sue, are you married yet? She goes, No, I'm waitin' for *you!* And like my pitchin' coach, y'know—

T.   You know what you're talking about? This is what everybody wants to do when he's a kid—that day when you can come back and do what you did, in front of your home town!

M.   Yeah! All right, all right! And here—all right, now, I look at my pitchin' coach, Fred Gladding. And like, he says, See what I told you? Him and the other pitchers. They go, Now we're in the town where you're *somethin'*. Where before, you were just good ol' Mark. Now you're *somethin'*. But yet, my town didn't

take it as that. Y'know, they took me as being, y'know—and not
the way *I* take it as. But we'd all just lived together. And everyone
saw that. But still, they're just sayin', *Lookit, now.* Y'know? That's
what was funny about it, y'know? But that was good. I mean it
was *so* good. I was in Fenway. I mean, I got a picture—I got a
picture at home that describes it to me. To *me,* if I look at that
picture, it describes my whole feeling of what I felt about that
game, when I pitched it. Because the guy just got me tossing up
the ball that I pitched in the game. Y'know? I'm just sittin' there
tossin' it, and the reporter's talkin' to me. The guy just took—the
kind of actions that I had.

    T.   A friend of yours took the picture, somebody you knew
from home?

    M.   Yeah. This guy I know, right? Like I went to school with
the girl he's—the lady he's married with, y'know? And she was
the one that was standin' there, too, when I told that Sue chick.
Y'know, I said, Hey—I was talkin' to *both* of 'em—are you two
married yet? Because I didn't really know that girl was gettin'
married to that guy. Y'know? And then we just—we just sat there.
And that picture—I'll never forget the picture because it was just
me sittin' there talkin'. Because I was—I wasn't *blasé*-in'. But I
was normally just sittin' there, y'know, goin' *voom, voom,* with
that ball. Just thinkin' about it. Talkin' to this guy, but really
thinkin' about the game. And he's askin' me—irrelevant stuff,
about the game. He's just askin' me things. Y'know, what's goin'
through your—what are you thinkin' about? Y'know, here you
are, pitchin' in Boston. Here I am, just tossin' the ball, goin' *voom,
voom,* fuckin' Boston beat me. I ain't even thinkin' about playin'
well. I'm just thinkin', One pitch! But that one pitch didn't blow
the game, though. That's what they say—that pitch don't blow no
one game. No way. But I'm just *sayin'*—y'know, here I am in
Boston. Y'know, seein' people that I haven't even seen—even my
cousins came out of the wall! Y'know? I haven't seen them in, say,
five, six years. *They're* comin' to the games now, y'know? It's neat.

The Writer Tells Me Why the National TV
Game Against New York Was Such a Big Deal

    T.   So six weeks after the game at Fenway—and you've won
six straight in the meantime—there's that game with the Yankees

on television, June 28. It seems like that one game on television is the one that really made people aware of you.

M.   Everyone picks out that game. Why? *Why* is that game —just 'cause it was national TV and I won? Say it was national TV and I *lost.* Right?

T.   Yeah, but it wasn't just . . . you know what it was? It was timing. *When* that game came. You know what I mean?

M.   Yeah, all right. But *why?*

T.   You were on a winning streak. You'd just won your seventh, four days before that—and all those games you were winning were close, exciting games. They were low-scoring, dramatic—none of 'em were runaways. They were all like 2–0, 2–1, 3–2. . . .

M.   Yeah, but I wasn't thinkin' of that, though.

T.   So right then you were hot. And then television came along. And then, when you were on, in that game on television, the truth about it is—

M.   You don't even know the truth, though.

T.   The truth about it—

M.   Even *I* don't know the truth about it!

T.   *I* know the truth that you don't know. And that is, I knew what it was like to watch this strange dude, who I didn't know from nowhere—

M.   All right, 'cause I didn't see—

T.   And, well, I follow things, but I'm not from Detroit. I'd heard a lot about you, but seeing that game—first of all, the way you work. It's super-fast. No stalling around between pitches, just *bang, bang*—really rapid. I mean, other pitchers have worked fast, but your concentration is totally different. It's like total. You're into your own moves. And you're right *there.* Y'know? And you express yourself—to the guys on your team, to the fans. And, like, you express yourself to yourself. It's like perpetual motion—animation! So television took all that, and combined the fact that you were winning all these games with—you were something *different,* you know what I mean? And even on TV you could see that the guys playin' behind you were right in the game with you. You could just see that—it was magic. It was something happening. even through the fact that it was just another television show. Like we were sittin' around watching that football game on TV today. If there was somebody in that ball game we were watchin' today who was totally different—like some quarterback who was doin' it different than we'd ever seen before . . .

M. Yeah, mmm. . . .

T. And so everybody just stopped and blinked a little bit. *What's this,* y'know? That game last June was like that.

The Guys Get Me Tight About National TV So as to Distract Me, All of Which Helps Get Me Up for the Game

M. But before I even walked out there—like, Tom Veryzer and I, we're comin' to the ballpark, right? And Tommy's goin'— grabbin' his throat and goin', like, *Choke.* To me. And I said, Whaddaya mean? And he goes, It's national TV tonight. I said, Whaddaya mean, national TV? He goes, Your friends are gonna see you at home, right? I mean, to *him*—he was always talkin', like, national TV. And like, y'know, his friends—but I mean, it could be TV, but not *national* TV. Y'know? I mean, like my first game against *Cleveland* they said it was gonna be national TV because the whaddayacallit—the other game was gonna get rained out, so it was gonna be on national TV.

T. Oh, yeah, the back-up. They had the Dodgers-Pirates on the main Game of the Week, so your game against the Indians only got shown in Pittsburgh and southern California. But it rained a little in Pittsburgh, so you came close.

M. Yeah, we were the back-up game. But they didn't get rained out, right? It didn't, but it was *going to.* They told us—they said, You're on national TV now. They told us before the game even started.

T. Not giving up a hit until the seventh like you did, that would've been—you could have nearly pitched a no-hitter on national TV in your *first start!*

M. Y'know, that's what they said. And before the game even started they said, Hey, it's on national TV, if the other game got rained out. And you're goin' through the locker room, and they're goin', *Choke!* Y'know, 'cause they were just—but they're just really gettin' me up for the game. They *knew* they weren't hurtin' me. They were gettin' me up for the game.

T. You probably got up so high for those first few games

that it helped you. I mean, you just went out there and looked like the original strike machine!

M. Yeah, it—that stuff *did,* y'know? But they were—it's just a joke that you do to anyone, though, that comes in and they got an important game. You *do* it to 'em. Because they're sittin' there walkin' around, thinkin'. Y'know? But then you just do that, and it's distractin' their mind. And it's helpin' them a lot. 'Cause it takes them *off* it.

When the People Called Me Out of the Dugout, It was Like a Great Welcoming

T. Even though it wasn't on national television, that game with the Indians was shown all around Michigan on the Tigers' network. So people back there got their first look at you. And then they started coming out to see you pitch. And then, was it after that Yankee game that they made you come back out of the clubhouse the first time? They wouldn't go home—they made you come back out in your socks!

M. Yeah, a couple times they did it, right? The first time they did it, I wanted the whole team to come out there, right? But they just threw me out. And they said, Go out and do it! Y'know? They said, We wanna get *outa* here, so go out and do it. I said, You guys *all* gotta come out! And they just all sat there and said, Okay, okay, we will. And they all like came down, and they got in the dugout. And I just went out. And those guys were laughin' their heads off, standin' in the dugout! And it made me feel *good,* y'know? It was *weird,* y'know? It was—it was a great welcoming, like. And it was cool. It was neat. And those guys were laughin'. And they were lovin' it just as much as I was, you know that? 'Cause that's what a few of 'em said, y'know, was—It's great, man. Y'know? Couple of the guys said, It's neat, I'd love to be in your shoes. But we were in it. It's somethin' like, y'know, when we won the World Series here—that's what it feels like to us. Y'know, again. It was good.

T. The last World Series in Detroit, that was '68. And back then Denny McLain was pitching for the Tigers. I heard that when he pitched in Detroit sometimes the fans called *him* back out.

M. Yeah. But like, they never call me out when I lose. You

know what I mean? That's what's good about it, y'know? They take the loss with you. But when you win, they're *there* with you, y'know?

Ralph Houk Kept Me Together
When I Needed to Be Kept Together

T.   How was Ralph Houk during all this? Did he talk to you at all?

M.   Nah, he was laughin'.

T.   You mean he was laughing when they called you out of the dugout?

M.   Yeah!

T.   But then, when things started getting a little heavy, he was there to help you out, to keep you together?

M.   Yeah, he kept me together when I needed to be kept together. Like when I lost, I was losin' my fourth straight, I'd go and talk to him. Y'know, just, after I came out, talkin'. It's like I went in there with a problem, I came out with the whole problem solved, not half of it. Y'know, the whole thing was solved. So that's what was neat about him. When it came down to that. Other than that, he let me do what I wanted to do, y'know? He never said, Hey, get outa here, do this, do that. He'd just—like if I was doin' somethin' *stupid,* he wouldn't—he really wouldn't say nothin'. He just let me go, y'know? He just—it was like he knew that when he wanted me to work for him, I'd work for him. And like after that—after I'm done workin' for him, he doesn't care what I do. He lets—like if I'm in the locker room, goofin' around a little bit, y'know? It's a time that—there's times and times. There's a time to goof around and a time *not* to. So I don't goof around when the time is *not* to. Y'know, you only goof around when you're winnin'. And usually no one says anythin' when you're winnin'. It's when you're *losin'* and you're goofin' around, *then* something's probably gonna get said. Y'know, like that. That's why I never really—I didn't goof around that much.

Tom Veryzer Educates Me
About Acting Happy When We Lose

T.   With the Tigers, let's face it, you were on a team that was losing a lot of games, which must have sometimes made for a kind of down atmosphere. If you're contending for second or third place, and then all of a sudden you fall out of that, it must be tough getting through all those games.

T. Yeah, well I really wasn't involved in the team at the beginning of this year. I wasn't pitchin' then. Y'know, I was just sittin' there watchin' everything happen. *Watchin'* it all, y'know?

T. How does that make you feel, when you're sitting on the bench between starts and the team's losing?

M. You got no feeling. It was like—all right, it's like, you know what it was? All right, Tom Veryzer, right? I was—one day, when I wasn't pitchin', it was like I came out and sat there and yelled and cheered. And goofed around, right? And like Tom Veryzer, my roommate at this time—we were in Baltimore. And we went—I went flyin' to get somethin' to eat, y'know? I mean, game was all over, we'd just lost a tight one again.

T. This was around the end of May?

M. Yeah, whenever. And I *flew* up there, y'know? I just ran —I like was in the back of the line, and ran by everyone, and got *up* there, y'know?

T. You beat everybody back to the clubhouse!

M. Yeah. 'Cause here I am—I mighta walked, if I'd played or was involved in it. I was involved in it, but yet I hadn't pitched enough yet to *really* get involved in it, y'know? So I ran by. And then Tom—that night we were drinkin', right? And Tom goes, Uh, Ralph told me that, uh—he didn't want to make any scene about it, y'know—but he told me to tell you, when you lose, *walk* to the lunch. Y'know, *walk* to get the meal, and stuff. Don't act *happy*. I went, Yeah, no way. He goes, Yeah, you did. He goes, We're just *educatin'* you, Mark, don't worry about it, y'know? Just don't *do* that, y'know—just *walk*. When you *win,* you can run out. Y'know, just—when you lose, don't.

T. You're not supposed to feel hungry if the Tigers lose, huh?

M. And then he told me a few other things, right? I can't really remember. But it was like—it was freakin' me the whole night. And, like, you've gotta know Tom. He was freakin' me with it, right? But then at the end, I said, No, are you kiddin' me? He *really* said that? And he goes, Tom goes, No, *I'm* just tellin' you. Because when you ran by *me,* you almost knocked me over! *That's* the only reason! And he goes, Didn't I get you *tight?* I had you tight, didn't I? I said, *Yeah* you sure did. Y'know, tight means he had me scared a little bit. He used to try to get me tight. 'Cause he's been playin' like a year or two. But it educated me, really. I told him, like—I said, Tom, I haven't played a *game* yet, I don't even feel like I'm part of the *team* yet, y'know? He says, Yeah, I could see that, too—but I was just, y'know, gettin' you tight. That's all. He was just goofin' with me, that's all.

T.   But didn't you feel by the end of the year that you were starting to be part of the team, and not a newcomer?

M.   No. No, I was—the minute I pitched my first game. The minute I pitched my first game, then I felt more a part of the team. Y'know, in the beginning I was just sittin' around, more gettin' educated—I didn't *do* nothin'. Except to shag baseballs and just sit in the dugout. I did not do a thing.

During My Hot Streak I Was
Bruce Kimm's Crutch, and He Was Mine

T.   Well, early in the year things were looking kind of tough for the whole club. They'd traded for a catcher, Milt May, and then two weeks into the season he broke his ankle. I mean, I guess that looked like a disaster at the time, but it's funny—when May got hurt, they called up Bruce Kimm, and he caught you in your first start, and you took off from there. He didn't catch the other starters, he just caught you, and he caught every game you pitched the rest of the year. Who decided that? Was it Houk's idea?

M.   Who decided on that? That's Ralph. Y'know? Because, well, we were hot, right? I mean, in the beginning. It coulda been —Hey, it coulda been Milt May! You never know what's gonna happen. It was weird—that, well, Bruce caught me in Triple-A. All right, Bruce was still in Triple-A, right?

T.   Him and Gene Lamont caught you at Evansville.

M.   Yeah, Lamont. They both caught me, equal-equal, y'know? It coulda been Geno that came up. Right? If they'd seen Geno before. I really don't know what happened there. It coulda been Geno or Bruce that came up. But that's what's weird about it. They said, Hey, y'know, Bruce is your crutch. And then you're Bruce's crutch. But yet, Bruce and I saw eye to eye. Y'know?

We're sittin' there goin', him and I—y'know, he's the catcher. He's trying to make his job as the catcher, and I'm trying to make my job as a pitcher. So we communicate. So we're hot, right? And he wouldn't have got his chance if Milt didn't get hurt. Right? So it would have just been one of us. But you never know. Something different could have happened, then. I could have been back down in the *minors.* You never know.

Say I Lost That Yankee Game, I Might Not Be Here Now

T. Well, you both were hot all right. But really, the way those early games, like all those games you pitched in June—in those first seven or eight games, you just seemed to be sneaking past those teams before they knew what hit 'em. It was like you were too quick for 'em—you came in and nobody was ready, nothing was prepared. Y'know? It was like, Who's this guy? So it was like a thief in the night—I mean, you were comin' in, and it was really quiet. And unexpected. But then it seemed like that Yankee game on TV turned everything around, made it all explode. I mean, could you feel that happening?

M. People point to that. But it kinda *built up* to that. Like, say I played the Yankee game the first game, and pitched like that. It probably wouldn't have been the same. Y'know? I was goin' good, it was probably—what, my sixth win in a row? Was that it?

T. Let's see, you were 7 and 1—that game made you 8 and 1. Seven in a row.

M. That woulda been my seventh win in a row. Y'know? So then, it just *hit,* y'know? Seven wins in a row, this guy's shootin' for. Pitchin' against New York, the number-one team—y'know, they built it up like that. Then all of a sudden they see what I *do,* they go, *Whoa!* Say I lost that game! Y'know? What the hell, I look at it and say I lost that one? What woulda happened then? Say I lost it 1 to 0, y'know? Nothing.

T. You might not be here now.

M. You never know. I still ended up 19 and 9, but that'd just be one of the games I lost.

12 Those Ballplayers, They Really Know That I Like to Play Ball (The All-Star Game)

I Get a Message from the President

T. Then you went to Baltimore for two days, after that Yankee game. Did you get a telegram from Ford? Or a phone call or something?

M. Yeah. Mm-hmm. Then, I even *asked* him about that in the All-Star game. I said, Did you send me—did you call, in Baltimore, did you call me up? He goes, Yeah. I just went, *Whooaaa!* I thought, y'know, someone was playin' a joke. I just said, Whoa. It was neat, y'know? I liked it.

T. What'd he say in the telegram?

M. It wasn't a telegram. It was just a phone message for me. Y'know, a message at the thing?

T. Congratulations or something?

M. Yeah. But no number to call back.

T. He probably had someone call you.

M. No, he said he called me. It mighta been him. But he just said, I'm not gonna leave a number. Just leave a message sayin', y'know, this.

T. And then you saw him at the All-Star game?

M. Mm. That's when I asked him. He said, Yeah.

T. Did you ask him about—did you talk to him about Jack?

M. No, I went up to—y'know, the President came by me, I was waitin' for him, standin' there waitin' for him. I shook his hand, said Hi. I asked him that question. And then we kept on talkin'. I said—I don't know, I don't wanna talk to him! What am I gonna talk to him about?—I said, Where's your son Jack, I wanna talk to him. 'Cause now you're gonna get a different atmosphere.

I Meet Jack Ford, Ask Him a
Question About Chris Evert, and It Gets Blown Up

T.   So you went and talked to Jack?

M.   I walk over to Jack. Hey, Jack, how do you *like* this? He goes, Well, I mean if your dad's the President of the United States. . . . I said, Can you *go* any place? And like, y'know, like he dates Chris Evert, right? So then I just said, Hey, how's Chris Evert? He goes, *Fine,* y'know? No big deal. Just, I used to go out with her once in a while, no strings attached. But—see, some reporter sees him there, with Chris Evert. And oh, automatically, *voom!* Jack Ford! 'Cause he's a big thing. Say he was just Jack Ford, his father wasn't President. Right? It would just—it woulda been no big deal.

T.   And then somebody found out what you said to him and wrote it up?

M.   So then, like everything blew up—Oh, Mark Fidrych wants to go out with Chris Evert! No intention in my mind! You think I'm gonna walk up to her and go, Hey, my name's Mark Fidrych? How are you? The only way—if I found her in a *bar,* I mean in a gin mill, *fine!* I'd walk up to her, say, Hey, how's it goin'? But in front of reporters? You know—you know what that's gonna *be? Stop the Press!* That's just what it woulda *been.*

T.   I couldn't believe some of the questions you got asked. Like it really was—they're following your every move!

M.   Yeah, oh, I mean! They go, Oh, what'd you say to Jack Ford? Yeah, I'm gonna say *right* to him, y'know, Hey, I— y'know, this and that, I'm gonna really say right to him. What I asked him—

T.   So Jack Ford was there in the All-Star locker room, he came in with his father?

M.   Yeah! That's when I asked him. I went over and talked to *him.* Y'know, the President, I didn't even vote for him and stuff. I said, Hi to him, is all. But I asked Jack, How can you actually go out with her, her bein' a celebrity, and your dad, y'know. . . . He goes, Yeah, that's true, it's just like *you* goin' out with her. I said, That's why I never want to meet her. And I never want to meet her in front of the press. If I'm gonna meet her, I wanna meet her in a *bar.* Or something excluded from people.

'Cause it would just get blown up, just like him. Y'know? He's really not *datin'* her. I mean they—he might just go out to eat with her! Y'know, or just go—y'know, the girl can't have any freedom now? But I just wanted to see his comment on it. And he wouldn't give me a comment. He mighta just gone out with her a couple times. Who knows, y'know? But my little *mind,* y'know? That's all I had on my mind. It was just I wanted to find out how it feels goin' out with a celebrity. But he understood it cool, y'know? And, like the reporters came up to me and said, Hey—came up to him and said, Hey, what'd he say? He said, No comment. And we started talkin' about scuba divin' after that. We started talkin' about different things. And like the reporters were just gettin' over there, they didn't even catch it in time! They missed the real thing! Unless one was standin' around lucky, y'know—you always get that *lucky* reporter, right? But it seemed like they were all missin' that. They hit *me,* What'd you say to him? So I go, Nothin', no comment. Just, How'd he like goin' out with Chrissie Evert. They go, Well, didn't you ask him somethin' *different* than that? What was everyone laughin' about? I said, I don't know. Then they go over to him—he goes, Hey, we were just talkin' about scuba divin', and this and that, y'know?

T.   Who was laughing, the Secret Service guys, or something?

M.   Yeah! And stuff like that, y'know? Like *him* and *I* were laughin'! And like, y'know, a reporter hears someone laughin', and all of a sudden I'm standin' over there—they wanna hear it, y'know? Yet if it was someone else laughin', they wouldn't have thought anything about it, y'know? But it was neat.

T.   Meanwhile the reporters are following you into the bathroom to find out what you said. . . .

M.   Yeah. So now, everyone thinks I wanted to meet Chris Evert, man!

Those Ballplayers,
They Really Know That I Like to Play Ball

T.   Well, once you get up to the top, everything about you is all of a sudden a story. Like just before the All-Star game, there were stories on all the wire services—there was one where Thurman Munson of the Yankees called you *bush,* or something. They played that up.

M. Oh, yeah, that don't bother me. Because those ballplayers, they know—they really know that I like to play ball, and that's just what I do. I was in the All-Star game, and that's where I really met—y'know, some ballplayers. 'Cause you really sat down—it was weird playin' with 'em. Like, they told me Munson called me a hot dog, right? So now in the All-Star game, he's gotta be my catcher. It don't bother me. I walked in, I said, How's it goin', Thurman, y'know? No big deal! And he goes, Hey, I didn't really call you a hot dog. I said, You coulda called me anything you want—you're playin' for the Yankees, I'm playin' for Detroit, you're my *enemy.* But tonight we're not enemies. Y'know? We're out to beat these guys. Because they were cuttin' us down, like. And I just—I didn't know, I wasn't about to pop off. Like Montefusco goes, Man, how come you don't pop off, y'know? A 1.92 record, man. Best pitcher in the league, and you're not even poppin' off! He goes, C'mon, *pop off!* And I say, Whaddaya mean, I'm scared, man, I'm not gonna pop off now. But if I pop off now, what happens *later,* y'know, when I start messin' around? I start losin', I can't pop off *then,* right? Fine.

T. Montefusco's got his own style, I guess.

M. Yeah, that's just what *I* got, too. But you know, you just —people don't *want* that.

Pete Rose Teaches Me Something

T. You got a chance to talk to a lot of the other ballplayers at the All-Star game?

M. Yeah, a lot of those guys, they *teach* you something. Like when Rose got up one time and he got a hit—it was a grounder —and then he come up against me again. I was goin' nuts out there. So I said, I'm gonna get you. I looked right at him and said that. And he looked right at me and just smiled. He just gave me a smile. And then after I got down to first base—it was hit to the first baseman, he threw it to me—and Rose goes, Now, see, you got me when you got *pissed off!*

T. Is that what he yelled back?

M. Yeah, and then he just walked off.

I Couldn't Adjust to the Atmosphere
of a Cement Mound at the All-Star Game

T.   In other words, Rose helped you by making you mad?

M.   In other words, sayin', I didn't—I wasn't pissed off when I was out there in the first inning. I mean, I *was* pissed off. Y'know, I was a little jittery. Like when I was in the bull pen. And even though it's an *excuse,* but yet it's not, really—because like when I go back on the bull-pen mound, they had this thing that stood up, it was cut like *that,* flat. And if you stopped—you couldn't, y'know, you'd fall off the mound. They stopped the mound so you couldn't come back to your full stride. There wasn't like a mound. There was like half a mound, right? And you'd try to pitch, to adjust to that, and then you'd get out there, and now you—you're doin' *this* in the bull pen, now you go out *there,* and you're doin' it the same way. But then *now* you can go all the way back, and then all of a sudden you're just throwin' your whole coordination off. That's an excuse, but yet, if it was different, and the same thing happened, there'd be no excuse. But you just—y'know, you use that for like sayin' an excuse.

T.   The mound there at Veterans Stadium, other people have complained about it. But maybe you were just jittery because you were so *up* to pitch—maybe you were just trying too hard.

M.   Yeah, but that mound was lousy out there. That mound —the guy comes in braggin' to me. He goes, Hey, how's the mound? Like he's supposed to be the best moundskeeper. That mound was like pitchin' on *concrete.* I had no hole to go in! I couldn't go out and fill the hole up, 'cause there was no hole to even start! There was just—I hit it with my spike. I said, This is like *cement,* man! I mean you, it's just—that kind of mound *stinks.* I mean, a cement mound. Maybe for those guys that are always pitchin' on it, fine. But they got Astroturf, they're not usin' real spikes like we are. They're usin' rubber spikes.

T.   That field is slippery and weird, anyway.

M.   Yeah. That's an excuse *I* can use. But normally I'm sayin', I just messed up. I should have been able to *adjust* to it. I'm a pitcher, right? You adjust to the atmosphere that you're *in.* So I shoulda adjusted to that. I shoulda blown that right out of my mind, said, *Forget it,* man, it's just *hard.* No big deal. Like, I got a mound where you throw, and when you land you suddenly go, *Whoa,* when am I gonna *hit?* Y'know? It's so long before you hit. That's why in the beginning I'll never come out there and throw hard. I'll come out there and just—*pfft*—toss it, to find out the footage. I've come out there at one time, where I've went to throw hard on the first pitch. And I felt *cocky,* y'know, so I went on doin' it. All of a sudden, you never find the end of the hole! And all of a sudden your arm's *here,* and then all of a sudden you *hit.* And you go, *Whoa!* Man, instead of makin' you feel good, you look like an *idiot,* 'cause the ball hits in *front* of the thing! You never landed—when your timing was right to land, you never landed. 'Cause I mighta had two seconds off. And that two seconds, man, is—even a *second* is off, y'know? That's how timing is.

T.   So that problem with the mound at the All-Star—that kept you from getting into your groove?

M.   Yeah. But I just said, Hey, I lost. That's it. I was out there, I had a good time, y'know?

I Had to Take the Pain

T.   Well, with that kind of competition, there isn't anything to be embarrassed about—I mean, just because you lost that one game.

M.   The way I feel, that's right. That's just what I said. I said, That's it. I mean maybe if we played 'em two out of three we might beat 'em. I mean, or three out of two. Play one game, do or die, fine. Someone's *gotta* lose, right? So I had to take the pain. So I said, The hell with it—I went back and drank three bottles of wine.

T.   Well, that game's supposed to be a good time, anyway. It's not supposed to be a game where you're at each other's throats. Lately, the National League talks it up like it's like that —but that's a game too, that's just talking.

M.   But they cut us down something *fierce.* They were sayin', We should just take two National League teams and play an All-Star game and we'll have a better game! I mean, how bad is that? Next day I'm readin' this stuff.

T.   That used to hurt some people's feelings, like Reggie Jackson used to get really upset about losing those games. Some people want to win every time.

M.   No, you *do*. Oh, I was upset. I was upset, but I said, Why should I take a lamp and bust it? Is that gonna get my aggravation out? I'll just grab a few beers and get my aggravation out, and then beat a pillow or something like that. Just gotta get it out of your mind, y'know?

It's War, but No One Gets Hurt

T.   Well, the All-Star game's entertainment, though. It's something for the people. It's something for the fans—to see everybody together, all at one time.

M.   It's like I drove back, I drove—I don't even know Looie Tiant, right? We both got a cab ride back to the hotel. And he just says, Hey, don't worry 'bout it, buddy, we'll get 'em next year. He says, Hey, don't worry, y'know? 'Cause he knew how I felt. And it was neat, y'know? I never talked to this guy, I mean, it was hard *understandin'* the guy. I was just tryin' to understand him the best I can. And, y'know, you *do*. And it was just neat. Playin' with those guys—I liked it. Even though they're your enemies when you're against them. They *are* your enemies. I can't see them— if you act as if they're your friends, then they're probably gonna take advantage of you. 'Cause you might have a little weakness there, y'know? So you have to take 'em as enemies, and then off the field they're friends. I mean, what the heck. I know other guys on other teams that got traded. You see them before the game, you say, Hi. But when they get up at bat, you throw all you got; y'know? It's me or them—so it's not gonna be me. I don't *want* it to be me. It might be me, once in a while. Y'know? That's the way I take it. It's *war*. But no one gets hurt. No one really gets hurt.

Pete Rose and That Little Gap

T.   You were talking about Rose. It's really beautiful to watch him play. He puts it all down there, every time, every second, he's just putting his whole thing right out there.

M.   Yeah, but, y'know, every ballplayer is like that. But he's just—maybe, like, you're in the minors, you don't make it. So he made it as a superstar, but yet you still got that mediocre player that's just as good as him. But he just made it a little bit better. He hits—one guy might hit .275, Rose hits .300. That's just that little gap that gives him a little bit more. He likes playin' for who he's playin' for, and when you're playin for a winner it's a hell of a lot easier than playin' for a loser, y'know?

**After the All-Star Game the
Board of Health Calls Me to Find Out If I'm Dying,
but Since There's No Cure for It I Don't Call Them Back**

T.   It must have felt good, playing in that kind of company.

M.   They treated me nice at the All-Star. And then they come tellin' me that I'm gonna *die*, man! How bad is that?

T.   What happened?

M.   At Philadelphia—they had that scare? With the bad stuff in the water?

T.   You mean you were staying there then?

M.   Oh, yeah! Same day! Same time! Here, the Board of Health calls you. Hey, how you been feelin'? Doc, doc, you mean I'm gonna die? Y'know?

T.   So you were there for the All-Star game at the same time the Legionnaires were there?

M.   Oh, yeah, that's when it was all *involved,* during the All-Star game! You know that place is closed down now? No one goes there. That place is closed right down.

T.   So you got contacted by the Board of Health—where, in Detroit?

M.   Yeah! Like when I come back, Vince Desmond says, Here, call the Board of Health.

T.   The Tigers' traveling secretary?

M.   Yeah. He goes, They wanna know if you're *dyin'*. But, y'know, it's funny. They wanna know what if you're dyin', but there's no cure for what they, uh—for what those people died from. Right?

T.   They want to have you on the statistics, though.

M.   Yeah! Sure, when I pass out, they'll know what I'm gone from, man! I didn't call 'em back. Y'know, I just said, Well, Ron —I looked at Ron LeFlore and Rusty.

T.   Because they were in Philadelphia too.

M.   That's right. And I just said, Hey, they got no cure for it, so we're dead anyways! So there's no point in sayin' much about it! And Ron goes, Yeah, that's true, too. 'Cause Ron got scared. He comes over—Hey, the Board of Health want to talk to you? I said, Yeah! They told me we were gonna die from stayin' in Philadelphia, man! From drinkin' that water!

T.   Did you feel any symptoms?

M.   I don't know. Maybe it takes a while to die, who knows? I could be on the borderline, man. But if you look at it this way, everyone in the hotel shoulda died. 'Cause you shoulda seen—oh, what a massacre that woulda been! All the people there? You couldn't walk—you think it's packed down *here* during a busy hour? You shoulda seen what Philadelphia was like! You could not even *walk.* I mean, it was like, Excuse me—hittin' people. You couldn't do a *thing.* I couldn't *stop.* If I stopped, I couldn't move. I hadda keep on movin'.

T.   You mean in the hotel lobby? At the Bellevue-Stratford?

M.   Yeah. I hadda keep on movin' right through the lobby.

By Perfect Timing I Meet Elton John the Same Night I Find Out I'm Starting the All-Star Game

T.   Darrell Johnson picked the All-Star pitchers this year?

M.   Yeah. It's good.

T.   Did they tell you a little ways ahead of time that he'd picked you to be the starting pitcher?

M.   Yeah, about three days ahead. Well, the day they told me I was gonna start was *one* day. The next day I was goin' to Philadelphia, and then the next day we played. Y'know? So I was —it was during a *baseball* game, I'm sittin' in the dugout, and all of a sudden they go, Ah! Right in between innings they go, Ah, we got some news here, Mark Fidrych is gonna be startin' the All-Star game. And I go, *Whoa!* I said, Where's a drink? And that night, I'm goin' to see Elton John. I mean it was—the timin' was just perfect. I was goin' to meet Elton John! And I get that news —the same night!

**Elton John Signs His Gym Shorts
for Me and Talks About Thurman Munson**

    T. You got to talk to him?

    M. Y'know. I met him. I'm sittin' there talkin' to him. I mean, *I* didn't know how to really talk to him. I was *in* there for like twenty minutes. But I was like shocked—

    T. Was he playing in town?

    M. Yeah, he was playin' out—like out at Pontiac Stadium. And we went into his dressin' room—this reporter got me in there, y'know? And I got in there, and I didn't know what to talk to him about! And he knew *me,* man! He goes, Oh, Mark Fidrych, how are you? How's Thurman Munson? I said, What? He goes, I read the paper, man! You're a very good pitcher! Y'know? And he goes, Thurman—What's Thurman say? Thurman said you were crazy, and you said, Oh, who's Thurman Munson? He goes, I know a little bit about you. I said, *Whoa.* He's shockin' the hell outa me. I even got it on tape, man. I brought my little tape recorder in, but it didn't come out that good. 'Cause it wasn't that good a tape recorder. I was lovin' it, though. And I sat there and had a bottle —a little wine with him. And like, he gave me a pair of his gym shorts and signed 'em. And I gave him a T-shirt, man—with a picture of me and him holdin' it. I got a poster of it, too, at home. And it's just me and him holdin' it—y'know, the shirt. What the heck. It was neat. I liked it, y'know?

**I Rap with Mike Love and
Get Drunk on a Helicopter with the Beachboys**

    T. Did you meet any other famous people?

    M. Then I met, uh, that Mike guy for the Beachboys.

    T. Mike Love?

    M. Yeah, Mike Love.

    T. Oh, yeah? Where'd you meet him?

    M. In Detroit. I went to, uh—we have Pine Knobs? I went out *there.*

    T. What's that?

    M. Pine Knobs. They got me—

    T. What's that, a golf course or something?

M. Hah? No, it's a concert place. It's outdoors. And like I rode to—in the limo with him, I rode all the way to whaddayacallit, to Pine Knobs with him. Sat in the back seat.

T. You mean with—

M. With Mike Love. And we just sat there and rapped.

T. What was *he* doin' out there?

M. Huh? Playin'. He was gonna sing.

T. With the Beachboys?

M. Yeah.

T. Were the other Beachboys there?

M. Oh, yeah. They were all there. I met 'em all. I got pictures taken with 'em—like, we're all on a helicopter, right? It went in *Creem* magazine, if you saw it.

T. I didn't see it.

M. Oh, I got it. There's a few things, articles in *Creem* magazine. Like when I met Elton, and when I met the Beachboys. And like we were just sittin' in a helicopter, all of us—we're just sittin' there with beers. Man, it was *good.* I got drunk with 'em.

Dennis Wilson Asks Me to Introduce the Beachboys, but I Tell Him Enough's Enough

T. So what was your impression of the Beachboys, meeting them?

M. Y'know, the funny thing about it is like that Dennis guy who plays the drums for 'em, right?

T. Oh, Dennis Wilson.

M. He comes up to me and he goes, Mark. He goes—he was *loaded,* man, y'know? He goes, Mark, you know what you're gonna do for me tonight? You're gonna introduce our band. He goes, These people like you. We—I like you. I think you're a pretty neat guy, even though you *do* play baseball. That's nothin'. And he goes, If you don't wanna do it, that's all right, I can understand. Y'know, because you play baseball, and we sing music. But I'd like you to go out there and— And I said, Hey, man, I can't do it. I don't know, I just, I *can't,* y'know? Enough's enough, bein' exploited. He goes, Yeah, I can understand. He goes, But man, you should think it over. If you think it over before the place starts, just come tell me and we'll do it. Y'know, no big deal. I said, Fine. I ended up sittin' up where the spotlights are, right? I ended up sittin' up there watchin' the whole concert. 'Cause the light guy said, Hey, you want a good seat so you don't get hassled? Come follow me. Brought a six-pack up, walked all up the catwalk, walked all the way around, and just sat there and listened to 'em. They're just as good as anything. I got what I wanted, y'know? I got to see 'em. Then after, we went out, and you know how they—we went out and had *dinner.* And goofed around. And it was good, man.

It Could Be the Way I Do
Things Is My Own Transcendentalism

T.   That's a good life, do you think? Being a rock star?

M.   Yeah. That's, I don't know—It was good, though. Y'know, we didn't really rap baseball. We just rapped, y'know, different things. Y'know, there really wasn't that much baseball, and it really wasn't that much music. He asked me if I drank carrot juice, and all that stuff!

T.   Did he ask you if you do meditation?

M.   Mike, he—Mike asked me if I was into that transcendental and stuff? I said, No. 'Cause he's into it. He goes, Just think, if it makes you a little bit quicker. I mean he was usin' these *fraction* things, y'know? And sayin' how much you'd make an improvement. But I just—yeah, I could *see* it, but I just, I'm not *into* it, y'know?

T.   Did you ever meet anybody else who was into that kind of stuff?

M.   No. Well, a lot of other ballplayers are into it. You gotta get involved in it. But if you're not gonna get involved, then it's a waste of time, so don't even ask. Y'know? That's what it is, really. You should get involved in it before—like karate, y'know? I went up to Benjy, I asked Benjy—I said, Benjy, I'd like to take karate, y'know? All that stuff you're doin'. And he goes, I'll tell you what.

T.   Ben Oglivie?

M.   Yeah. He goes, Take it. And then you and I can goof around. But he goes, You'd better take it, and take it like— y'know, go every day and *do* it, and learn how it's done. Either that or don't even try it at all. 'Cause he goes, That'd be a waste of your time. 'Cause you gotta do it every day. Y'know, you gotta be dedicated to it. So I go, Well, *that*'s out. 'Cause I can't, y'know, be around every day.

T.   A lot of people came around and asked if you did transcendental meditation and stuff like that?

M.   Yeah, I had like—I just don't. I said, What *is* that stuff, y'know? Like, oh—Reggie Sanders. All right, I got into spring training. They were just startin' all that at Tigertown—the first year they really had it, exploited it in Tigertown, right? And so someone says, Hey, Reggie, you takin' that? That, uh, transcendental medication? He goes, No. He goes, I been playin' ball somethin' like fifteen years now. I didn't know about it for fifteen years. If I start now, I might hurt myself! Y'know, that's just— you say, Hey, it might help me some ways, it might not. Who knows? People still do it, though.

T.   I think people thought that you were into it because of your concentration when you're pitching.

M.   The way I do things. It *could* be that that's my own transcendentalism thing, though, you could say. Right?

T.   Sure. You don't have to go to school to learn that. I mean, the people that teach it are the ones that've *got* it—and the ones that want to learn it are the one's that don't have it!

13 I Get in a Bad Train of Atmosphere in Cleveland

A Bad Train of Atmosphere in Cleveland

T. So, okay, then came the period when a little transcendentalism might have come in handy. Right in there after the All-Star game, that was the time when everything was just blowing up for you. Everywhere you went. And I take it all the reaction you were getting then—it was starting to make it hard to concentrate. Like in that Saturday national TV game against the Indians, in the middle of the summer. Let's see, July 24. Those guys on the Indians bench, what were they doing? Just getting on you, trying to agitate you and break up your concentration?

M. Oh, yeah. But that wasn't—

T. Because you looked like you were getting pissed off out there on the mound.

M. I was!

T. Ralph lifted you in the fifth—I think it was the first game you didn't finish in something like five weeks. Or maybe only the second time all year. On your way out it looked like you yelled something back at the Cleveland bench. But those throwing errors —what hurt you there, really, were a couple of throwing errors in the fourth. They got two runs off it, and you looked pissed.

M. No, that's what—all right, that's when you gotta keep your composure. Right? Like you just said, okay, the game was —it started gettin' screwy. But still, then they started throwin' the ball around. They started, y'know, just throwin' everything around. *That's* when you had to get your composure back, sayin', All right, we gotta relax things down. Slow things down a little bit, let everyone get their heads back together, y'know? Because we were all—we weren't functioning good together, at that point. And they knew it. Everyone knew it. 'Cause when we came *back* to each other, y'know, there, we'd all say, we'd come back and we'd say, Hey—*voom, voom.* Y'know, we're all set. We just came back, and they said, Mark, don't worry about it. And I said, I ain't worried about it. There's still a tie score. And they're sayin', Yeah, this and that. And—but yet, I was goin' *too* nuts. So where he's —Ralph mighta said, Hey, it's time to pull this kid before he blows. I was ready to blow. I mean just because of the train of atmosphere. But after I settled down, I wasn't ready to blow. I mean, after I talked to the guy. And he said—y'know, I said *bullshit* on the air, and stuff like that.

You Can't Do That on TV (I Expressed My Feelings)

T.   You said that where, on the radio?

M.   No, it was on the air. On the air—the guy comes up. You know *why*—because, see . . .

T.   What, you mean after that game there was an interview?

M.   Yeah. See, after the game, this guy—he comes up. Y'know, because it was on national TV. He came up, and goes like this to me, y'know? He goes, It looked like you were about ready to crack. During the game, y'know, when he pulled you out. When they knocked you out.

T.   Was this Tony Kubek, or one of those guys?

M.   Ah, one of those guys. It wasn't Kubek. I forgot who it really was. It might have been Kubek. But I just, y'know, I looked at him, and then I just remembered—I went back, I flashed back to like when I was in high school. And I said, Wait a minute! You ain't gonna cut *me* down on the air like that any more. Y'know? He said, It looked like you were gonna cry. I just said, No, I wasn't about to cry, I was just *bullshit.* I just—you know what I said? I said, *I was just bullshit.* That's what I said. And then I said, Excuse me. I said, I didn't mean to swear on the air, but I just showed you my feelings. And I dropped it right then and there. I didn't explain, I'm just sayin' to him, Hey, you shouldn't have said that. Y'know? You *knew* what kind of an atmosphere I was in, man. You don't go and say things like that on the air. If you're gonna come down and get on *me* like that, I'm gonna get *you,* too. Y'know?

T.   Yeah, they were just patronizing you, so—

M.   But then after that was over, like, I come back—because Ronnie and I were on. Ron LeFlore and I were on the air. And we come back to the locker room, right? And those guys, y'know —they said, *Whoa,* I don't believe you *said* that!

T.   What guys?

M.   Y'know, the guys on the team. They heard, they thought —they heard I'd said *fuck* on the air. And I said, No, I didn't say that. I said to them, I didn't—I said, Hey, I did not *say* that. I don't remember sayin' that. Y'know, if I *did,* I'm sorry. I didn't say that! They said, Hey, man—they pulled me over and they said, Hey, you can't do that. When you're on national TV, or anything, you can't swear like that. They said, Hey, Bowie Kuhn I betcha ten to one is gonna *fine* you for that! I said, *Whoa,* that guy can't fine me for that, man! He's got no—he can't *do* that to me!

T.   Did it make it on the air?

M.   Yeah. Oh, it made it! It's like, y'know—it made it! I *did*—

T.   It came and went fast, eh?

M.   It came and went—oh, my dad! I talked to my dad, my dad was *angry* at me! Y'know? He said, Don't say *bullshit.* Say somethin' else! Oh, he—oh, damn! Oh, he . . . it was on the air. Y'know? And now I got *scared.* I said, Oh, damn! Right? So—

T.   All you were doing was being yourself.

M.   I expressed my feelings! I expressed my feelings, that's just what I did, I expressed my feelings to myself. But then they said, Oh, God, Bowie Kuhn's gonna fine you! If anything. You're gonna get fined probably, because you—they want to teach you. Or somethin' like that. I said, No way, no way!

I Get a Telegram from Bowie Kuhn

T.   But you didn't hear from Bowie Kuhn?

M.   Next day—all right, we're playin' in Cleveland. A doubleheader, right? Here I am. I come to the ballpark, we play the first game. We win. All right. The clubbie, the clubbie played— they all played it great. They were actin' it out, they played it great. I have to admit that they had me scared!

T.   What, the clubhouse boy in Cleveland?

M.   Yeah. All right, clubbie comes up and goes, Hey, you got a telegram. I said, Hey, no big deal. I said, It's probably one of my friends, sayin', Hey, don't worry about it. Opened it up. Bowie Kuhn! Fines you two hundred and fifty dollars! I'm sittin' there goin', *Whoa!* I dropped everything. I had a sandwich, milk—I dropped everything! I said, Ralph, Ralph! Where are you, Ralph? I was screamin' for Ralph, man. I mean I said to John Hiller, who was right next to me—I said, John, can he do this? John goes, Yeah, he can, we told you that yesterday, y'know? And I said, No! He can't fine me like this! I said, I can't afford two hundred and fifty dollars! I said, I ain't *goin'* that good, I can't afford it! I said, Come on, he can't get me for a *mental* mistake! I went, Ralph— and Ralph goes, Hey, I can't say anything. I mean, if he fined ya —that's one of the things you have to find out. Y'know? He goes, you know how you live life, you gotta find it out the hard way? He goes, You just found it out the hard way. I said, Come on, Ralph, pull some *strings!* He goes, I can't pull any strings. I said, Whaddaya *mean* you can't pull strings? He said, Hey, he's the commissioner, right? I said, *Wow.* I said, I ain't payin' this, man. I said, No way. He goes, You're payin'. Wow, I'm goin' crazy— we had twenty minutes, and I'm goin' nuts. And everyone else is *laughin'*—goin' Ha, ha, ha, we *told* you so! And a lot of the veterans are comin' up, ridin' me, y'know? Goin', You loved that two hundred and fifty bucks, y'know? And they're ridin' me, gettin' me goin'. I had some cheesecake, I took the cheesecake in my hand and I went, *Boom!* I threw it in the trash. I said, *Hell,* they can't do this to me! I said, Where is he? I wanted to *call* him, man. And Ralph says, Talk to him Monday. Y'know, this was Sunday. And he said, Talk to him Monday. He might be home, y'know? And I said, Where's the telephone? I was goin' nuts, right?

    T.   I bet nobody would give you his number!

    M.   I mean, they *knew* I was blowin' it. But they let it go to where they'd had their fun, y'know? They'd literally had their fun. And then John Hiller came up to me. And he goes, We played a joke on you. And I said, *Whoa.* I said, You *what?* He goes, We played a joke on you. We set it up. Y'know, you made the mistake. But it was such a thing that we could set it up, because you didn't know anything about it. We set it up on you. And I said, *Wow.*

But they blew my mind for like twenty minutes. And they were havin' such a good laugh. Everyone knew it! Everyone knew it! But they'd typed the telegram up *so* good—it was great, they'd had a reporter type it up, right? And sent it down in a Western Union telegram, and everything. I mean, it was set up. Because I looked, and I said, No way. And I *studied* it, because I saw a lot of telegrams in my life. And I said, Hey—he's from, y'know, *there,* and it *came* from there. And I said, *Whoa.*

T.   They were trying to teach you a little lesson?

M.   That's what I mean, y'know? That's just what I mean. They taught me a lesson.

T.   So you figured they were doin' that for you?

M.   That's right. But yet it scared the shit outa me!

T.   That's a lesson.

M.   A *good* lesson. Y'know? And now, I look at that as a joke to tell people. Because it's a joke that I was so scared, man.

T.   And later, you could laugh at it?

M.   *That's* what I mean about that joke. It was so good, and such a set-up. And after—after they'd told me, they even laughed harder. I mean—and *I* even had to crack up laughin', and say, *Wow,* you S.O.B.s did this to me!

T.   So it worked—they took you down out of your tension about it.

M.   Yeah! Oh, I was in *such* tension! Two hundred and fifty dollars! But it's just—that guy just hit me with the wrong atmosphere about it.

My First-Base Coach Finds Some Words on the Baseball

T.   The TV guy hit you with it, yeah—but you were already upset by then. Where you really blew your cool was in the game.

M.   That's right. That's what I was sayin', that's what I told you from the beginning. I was blowin' my cool.

T.   What were the Indians yellin' at you? I mean, out of their dugout?

M.   I don't pay no—I don't hear 'em yellin'.

T.   Did somebody write something on the ball? I heard the Indians wrote an obscene note to you on the ball.

M.   Oh, on the baseball. I didn't get the baseball. My first-base coach got the ball. He didn't tell me anything about it.

T.   Who's that, Tracewski? Dick Tracewski?

M.   Yeah, he got it.

T.   At the beginning of the game, or between innings?

M.   The beginning of the game. And like, they didn't tell me anything about it, right? And like, he just let it slide. He just grabbed it. He didn't want me—he figured if I saw it it might blow me, right? Probably—in his mind he was probably thinkin' that. So he grabbed it. He intercepted it.

The Twins Throw Thirteen Pigeons at Me

M.   Just—like, and the Twins. Just like the Twins threw those, uh, pigeons. Thirteen pigeons! They go, Oh, this is your thirteenth complete game. Or your thirteenth start. They did—I mean, they tried to do that to blow my concentration.

T.   That would have been your thirteenth start, July 20. But I didn't know they did this with the pigeons before the game.

M.   Yeah. Before the game. It was in Minnesota. And they went and did that, right? And so, here I am, y'know, pitchin' the game. And like, I'm warmin' up—

T.   Where'd they have the pigeons?

M.   They had 'em on the *mound!* Before the game.

T.   How'd they get 'em there?

M.   Oh, they kept—they were homing pigeons. Some guy brought his homing pigeons there.

T.   Did the management think it up? It couldn't have been the players!

M.   No, the management. Uh, one of the—like, I guess the head man.

T.   Like a stunt, you mean? A promotional thing? Because I see they drew something like thirty thousand in that game, on a Tuesday night—biggest crowd they had all season.

M.   Yeah, it was just like—it was like a *circus,* man! Here I am, gettin' ready to pitch for the circus! That's why I said, What the hell is this? This ain't no baseball game, a guy doin' this, right? Here's this guy—it's like the ticket guy. So he's doin' this to draw people in, right? So here I am, I'm gonna pitch against the Twins. And I'm sittin' there, y'know, warmin' up. And all of a sudden they start talkin'. They bring the thirteen pigeons out, they bring all the guys out, right?

T.   You didn't hear about this before it happened?

M.   I didn't know it was gonna happen. All right, they bring it all out. And they do all that, and they put it on the mound. They put 'em on the mound. And I'm warmin' up now.

T.   The p.a. system's goin' on all this time?

M.   Yeah, the p.a.—oh, they're talkin', man, they're doin' all that. They're sayin', Hey, this is Mark, and this and this. And all of a sudden—I'm there, *Wow,* y'know? I'm just throwin'. And like, the guys down there, a lot of the ballplayers—*my* ballplayers, they're goin', Yeah, they're just *harassin'* you, man. I said, Yeah, I know. And that's just what they were doin'. But like, it's not the same harassment as the other ball team'll give you, y'know? It's different harassment with these guys. I'm sittin' there goin', They're—y'know, it's just that they were exploitin' me more than what was bein' made.

T.   Did Ralph say anything to you about it?

M.   Ralph's just sayin', Hey, don't worry about it. Y'know? And they set the thirteen pigeons off. And then just before I was ready to pitch, there's this silence. And it was cut. Y'know, Bruce threw it down to the second baseman. I got the ball. And the silence was cut, when I was just gettin' ready. And the announcer, just before the game started, when I was ready to pitch to those guys—he goes, Mark, I hope this doesn't scare you, I mean this is your thirteenth complete game, I think it was he said. Or, your thirteenth start. Somethin' like that. And he goes, I hope it's not a jinx on you. And all that. And like, I just *turned*—and I stopped everything I was thinkin' about and just freaked out and listened to this guy. And I said, *What* the—

T.   And just then they let the pigeons go?

M.   No, they let the pigeons off *before* that. But he announced it then—

T.   Ah, I see! And they put it together for you by sayin' that—

M.   Yeah, yeah, they put that together. Right at the beginning of the game. And then I ran out—the National Anthem was played, and I came out to pitch. At my time, right? And then, that's when everything started. And then he hit me with *everything*. Like he was just talkin' to *me!* And I just looked up, kinda, at the guy. Y'know? I was—I just went, *Wow,* and he talked to me. It was like he was talkin' directly to me, and everything else was quiet. I think you coulda heard a pin drop, it was so quiet. And he just announced to me. And I just went, *Wow.*

We Beat Their Thirteen Jinx

T.   All that must have flustered you a little, at least—they got three runs off you early. But you hung on—

M.   And then, all right, I had—one of their guys, right, some reporter sent me a picture. I got the guy's name at home, on an envelope—he sent me a picture that he took. It was like, in the seventh inning, they put up, on an electric billboard—*THANKS A LOT, BIRD!* Y'know, for bringin' so many people in our ballpark. And then, like, they dropped it. They knew they were beat, man. They dropped it. Because we were losin' three to nothin'—they were beatin' me, too. Y'know? And it like blew my mind. They were beatin' me, man. But then all of a sudden, my team said, Hey, screw them. They knew—probably they *knew* it kinda blew my mind. And *voom,* we beat 'em 6 to 3, y'know? I mean, they got three runs, and our team came up with six. I mean, three here—I mean, four, or three or somethin'. But we came up with six runs.

T.   It was eight—you won 8–3.

M.   Yeah. But they didn't get—after we went ahead of them, they didn't get any more. Because the team said, y'know—guys were comin' up to me and sayin', That's bush, what they did to you, man. They shouldn't have done that. That's bush! Y'know? I mean other people were comin' up, and all the reporters came up and said, How did you feel about it? I said, We beat their *thirteen* jinx! They thought it was gonna be a big jinx. The guy—they made a *promotion* about it, y'know? A big thing about it. And that promotion *fell.* That's what I loved about it. It *fell.* It would have been great, if they'd won. But it fell. That's what was great. That's what my victory was, and that's what our victory was—that they fell. Y'know?

Those Losses Were Mental Lapses

T. You ran into this kind of stuff everywhere you went?

M. Oh, definitely. Like, Cleveland did it. Yeah, all that—they try to blow your mind!

T. And was it buggin' you?

M. No, not buggin' me. Not really buggin' me. Just, some teams. It was a good antic. You could laugh if you beat 'em. But if you didn't beat 'em, you didn't laugh.

T. Do you think that at a point in there after the All-Star game—do you think there was a period in there where it was getting so intense, and weird, and strange, that it was getting to your head? I mean if you look at the record—like up to the Fourth of July you were 9–1. And from then until the middle of September you were only 5–8, so something was—all that publicity . . . maybe it was getting to your head.

M. Yeah, it mighta been, It was—it was a mental lapse. That's all I can say, is those losses were mental lapses. They ain't that you didn't *pitch* good. They're just mental lapses.

I Blow My Mind and Throw
Butch Wynegar One Change-up Too Many

T. There was another game against the Twins, near the end of August—August 21, right? Where you lost 7–3 in the eleventh. Or the tenth, I guess it was. You held 'em for like seven, eight innings, but then in the tenth—

M. Yeah, I remember that game. It was at home.

T. It was 3–3 going into the tenth. They got two guys on, you walked Carew on purpose to load 'em up, then hit a guy to force in a run. And then Butch Wynegar singled in two more, and somebody else doubled *him* in . . .

M. Yeah, I was messin' up. I was blowin' up out there, and they took me out. I didn't complete the game, they took me out —no, I *mighta* completed that game . . .

T. You completed it, but they got four runs in the—

M. Yeah, like in the eleventh inning I blew up. It was like —you know what it was? In that game, they got their one run that got 'em ahead in the game.

T.   You hit Ford with a pitch to force in the run—

M.   Yeah. And then I just said, *Wow.* I was so upset about myself, I was throwin' crap. Y'know? Instead of throwin' a fastball, I threw a slider. Y'know? Or I threw a change-up. Like Wynegar, I remember that time—I threw him a change-up. I had got him on change-ups before—earlier in the game I had got him on a change-up. So now I come with the change-up again. I just, y'know—Bruce called for a different pitch, I said, No, I got him on a change-up before. So I came with the change-up. And *voom,* he got a hit, y'know? And they scored the runs. And then it just —it started blowin' my mind. And then Ralph came out, and we got outa the inning. He said, I'm gonna leave you in the game. Because now we need more, right? He just—*voom.* He knew I blew my mind. I *did* blow my mind.

T.   But once a game like that's over, you've just got to bounce back and forget it, right?

•   M.   Y'know, I just—it was just one of those games. But yet, now you could talk to your teammates. Your teammates help you about it, y'know?

What More Could They Do?

T.   Well, everybody's gotta go through that now and then. You've got to lose a few.

M.   You do! And like I'm sayin', Frank went through it earlier. I'm just usin' him for an example. Frank went through it earlier, before he even got a win.

T.   Oh, Frank MacCormack? You mean doing so badly when he first came up?

M.   Y'know? He went through it. If he had a win and went through it, it might be different. Right? It's just, y'know, the whole thing of the game. You gotta get your first win—it's like gettin' your first hit.

T.   But as far as you're concerned, you've got the confidence of what you did early—of getting your feet on the ground, beating people, then losing a few, but coming back strong. Maybe that bit of experience insures you against trouble next year. I mean, people say, Next year—okay, you know you've been through the first one. That can't be anything but an advantage. I mean, what more could they throw at you than thirteen pigeons! What could be more bizarre than that?

M. Yeah, that's what I'm sayin'!

T. Like suppose they called you "The Lizard," and just before you were going to pitch they let thirty lizards out of the dugout! What *more* could they do?

M. Right. I mean, right now I'm just sayin'—they're hittin' me with sayin', Next year there's gonna be so much pressure on you. I said—

T. There already was!

M. It was there. And it's—

T. There'll never be so much—

M. It can't be any more. It can't *ever* be more.

T. I mean, when they're talking about pressure, and the sophomore jinx—could that possibly be more than what this year put you through, and what you had to put up with?

M. No. I don't know. Maybe it came out now, and that's that.

T. I bet in two years from now, if you got into a World Series, the pressure wouldn't be as much. Because by then people would know you and be used to you.

M. Yeah, y'know? You just realize you gotta find out what they're tryin' to do with you.

I Spend Two or Three Days in a Bird Cage in Anaheim and Get My Little TV Out of It

T. Along those lines, was there a thing in Anaheim where they made some kind of a cage to put you in to sign autographs, like a big bird cage?

M. Yeah.

T. And then it broke down or you got locked in or something? Somebody said that.

M. No, it didn't break down. Whaddaya mean, break down?

T. They put you in it before the game?

M. Yeah, the guy came up, he goes, We're trying to make a million people. Right? And he goes, You're a good drawing card. Would you please come up and sign autographs before the game? I said, Okay, I'll sign autographs from seven o'clock till seven thirty. And like, he went through Ralph. And Ralph said, I know the guy. If you want to do it, do it. Y'know, *I'm* tellin' you you can do it. I said, Okay, Ralph, I'll do it for the guy. And I did it for him. And, y'know, it was just—y'know, I did it, and they blew a big thing up about it. But I did it because, y'know, they were askin' me to do it. And I said, Fine. You wanna get this and you wanna get that, fine. Y'know? It ain't gonna hurt me. What am *I* gonna be doin'? I'm just sittin' around. Maybe I'll get lucky and find a lady that comes through, y'know? That's all I'm lookin' at too, y'know? Maybe I'm gonna meet somethin' that's gonna benefit me as much as it's gonna benefit you. Right? That's the way I look at it.

T.   They put you in a cage to do it?

M.   Yeah, I mean they—no, they had, like they were takin' infield, right? So I wouldn't get hit by infield, they just had a cage around me, y'know? But I mean, other ballplayers could see me doin' it, too. Like the guys on my team were concerned. They said, What are you gettin' outa this? They said, Hey, you better not be doin' that for nothin'. And I said, Don't worry, I ain't doin' it for nothin'. They said, you better not be doin' it for nothin'. If you are, you're crazy. Because you're takin' *your* time. And they said, Make sure you get somethin' out of it. Y'know? And I got my somethin' out of it. I got, y'know, what I wanted. I got my little TV out of the deal.

T.   Oh, yeah?

M.   Y'know? It was nice. So, I spent two, three days, I think —I don't know what it was, two days or three days, y'know? An hour at the most. So I got my little TV out of it. It didn't bother me. It didn't hassle me. I met, y'know, different people. Y'know, a kid comin' up to me, and goofin' around with him? I didn't mind it, y'know? It didn't bother me at all. I just was happy doin' it.

T.   They gave you a television set for it?

M.   It was neat. At the end—I mean, like I didn't really know what kind of a TV I was gonna get. But when I got my TV, I was satisfied. He coulda sent me a little console like that big. Instead he sends me somethin' like *that,* y'know?

T.   What, like twenty-inch?

M.   Yeah! Y'know, I mean it was just—I went, *Whoa!* I mean, like they treated me—y'know, fine. Just like Ralph said they would, probably. But yet other ballplayers, guys on my team, said, Hey, you don't have to do that. Because they knew. They said, Don't let them take advantage of you now. I mean, there's a point to draw the line. And they said, You just went over that point. Because I did, y'know?

They All Ask the Same
Questions, so They All Get the Same Story

T.   Talking about taking advantage . . . around that time, when you'd come into towns with the team, would a lot of people come and want to interview you and talk to you?

M.   Oh, yeah.

T.   Ask you the same questions every time?

M.   Oh, yeah, every single one of 'em. That's why I always wanted to sit 'em all down at once. Like in New York, right? *This* guy'll hit you, and then *this* guy'll hit you. But they all get the same story. Because it's all the same questions. Instead of every individual hittin' you, y'know? You're more excited talkin' to them if they're all around at once. Y'know? Instead of takin' ten individuals, *voom,* you take all of 'em. And you just rap to 'em. And they ask you a question, you answer 'em. But if I can't answer, I'll say, I can't answer you. It's as simple as that. Please rephrase the question, I can't answer it. I don't know what you're talkin' about. Y'know? I'll do that. And they'll respect me for it. Because then they'll come back with a different—y'know, I'll say, You used too big of a word. All right, what do you mean by that word? Y'know? Because words mean a *lot* of different ways. Depends on how you put 'em, right? And they'll hit me with a big word, and I'll say, Hey, I don't know. *Voom!*

T.   So they didn't get in your way too much?

M.   No. They were all right.

I Blow Up at Some New York Reporters
Until a Ballplayer Reminds Me That They Made Me

T.   At least most of the reporters seemed to be on your side, which helps.

M.   Yeah, well. One time, like I was sittin' there. And I—I lost against New York, right? They hit two home runs in the game, I think.

T.   Yeah, that was August 3, Yankee Stadium. They came back and beat you 4–3 on that homer by Gamble in the seventh.

M.   Y'know? It just—everything blew up. And like we were ready to leave. We're goin' out to leave the next day, y'know? I mean *that* day. We were gonna leave right after the game. I was really upset. I was just gettin' ready to leave. And like, the reporters wanted to talk to me and find out, y'know, how I felt. And I said, I ain't—before they even walked in, I said, I ain't gonna talk to any one of those guys. And one ballplayer hits me, he goes, Hey, just remember—*they* made *you* just as much as you did yourself. I said, Yeah, that's true, too. It started hittin' me then. Y'know? I mean I was *blowin' up*—y'know, still. But I mean if he didn't hit me with it, I would've gone out—I know I would've gone out and said, Hey, screw you guys! I woulda just split. I woulda left. But since he broke my train of thought and said *that,* right? *Voom,* that stopped me, and I thought about it. That made me think about it, harder. Y'know? Instead of just really blowin' your mind. Y'know how someone—you got one train of thought, and all of a sudden it gets cut down, and then it stops you? And then you start thinkin' about *another* train of thought, *voom!* So it did. It started me thinkin'. I said, Okay. So then I sat down with all those guys and started talkin' again. Y'know? And started feelin' things out. And then they were all done. And *then* I left. Y'know, I told 'em—I said, I didn't want to *talk* to you guys! And, y'know, they started laughin'! Y'know, they said, You had—we can imagine what you feel. Y'know, and stuff like that. And then you just start gettin' more involved. And yet, here I am—I lost, and yet I say a few words, and those guys start laughin'. So it gets *you* kind of a little laughin'. And here I am, I just *lost!* I shouldn't be laughin', man, I just lost! Y'know? But then, I just let it go after that. I just sat there and drank some Jack Daniels. And, y'know—that's goin' from *high,* to *low,* back up to *high!* I was upset, but things like that happen. What are ya gonna do?

A Book All About Newspaper
Clippings, but You Got Nothing Out of It

T.   You even had a book written about you before you'd won ten games in the big leagues—*Go, Bird, Go!*

M. Hey, fifty thousand copies were written of that book, and I haven't even read it yet! It was written in a book, all about newspaper clippings. Fifty thousand copies were sold, like *that.*

T.   In one week?

M. They sold out before they—they couldn't put out enough. And now I'm sittin' there goin'—I woulda sat *down* with the guy. And just told him everything I know about life and be done with it, y'know?

T.   You mean the guy didn't talk to you?

M. No, y'know, like when they put that book out I just said, Hey, why not just, y'know, forget about that, big deal, because they couldn't *do* that if you weren't playing baseball. And just remember baseball's, y'know, the thing that got you that book there. But got you nothing out of it, though.

T.   So you just weren't consulted when that book was being written?

M. No. That's why I say—that's why I really didn't *read* that Bird book. 'Cause I had nothin' to say in it. I said, Hey, what they say—and every time anyone comes up to me and says, Whaddaya think about that Bird book? I just say, I didn't read it. I have nothin' to say about it. That's all I say, and I drop it right then and there.

I'm Doing What I Always Did, but Now All They Want to Hear About Is Talking to the Baseball

T.   So what'd you think of the image that got created of you in the media by that book and all the other stuff people wrote? Like some funny cartoon character—this flaky, nutty guy who talks to baseballs?

M. I ain't flaky, nutty. I just—that's just the way I went through the game. Like I told you, I never knew anything about it, until they started mentionin' it. Y'know? Like—This guy's talkin' to baseballs. And then they say, Did you do it in Little League? I look back to Little League—did I do it? I seriously look back. And I say, Dad, did I do it? And he says, Yeah, you did it before. I go, *Wow,* I did? Y'know? Now they're startin' to make me think, What did I do? Y'know? But yet I was doin' it all along and didn't know it.

T.   Well, it isn't something you can consciously think about.

Like saying, Today I'll go out and I'll talk to this baseball.

M. Hey, there's been many games that I've gone out and I haven't talked to the baseball. If you're gettin' down to talkin' to baseballs—in the beginning I was just pitchin', and I was feelin' good, and I was pitchin'. Y'know, it was just the first game I started in baseball. The second game, I was still talkin' to the baseball, but maybe not as much. But still I was doin' it. And every game I do it. It just depends what kind of atmosphere I'm in when I'm pitchin' that game that you're gonna get into. It's just like, any kind of time you do work—if you're doin' good, you're gonna stay in that atmosphere, right? And then somethin' different comes up, and you're still doin' all right. Y'know? Some days you don't talk, some days you do. Like, after you lose a game, they say, I don't think you talked to the baseball that much! Y'know? Whaddaya mean? I did the exact same things as I did when I went there the first time, as I did the second time. And you just—you just say, Well, maybe I should have talked more. And then you say, *Whoa,* wait a minute, this guy's tellin' me I didn't *do* it, now. Then you go, *Whoa.* You say, Wait, wait, I was out there, I did what I hadda do. I didn't win, but I still did the same things I did the *first* time out, y'know? But just the breaks went the other way! That's normal! But just because this guy said, Maybe in the third inning you didn't talk hard—you didn't say three words to the ball. Where you might not have talked to it, you might have just pitched and didn't say a thing—you just, y'know, walked around and didn't do nothin'. But that was the time to walk around and do nothin'. You were just thinkin' in your head. But then when it got down to the bare facts of bein' more explosive—y'know, to blow up a little bit more—*that's* when you started blowin' up at yourself—and *voom,* they start talkin' about the ball. But it's—hey, third inning, if I didn't give up any runs, they wouldn't have said it then. They say, You gave up two runs. But you weren't talkin' to the ball. If you were talkin' to the ball you wouldn't have gave up the runs. And then you start lookin' at the guy. Thinkin', What the hell, man? You start lookin'—you start *thinkin'* about a person then, Y'know?

At Least I Showed Up Every Time

T. What was your reaction to that kind of thing? I mean, how could you explain—

M. I just—I said, *Wow,* y'know? I went out there and did what I had to do. Y'know? I at least *appeared* for the game. As one pitcher told me, Every game they asked me to start, I started. I didn't come up with any ailments so that I couldn't pitch. I didn't come up with this, I didn't come up with that. I started it. Maybe I didn't finish it, but I at least *started* it. That's more than a lot of people can say. Y'know? Because I took the agony. And I took the defeat. And I at least came out every time to show up. I didn't hide. I came out. I coulda said, Oh, no, I don't feel like playin'. Y'know, or, I can't pitch. Or somethin' like that—I coulda done that. But I was out there every time. I was out there to start the game—maybe I wasn't there at the end, but I was out there at the start. You gotta have someone to start it.

14 The Girls Really Do Sit Down in the Halls and Wait for You

A Magazine Article That Keeps a Lot of the Ladies Away

T. So by the middle of the summer you'd been interviewed by so many people it probably got hard to remember what you'd told the last one. Didn't you say you told one magazine that you only go out with girls when you're horny, and that it got you in trouble with the girls?

M. See, y'know, I *said* that. You know that? But, y'know, it's weird. When I was at the airport—the other day, I was comin' out here. And this girl who works there—I went through that inspection thing? And she goes, Oh, you're Mark Fidrych! And I go, Yeah. And then, I was just sittin' there, and the buzzer went off and I took all my junk out. She goes, Oh, I read that thing you wrote in that magazine. And I said, What—what's that? She said, Somethin' about you only go out with girls when you're horny. And I said, Yeah, that's true, you want a date? She goes, I'd *never* go out with you! I just—I said, Fine. No big deal. And then the girl beside me, checkin' all my change and junk, *she* goes, That shows where *her* head's at. *I'd* still go out with you. She goes, Big deal, you could always say somethin' to a magazine, y'know? I said, Well, see, my thing worked. That keeps a lot of the ladies away. 'Cause now they won't come out and hit on me so much!

T. So this interview—what magazine did that come out in?

M. It was a woman's magazine.

T. What's the name of it?

M. I don't know. She told me the name, I just don't—I don't think of it, y'know? I'll give people hours and I won't even remember who it was. There are so many of 'em at any time.

**Ball Four Told It Like It Is—In the Big Leagues the
Girls Really Do Sit Down in the Halls and Wait for You**

T.   Well, *whatever* the magazine was, I don't think that was
such a bad thing to say.

M.   No!

T.   I mean, just for being honest—but you wouldn't be the
first guy who ever got in trouble for telling the truth!

M.   No, y'know? But, like here—it's like this book. You
could make this a kids' book. And you could make this an adults'
book. You know what I mean? It could be like *Ball Four,* if I
wanted it to be like that. I never read *Ball Four* in my life. But
it could be *exactly* like that, y'know? And story-wise. Or you
could just make it, y'know, a kids' story. What'll you make it? You
know what I mean?

T.   I think it's probably closer to *Ball Four.*

M.   That's what I mean. But like you look—you look at this
kid that's ten years old now. He's gonna start readin' it, and he's
gonna go—*Whoa,* I got a different head on this guy now. It might
blow a lot of people's minds. They'd say, *Whoa,* is this what he's
like?

T.   I think kids are sort of hip, y'know? The kids are maybe
more hip than—

M.   Than the grown-ups think they are!

T.   Well, the kids are probably going to be less of a problem
than—I mean, a lot of people have their own idea of what you're
like. What if you tell your story in your own words, the way it
really is, and then they say, Listen, Mark, you probably shouldn't
let it out this way, y'know, you probably should be much more
careful?

M.   I can't see that. Hey, why change it? I mean, *then* they're
gettin' a false atmosphere. And then *I* gotta live with it. I mean,
it's a *trip* to me. How many of your friends have ever had a book
written about them, y'know?

T.   Right.

M.   I'm just sayin', if they're gonna go and say *that,* they just
do what the other guy did—just write the book, y'know? Why
even get the guy's views? Here you're gettin' the guy's views.
We're sittin' down and you're gettin' my views.

T. But you brought up *Ball Four.* I don't think *Ball Four* —*Ball Four* was meant to be an exposé, y'know? Whereas here you're just telling your story, you're not intending to write an exposé.

M. What do you mean, an exposé?

T. Bouton was writing about his experiences over the years and trying to make baseball seem—I guess he just wanted to make it seem more believable.

M. Yeah, well, that's how it *is!*

T. And to tell the truth.

M. Well, that's just—that's just how I learned this to be, when I got to the big leagues. The minors is a whole different atmosphere of baseball. The *game*'s still played the same. But, when you got to the big leagues—it's *true.* They *do* actually sit down in the halls and wait for you. And they *do* actually call you up and ask you to go out. Y'know? And it's—it was, y'know, weird. First stage around the road trips, I didn't do nothin' but go down to the bar and goof around. Second time around, after they knew me—it was something. Like, y'know, *voom,* they were *there.*

T. Who was—you mean the reporters calling you up?

M. No! *Girls.* That's what I'm talkin' about. I mean, y'know, it was just *like* that.

T. Oh, you mean like *Ball Four?*

M. Yeah!

My Roomie and I Meet the Baby-Oil Lady of Baltimore

T. So you're talking about what happened this summer? Like, starting your second time around in the league?

M. Yeah. I mean, like that's—That's when it really started, y'know? And like I couldn't really believe it was gonna happen like this. 'Cause they told me it was gonna happen. They said, You just *watch.*

T. But doesn't it sort of rip off your energy to try to deal with everybody that calls you up?

M. Mmm. Oh, yeah, but I mean, that's what I—

T. Did you ever *try* to deal with everybody who calls you up?

M. Yeah. If I don't *have* something, I would. But then if you saw it and you don't like it, you go, *Pfft,* see you later. But still, it got to the point where it was, *Wow,* y'know? Here I *am,* y'know, my roommate and I—two chicks come up, one chick gets sick and the other just takes on *both* of us! And we're sittin' there goin', *Whoa.* I'm lookin' at *him,* y'know, and he's lookin' at *me,* and we're goin' *Yeahh!* Like, we called her *Baby-Oil Lady,* because she liked baby oil. Y'know? I'm just sittin' there, *Whoa!* Y'know? I'm *trippin' out* at this!

T. Where was this?

M. This was *Baltimore!* And like the chick goes—I go like this, I go, Do you *like* this? She goes, *Yeah,* I like it. And I said, *Whoa!*

T. Was she young?

M. Yeah, she mighta been young. She was only about— maybe four-foot-ten.

T. A ballplayer groupie? Who hung around the ballpark?

M. Every time I came to Baltimore she was there.

T. I take it she wasn't the only one?

M. No!

A Girl Back Home Changes Her Tune
(Now It's a Whole Different Atmosphere)

T. That's got to be a funny feeling—I mean, it's a little hard to respect those girls' motives, huh?

M. All right, that's like—all right, I'll go home, right? Went home for Thanksgivin', I'm sittin' there—y'know, I went to a bar with my buddy. I'm sittin' there drinkin' away, and stuff. Y'know, meetin' all your old school people that you went with—y'know, when I was a senior? And meetin' a lot of chicks, y'know? And this one chick comes up and she goes, Mark, I don't know what it is, but I *still* don't like you. I don't care *who* the hell you are, I still don't like you. And I go, Diane, that's all right, I don't like you either. Like that. She says, You—and then she sat down and started *talkin'* to me. I'd never really talked to this chick before. But then we started. Like I kinda brought *her* head up—sayin', Hey, bitch, I don't need that, y'know? We started talkin'. I said, Diane, I'd still ask you out even if you *don't* like me. She goes,

I'd probably still go out with you, too. I don't know what it is, why I said that. She couldn't give me an answer, really, why she said it. But it was neat when I said that. 'Cause her eyes just looked and said, *Wow!* I'm sayin', like, Where's *your* head at? I mean, that high school shit's over with, y'know? Now you're talkin' about *life*. I mean, if you don't—I mean, there's been many a guy I didn't like, or I just didn't hang around with in high school, and I hang around with 'em now. Like, if I go home, and they're in the bar, I'll say hello to 'em and have a few drinks with 'em. Y'know, go out and goof around with 'em for a while. And yet, before I wouldn't have. But now I do, because it's a whole different atmosphere. You're not in school any more, y'know? *He's* out workin' hard. You know what *his* feelings are, too, y'know? That's a lot different. But like she took it as, y'know, still in high school. And I said, Get outa here.

T.   And yet, now she'd go out with you—so she changed her tune!

M.   Yeah, that's just what I'm sayin'.

T.   It must be a little strange when you don't know what people are after. They're after you for something that—it's half you, and it's half something else.

M.   It's what they want.

T.   But for them it's a connection, through you, with something else. With whatever fame is. You think it's like that for everybody?

M.   Oh, it is for everyone that makes the majors. It is, when you go home. Like when I was in the minors, and I'd go home, no one knew you.

T.   But suppose you were pitching for the Tigers, and you were just another pitcher.

M.   Oh, they'd know me—at home.

T.   So it'd be the same?

M.   Oh, yeah. It'd be the same. You might not be *exploited* the same, but it's the same. Because you're playin' major league ball, right?

Now I Can't Even Act Comfortable

T.   At first all that attention's probably a real kick.

M.   Yeah, it was. It was a trip. Y'know, here I am in the

major leagues. But then—it kept on goin', y'know? The ride is still goin'. And it's still there. But you're gettin' a different atmosphere on it now. You're sayin', *Whoa,* I gotta—

T.   Be a little more selective?

M.   Yeah, you gotta say, *Whoa*—I gotta do *this* now, I gotta do *that.* Y'know, I'll let *that* one go.

T.   So you started picking things out—

M.   Yeah. That's what they told me to do, y'know? Don't take everything. But at first, though, you *do* take everything. Because, y'know, your head's just *blown* by it. And then you just finally say, *Whoa,* I can't handle everything. Y'know? It's like you said with the ladies, Do you take every single one? No! A lot of times you say, Hey, I can't—I just want to come up and have a few beers with my buddy, and that's *it.* I don't want to, y'know, act, and talk to you. But like now I go home—before, I'd go home, go to the same bar. Y'know, it'd be nothin'. I mean, I'm not talkin' about *my* town. Any time I go into my town, they knew what I was doin'. But I mean outside of my town—like, say, Worcester, right? I went to Worcester, right? And I went to a bar. *Voom!* One kid knew me. One person said, Oh, how's it goin', Mark? And he told his friend—Oh, that's Mark Fidrych. And all of a sudden they told their friends. And all of a sudden the whole bar knew about it. And *now* I can't even act comfortable, can't even get drunk. Y'know? I mean, to where I want to. I can't—y'know, say I wanted to yell something, goof around, right?

T.   You'd probably have to get a little farther away from civilization and television—a little farther away than Worcester, before you'd find places where you could go and nobody'd recognize you.

M.   Yeah. But then, really, you *could* yell and goof around and stuff. *Now,* I get to that bar. And then the guy—like there was a one-man band up there, just playin' music and stuff? And he exploits it. The guy goes, Oh, boy, just think, we got a big celebrity in here, y'know? He goes, Just think, I'm playin' in a big celebrity place. And I felt like yellin' at him, You're an asshole, buddy! Why don't you just let me come here and have a few beers with my buddies? I go in with three buddies. I'd just got home, y'know? And I said, Bill—before we even get in, I said, You watch. Someone's gonna know me. He says, Nah, I can't see that. And then

Timmy Ellsworth goes, Nah, I can't see that. And I said, Tim, you haven't been around it. McAfee's seen a little bit of it, you haven't. Like, Tim, I'd never really hung around with—he'd been married and just come back for Thanksgiving, y'know? He works down on the Cape. And he goes, *Nah,* no way. I said, You just watch. I'll give me ten minutes in that place, and everyone's gonna know me. And I said, I'll throw any kinda money you want on it. I mean, that's how *sure* I was when I'm goin' into it. And I walked in, I got a beer, I'm just standin' there. And I'm sittin' there—*Mark,* you see those people over there? They're lookin' right *at* us! They're tryin' to discover, Is it him or isn't it? And they *were.* And like my other buddy's sittin' there—so I go, Timmy, it didn't even take ten seconds. Look over here, see those people? They're discussin' what we're doin' right now. And all of a sudden, *voom, voom,* just like that—Timmy looks at me and goes, Jesus, you're right! I said, That's true.

T.   Ten seconds, that doesn't give you much time to relax and get natural.

M.   No! And so, you know what the bartender did? I mean, this is how *weak* the bartender was at the place. He goes, I tell you what, I'll give you a free beer if you give me an autograph. And here I am! I look at the guy. I said, No, I'll take four, please, and here's the money for 'em. I said, Man, I got the money for 'em, I don't have to sign—and he goes, You won't give me an autograph? I said, No, not the way you—

T.   He tried to buy it—

M.   I said, I'll tell you what, I give you an autograph and you give me *four* beers. I'm gonna make you *pay* for it now, if you're gonna be like that!

T.   The price just went up!

M.   Y'know? He coulda give me the beer, and I woulda just paid for it. And he coulda just *asked* me for an autograph, and I woulda signed it. Just like other people in the place were doin' that. And then the bartender hits me—I just cracked up. Y'know, this guy—you gotta be kiddin' me!

When I Dance, *Then* Come Up and Ask Me

T.   I could see how that kind of stuff would drive you nuts sometimes, when you just want to take it easy. It's okay when you want to be sociable, when you want stuff happening. But when you want to lay back—

M. Yeah! Let's say—then, like, I go to that bar. And say I'm rappin' to a nice chick, and all of a sudden this *mullion* chick comes up and says, I want a date, right? I mean, all right—I'm in Detroit, I'm on a date. I *like* this chick, y'know? And I'm on a date, takin' her out and havin' a good time, y'know? Sittin' at a bar, you can dance and have a drink, her and I are just rappin'. All of a sudden this chick comes right out of nowhere, *jumps* in my lap, starts kissin' me! And I'm just sittin' there goin', *Wow,* I don't even *know* this girl! And I look over at my date—I look at the girl, and I go, *This* is the girl I came here with. This is the girl I want to *be* here with. I said, Hey, I haven't even danced with *her.* So I ain't about to dance with *you.* So, I mean, when I dance, then come up and ask me. Until then, I'm already occupied, if you don't mind. The chick—*weeooaw!* It blows her mind. I said I don't —I don't need it. Ten minutes later, the exact same thing happens. And my date's goin'—she's just *lookin'* at the chick, goin' . . . can you imagine what's goin' through her mind? How she *feels?* Like —God, if he's like *this,* I can imagine what he's like on the *road!* I mean, there's no way I'm gonna go with this character, man— he's out with every Tom, Dick, and Harry! What's he gonna give *me?* Y'know? And that's just—that's the only thing that's weird about *that.*

They'd Leave Me Alone if I Was Married

T. Do you think it'd make any difference to them if you were married?

M. Chicks?

T. Yeah.

M. Yeah, it would. If I got married, and they came and started foolin' around, I'd just say, Get the hell out of here—I don't need it.

T. I mean, would it make any difference to them?

M. Oh, yeah, I think it would. I do, for some reason. Because they know I'm not married, y'know?

T. Right, so then there's always that chance.

M. Right. They'd find out if I'm married. Then I think they would, y'know, say, Well, leave him alone, now. Y'know? My wife, I mean, you're not gonna go over—you're not gonna have fifty million chicks, I mean, a girl's gotta be pretty stupid if she's gonna come knockin' on your door when your *wife's* right there, y'know? I mean—Remember me, Mark, before you got married? When you dated me? I'd be goin', Oh, God!

Why Not Experience This While I Can?

T.   But like at Evansville, or somewhere, that just wasn't around?

M.   That stuff was never there, man. I mean, I never had any problems doin' nothin'. I'd go down the street, nothin'. I wouldn't call 'em *problems,* either. Goin' to Detroit, I—that's why I'm *stayin'* in Detroit. I still *like* it, y'know? If I really, really, absolutely wanted to get away from it—from it really, really blowin' my mind—I'd be away. Because why aren't I home, y'know? And then fly out here from home? 'Cause, home's the same to me. My friends are there, and it just hasn't changed yet. They're all doin' the same jobs. So when I end up *here,* then I always get to go home. It's always gonna be there. So why not experience this, while I can? That's why I live in Detroit, y'know? There's a lot for me to do out there. And I can do it.

T.   Well, I think you handle it great. I mean, you've survived it!

M.   Y'know? I *am* relaxin'. Like, I moved out of my other apartment because I had no—I had, I couldn't even have five minutes to myself. So I got this new apartment now, and no one comes around.

T.   Now you've got better security, or something?

M.   Yeah, they got security there. And no one can get in the front door without buzzin'. Y'know? And then they gotta go on up to *my* door.

T.   Is it in the suburbs?

M.   No, it's out of the suburbs. Y'know? It's in the suburbs, but I mean, it's on a high—you drive on a highway, I-94, and you just take a left, and you just, *voom,* y'know, you're on it. But it's still—I could sit home now, for a whole night, and just sit there and watch TV and not have to worry about someone knockin' at the door for an autograph. I could get drunk now, and not have to come to the door and just, y'know, look at a person. I could buzz down.

Mickey Stanley Tells Me I Ought to Put Out Numbers

T. Did you ever stay over at the ballpark? Like sleep over there?

M. No. No, I never had to do that. But it just got to a point, y'know, like I'd have a chick over to my old apartment. Y'know, come home with one? And like, you'd come *home* with a chick, and there's these . . .

T. They're there waiting?

M. This is at one thirty in the morning! Two o'clock in the morning, now, right? You'd come home with a lady or somethin', and there might be three or four ladies sittin' there! Or a couple *guys* sittin' there, wantin' an autograph. Somethin' like that. It was weird. And like my buddies, we just sat there—and we'd laugh. Goin', *Wow,* y'know? And then, one time, I brought Mickey Stanley over, right? I came home with Mickey Stanley— it was in the afternoon, right? Mickey Stanley just came over. And he goes, God damn, you oughta make it a meat shop. Put *numbers* out there, it's so bad. He goes, How the heck do you *live* like this? I said, Man—y'know, they're there, they don't get in my door. Some of 'em *do* get in my door, y'know? But they're all like waitin' their turn to get in that door! When they get in, I mean, it's like *that.* They're just—and it's weird, y'know? I mean, girls are *funny,* man. I mean, that's why I got a different atmosphere on it now.

Ralph Houk Tells Me to Stay
Home and Let 'Em Come to Me, and I Do

T. You just want to make sure none of this starts hurting you in your work, right?

M. It's just, I don't know—that's the main thing. Like Ralph told me, before the season even started. He goes, There's one thing I got to say to you. He goes, You're a pitcher—stay a pitcher. But just watch out for the booze and the ladies. He goes, Drink your booze at home, and stuff like that. And have your ladies at home, and stuff like that. But just don't go out chasin'.

Because you could stay up all night and come home with nothin'. So now, all right, I don't—I'm in a bar, I don't *chase* chicks any more. Y'know? They actually come to you, now, come up and start talkin' to you. And you just start talkin' to them. And then you just say, Hey, I'm leavin'. I'm goin' home. Like to come? They go, Yeah. Right, y'know? I'm not goin' up to them, now, and have to—y'know, find some kinda *rap* and shit? All I do is go to a bar, and go to a pinball machine, or play pool—just sit there and just do that. Or just stand, or sit at the bar, right? And that's it. They come up and rap to *you.*

T.   One of these days you're gonna meet one of 'em that sweeps you off your feet!

M.   Yeah, that's just what's gonna happen. But I bet you ten to one I hustle her up before she hustles me up.

T.   Yeah, undoubtedly.

15 When You Get Down to Real Life, the Bird Was Just a Symbol

On the Road Your Body Gets Tired

T. Even though you've got all these diversions in the big leagues now, isn't it still mostly just life on the road? I mean, okay, you're flying, but isn't it still a hassle, all that flying? All those hotels?

M. Is it a hassle?

T. I mean, do you ever get tired of it? Your body gets tired?

M. Yeah, your body gets tired. 'Cause you get tired, 'cause you wanna—you're just sick of bein' cramped up in a room. Y'know? You wanna like have your apartment, where you got your music, y'know? Where I can look outside, now. Or just get in my car and take off and *go* someplace. Y'know, say, I've been in this room for twelve days—it's startin' to be like a jail, y'know? It's not the same as playin' baseball. You get to go to the park, and stuff. But still if you go home and listen to your . . . but, too, when you go on the road, it breaks up the monotony of stayin' *home*. y'know? Stuff like that. I don't mind travelin'. but when you get on the road twelve, fifteen days, you are *dead* tired. You are.

T. Even when you're flying.

M. Yeah, even *though* you're flyin', is right. But you just get tired of sittin' in the hotel. You get tired of goin' out to eat, y'know? You're not sittin' home and eatin', like in front of the TV. Or, y'know, you're just not home—where *home* is, y'know what I mean? Like, you just mighta left somethin' *exciting* back in Detroit. And now all of a sudden you're on the road, and when you come back you never *see* it, y'know?

197

T.   Yeah, I guess it's really different. Even though there's people there on the road, and women and stuff, it's maybe not the one you wanted at the time. Maybe they're not the people you want to be around at the time.

M.   You run into some weird people, man.

On the Road You've Got
Nothing to Do, You Just Want to Conk Out

T.   So when you're on the road, your phone rings and it's some girl you don't know on the other end. But what if it doesn't ring? What else is there to do?

M.   You got nothing to do.

T.   Not much else *to* do, is there?

M.   No, not really. You can go duckpin bowlin' in Baltimore.

T.   *What* do you do in Baltimore?

M.   Duckpin bowlin'.

T.   What's that?

M.   Instead of tenpins. They're not as big as the regular things, y'know? It's a smaller ball and smaller pins. It's a good game.

T.   Any other cities where you found things to do?

M.   Not really.

T.   Not much to do anyplace, huh?

M.   No.

T.   So, in other words, it's a lot of dead time on your hands, really.

M.   Yeah. But you gotta—that's why you gotta find somethin' to do. Y'know, people say you got so much time on your hands. You *do*. But a lot of that time you wanna relax. Y'know, just sit in the room and conk out for the whole day, 'cause you don't want to be hassled.

T.   But the ballpark's where the business is at, so that's what you get yourself up for.

M.   Yeah. Get ready at five o'clock, and then I go to work.

Some Things to Do at the Ballpark

T.   What do you do when you get to the ballpark?

M.   Get dressed and go out and shag baseballs. And then

come in, sit down, and wait for the game to start. That's all you do, y'know? You do that.

T. You keep things active in the clubhouse and stuff, though?

M. Oh, I do. You walk in the trainer's room, sit with the guys, and be in there tellin' jokes or just goofin' around, y'know? And then when that gets boring you go outside and sit around. Either that, or a lot of times you go sign autographs. Either that or maybe one of your friends will pop up, that you used to know. Y'know, here, like when I was playin' against the Twins, a kid that used to live in our town—well, he lived in Southboro—he was on his way out to California with his older brother, and he stopped, 'cause he knew we were playin'. He went to the game. And I just said Hi to him and rapped to him. And like when I was out in— like out here in Anaheim, Pat Murphy, I see him. And then—a lot of times you know people. Baltimore, I know someone at. Most of the towns you do. Come home to Boston. New York, my friends come. Y'know? And . . . Cleveland? I don't know anyone in Cleveland. Oh, yeah, well I knew a guy there—I only saw him once. Kid I used to play baseball with. First time we were in Cleveland, he was out in center field. And we just—he said, Hey, how's it goin'? And I said, *Wow.* 'Cause I was in shock from seein' him, 'cause I'd forgot all about him, y'know? Like when I was playin' Triple-A, he was playin' A ball.

If You Just Sit There on the Bench the Whole Game, It Gets Boring

T. When the games are goin' on, it looks like a lot of the time you're down at the edge of the dugout, yellin' a lot and kind of keeping yourself in the game.

M. I'm yellin'. I'm like—it gives you somethin' to *do,* y'know? But yet you're havin' fun at it. Like when we're out in the field, I might run in the clubhouse and get somethin' to eat. Y'know, like just grab a cracker, somethin' to break the monotony. And then come back—y'know, go up there again, come back. There's just different things like that, y'know? But you gotta do it. Because I can't just sit there and sit on the bench. I mean if you just sit there the whole game, it gets boring. You gotta fool around a little bit. But then, you can only fool around if you're winnin', y'know?

T.   You've got to sit still if you aren't winning?

M.   Oh, yeah. You don't *want* to, really—you're gettin' beat ten to nothin', you don't want to yell no joke out. No one's gonna *laugh,* y'know?

When I'm Out There Working, There's No Need for Me to Yell

T.   One time Ralph said that in the dugout you always made a lot of noise, *except* when you were pitching. He said you were totally silent when you were pitching.

M.   Yeah. 'Cause then, there's no need for me to yell. I'm out there *workin',* and it's like—y'know, I'm out there, I'm thinkin' about the *game* now, and what's goin' on. When I'm *not* pitchin', *that's* why I'm yellin'. Because *those* guys are up there bustin' their ass, and now I can give *my* percentage on the bench. Because I'm not—I can't give my percentage out in the field, y'know? That's why I fool around like that. I just sit back, watch the game. Oh, I yell once in a while, if somethin's startin' to go wrong, I'll get—y'know, I'll get a little riled, y'know?

They Call Me Bird when They Want to Exploit Me

T.   Do the other ballplayers—I mean, your buddies don't usually call you Bird, do they? I mean, except as a joke?

M.   Oh, you mean like Lance Parrish was callin' me Bird, here? But, hey, two seconds later he might call me Mark, y'know? Like when he first introduced me to all his friends, he introduced me as Mark. But then he started gettin' drunk, and he called me Bird. So you look at that. And you say, Hey, it's a nickname. Y'know? Because when he introduced me to his friends he coulda said, Mark, uh—this is The Bird, y'know? He coulda done that. But he said, This is Mark. Y'know, he didn't exploit it out. Because he knew I didn't want him to exploit it out. But yet his friends knew me! Before I even went over there, I bet you ten to one they knew me.

T.   You mean those dudes sitting around the place?

M.   Yeah. I just, y'know, it's because I played ball with

Lance. Y'know, what they know about Lance they gotta know about all the other ballplayers, too—guys he plays with. 'Cause he'll mention it, y'know? Like if he writes to them, or talks to them, he mentions it. Just like I go home—and just like I met you, I mention it to a lot of guys, right? Just like they mention a lot of you in their home towns. Because they want to exploit you, y'know?

When You Get Down to
Real Life, the Bird Was Just a Symbol

T. So you'd just as soon pass on out of that Bird stage of your life? You were saying you don't want that name in the title of your book.

M. I don't want anything to do with Bird in it. It's just, y'know—people are gonna know it.

T. What's going to happen, man, is that in ten years, you're going to be—you're not gonna be a joke. So why not start not being a joke right away? I mean, because The Bird is sort of a joke, y'know?

M. It's not a joke. It's a good nickname. And it's got every —it's got all its points. But when you try to get down to real life and gettin' across it, y'know, that was just a little symbol. You gotta get down—you gotta get down to the real life now. I mean the tactics of what did it there. I mean everyone's got their nickname. Say my nickname *wasn't* Bird and I did the same thing. Say they used *Fid*. When I go home, you think they call me Bird? They do it jokingly—they go, *Hey, Bird!* And then they laugh, and they go, C'mon, Fid, let's get outa here. They call me Fid at home.

T. Since high school?

M. Oh, since—since I been a little kid. Since I been goin' to school it's always been Fid. Right? But then now it became Bird. But it's just—it was good, y'know? Like in New York, I went out with Big Bird and all that. Do you think I *wanted* to do all that?

Goofing Around with the Real
Big Bird in Yankee Stadium Gives Me a Rush

T. How'd they get you into that—did the William Morris Agency set that up? Steve Pinkus, your agent, called you?

M. Yeah. Steve goes, It's gonna be good for your image. All right? And I said, Yeah, that's true—but for *them!* For *Sesame Street.* It was like doin' a free commercial for *Sesame Street.*

T. Where'd you go to do it, a studio?

M. No, in New York! In New York, before a game! Oh, they filmed it and they did all that stuff. Can you imagine gettin' your picture took with—I liked it! I had a good time doin' it. You know why?

T. So they had the actual guy out there at Yankee Stadium? The guy who plays—

M. Big Bird—the guy that did it and everything. But, you know why? See, I said, *Whoa,* before I even do this, I'm gonna meet the guy. I went and met him. And he was a neat guy.

T. The guy inside the suit?

M. Yeah, the guy inside the suit. I met him, I said, Hey, how's it goin', buddy! I said, You and I are supposed to go out there and mess around now, y'know? He goes, Yeah, it's true. He goes, Just goof around. And I did. I just went out there and had a good time. I said, All right, they wanna make it entertaining, so we'll just fool around. And we *did,* y'know? Stephen gets to walk around the field in Yankee Stadium.

T. Did he get a kick out of that?

M. Oh, I *know* he did! I know he was rushin' on it. 'Cause *I* was rushin' on it, too. So he's gotta be rushin' on it. Stephen's *gotta* be feelin' somethin'.

M. Well, being on the field at Yankee Stadium's a thrill if you grew up in New York.

M. Y'know? Like he tells me, I mean every time we're out with people, he always goes—Jim Campbell gave me his box seat tickets for the World Series! So, see, Detroit's treatin' *him* good. And now, see, he's helpin' *me.* See, Detroit said, *Whoa,* we got a good ballplayer here, man. Now here, we'll be nice to you. Please help him out because we just want him to play baseball. And don't mess his mind up, and don't let people mess with him. And that's what's good about it! Y'know? It all works in a certain—but he tells me all like that. And he's—he's excited, man, too. Y'know? He's *super*-excited. What the heck, I don't blame him. 'Cause *I* am. I mean, all right, I was goin' with that Big Bird and goofin' around with him. So what? I said, Well, I'll look at Channel 2—

I mean here's my little sister used to always watch it. Right? My little sister, Laurie. I mean, here *I'd* be, watchin' a program, and it came on—like I think at four o'clock. She'd come runnin' in and turn it up! I'd say, Hey, you can't do that! But then—It's educational, Mark. I said, Okay, fine. And I'd just go off and do somethin' for a half hour. She used to love it. Y'know? And *I* used to sit there and watch it, once in a while. And now here I am seeing that actual Big Bird and messin' with him. Just because back in '74 this guy called me Bird.

My Dad Always Said,
Keep It Level and Dig Your Own Little Hole

T.   You were talking about your image. Every little thing you did got blown up.

M.   Yeah.

T.   People went on a lot about the way you get down on one knee and pat the dirt into shape before an inning. But actually a lot of pitchers work on the mound with their spikes—instead of using their hands, they just kick out a hole.

M.   Yeah, well, see, I fill it up because I've always filled it up, ever since I been a little kid. Y'know? My father—I don't know, he always said, Hey, you're goin' down in a hole, and then you're gone. Keep it level, and *dig* your own little hole. And then fill it back up, and *dig* your little hole. Y'know? But yet a guy—some guys love to pitch out of a hole. They pitch better. If they have it full, they can't pitch. It's just in their mind! 'Cause they can— but the coordination you have all the time, you're always doin' the same coordination. And if somethin', like if you get on the mound, and all of a sudden you step back and it's cut *deeper*—you go back, and then you come up, and now you gotta readjust yourself! Because you're steppin' back too far. Where one mound might be all the way flat, so you're comin' back flat. Where the *next* mound you come in and you're goin', *Whoa*—down, and then up again. Y'know? That's two motions instead of just one. So that's just two whole things that you got different. Y'know, then you gotta readjust.

T.   Do you ever go out and find out the other guy likes it flat too? The other pitcher doesn't dig?

M.   Yeah. Oh, yeah, if he don't dig it. He let's the—he just let's the hole get bigger and bigger. He just don't *do* nothin', y'know?

T.   I notice some guys like to dig big enough holes so that they can land in 'em and use the hole to hold their foot in.

M. Yeah.

T.   But you come out of it anyway, I mean you pull your foot out?

M. Yeah.

T.   So you've had pretty much the same motion since— what, years, huh?

M. That's right.

I Never Did Talk to the Ball, I'm Just Trying to Control Myself

T.   Getting back to the talking-to-the-baseball thing, some of the games that I saw you pitch it looked like you were really talking to yourself.

M. I am!

T.   So what you're saying—the instructions are to yourself, not to the ball?

M. No, no—see *they* related it to me talkin' to the ball. I never did talk to the ball. I might have the ball there, and just goof around. But I'm sayin', Come on, Mark, you gotta throw a strike! Y'know, Let's get the thing *in* there, I mean, what are you *doin'* out here, y'know?

T.   Psyching yourself up, then.

M. That's just what I'm doin'. And it's just like that *other* guy. They asked me, y'know—I forget, I don't know who he plays for, that left-hander? That relief pitcher? He comes in, and he goes in back of the mound and psyches himself up.

T.   Oh, Hrabosky. Hrabosky, of St. Louis.

M. Yeah. And they asked me, Did you get this from Hrabosky? I said, Who's Hrabosky? I mean, I just—I came up, and they said, Oh, you're talkin' to the ball. And I'm *not* talkin' to the ball. But they still tell me this—they try and tell me I'm talkin' to the ball! But I say, No, hey, I'm not talkin' to the ball, I'm just tryin' to keep myself under control. I ain't gonna look at the ball and say, Hey, c'mon, ball, c'mon, ball! Y'know?

Taking a Picture of a Spot and Aiming for It

T.   Maybe it's—maybe they think that, because you've got this habit where before each pitch you hold the ball out in front of you and kind of zero in with it. You've got it in your hand, and you're aiming with it. Maybe that's what makes people think you're talking to it, where really you're just talking, and kind of zeroing in on—

M.   You mean I'm goin' like *this?* With the ball like this?

T.   Yeah!

M.   Well, I'm doin' that—see, my pitching coach when I was in the minors, I used to throw, and he used to *always*—

T.   Who's this, Grodzicki?

M.   Yeah. He goes, When you let your slider go, if it breaks too far in the middle, then you know you let it out *here.* And he goes, When you throw your fastball, if it's high, you know you let it go way up *here,* instead of down *here.* So he goes, Just tell yourself, Bring your arm *down,* and throw. Instead of havin' it way up here. Like if I throw a high fastball, I'll go, Damn it, bring it *down.* Y'know, you're keepin it *up.* 'Cause I know I left the ball up. That's like if I'm gonna throw a slider over here—if I throw a weak one that's breakin' over in the middle, right? And I go, C'mon, right in the *middle* there! So now—

T.   So in other words you're kind of true-ing in on this spot out in front of you, where you're holding the ball up before you deliver? Like visualizing a groove and then throwing into it?

M.   Yeah! So now, I'm gettin' ready. I'm lookin' at the spot I want. See, now, right in front. So now, when you're ready to throw it, just when you're ready to leave the ball go—and your mind goes, *Now. Voom.* Because you really do know when your body's *there.* Y'know, you've just got the feeling your body's there. You say, *Now,* in your mind, and you let it go. That's what it is, and that's what Grod explained to me. And if you sit down and think about it—

T.   It's like you're seeing the pitch before you throw it, almost?

M.   It's like—but you still—your eyes are right on the catcher's mitt. 'Cause he's got it right where you want it. And now, you're just takin' a picture—up here, like if you're throwin' a breakin' ball—takin' a picture of a spot. And aimin' for that. But you're really aimin' for his glove. But then you aim for that spot —because you know it's gonna hit his glove, 'cause you know your break. And then *voom,* it goes in, like that. You think—now I'm thinkin', I'm gettin' technical about it, right? But when I'm out there, it ain't technical. It's just, I throw it—if it goes, it goes. I mean, it might break—it might break ten feet, or it might break two feet. Y'know? I don't *know.* But I'm just aimin' for the outside corner, any time I throw that slider. Y'know? And you adjust yourself to the way it's breakin', all through the game.

T.   Right. So in a sense, you do know where it's gonna go, by where it's been going.

M.   You don't *know.* You hope it is. Y'know, you just hope it is. I mean it's like I told you, it's—this game, it *is* luck, man. It is—whose ever cards are goin' that day. I mean, it's not skill. It *can't* be skill. If it was skill, I could go out every day and *voom, voom, voom*—no one'd touch it, if it was skill. But it's gotta have luck. It's just not skill. There's no—no game that's skill. It can't have skill in it. I couldn't throw ten strikes in a row. I tried. I actually tried. I got in the bullpen, on the mound, and got warmed up. I said, Okay, I'm gonna throw as many strikes as I can. Y'know? I couldn't throw ten in a row. I mean, and be actually strikes. And throw to where you wanna throw, y'know? I mean, maybe I could sit there and steer it, and maybe get ten. But I mean just really sit down and *throw* it, y'know?

My Dad's Always Said, Throw to the Knees

T.   A guy I know's a friend of Graig Nettles of the Yankees, and Nettles was telling him that he didn't think you threw the ball any harder than anybody else, but that—he said that the rare thing about you is that a guy as young as you could throw so many strikes between here and here. Between the knee and the thigh.

M.   See, that's what they drive through your mind. I mean ever since I been pitchin', my dad's always said, Keep it low. Throw to the knees, throw to the knees. Y'know? Tell your catcher to bring it right down. But now, you get up here and the catchers are always right there, man. They're always, y'know— it's *there.*

T. In the majors they're always down low, giving you that low target?

M. Yeah. And they know that's how I throw, is low. Because they're gonna have to swing *down* at it, now, if it's *low,* right? So they're gonna hit it on the ground, and all that. That's why I'm not a strikeout pitcher. That's why you get Nolan Ryan as a strikeout pitcher. He throws the ball—what, ten, fifteen miles faster than me.

But Nolan Ryan Is a Strikeout King

T. Sure, Ryan throws awfully hard, but he's never too sure where the ball's gonna go. Think of how many pitches he has to throw every game because of that.

M. Right! But he goes—he goes three and two on batters, y'know? But then he throws that strike, where it *looks* like a strike to a batter. And it mighta been a ball, but the batter still swings at it 'cause it's three and two, and they know Ryan—y'know, he's got his strikeouts. 'Cause they gotta keep *that* in the back of their mind. But *voom, voom*—he's got that heat. But yet, here I pitched against him, he lasted six innings, y'know?

T. Because he's throwing so damn many pitches!

M. But I mean we had rain that day, we had a delay here, a delay there, and stuff, y'know?

T. Right, that was June 11—you beat him, 4–3. He struck out nine guys, you only struck out four—but you didn't walk anybody, and he walked four and had a wild pitch, and only lasted five innings.

M. But it's no big deal. It's just, *voom*—when I saw he hit three thousand strikeouts, I think it is, and I look at my fifty, I just said, I got a long way to go!

T. Yeah, but this year you walked fifty guys, and he walked about a hundred and ninety.

M. Yeah. But yet, y'know, he's a strikeout king. Right?

I Want to Walk Out of There and Say, Hey, I Beat Tiant

T. Did you notice that a lot of teams—I don't know if it just worked out this way by coincidence, but in most of the games you pitched, you were up against the other team's top pitchers. Maybe it was just the luck of the draw, but you pitched against a lot of top pitchers—Blyleven, Ryan, Perry, Tiant, Tanana . . .

M. That's just the rotation. That's just what it was.

T. Well, you drew some pretty fast company, if it was just luck. You were usually up against good pitchers, and may be because of that, you were in a lot of low-scoring, tight games. A half dozen of 'em went extra innings. I think maybe even the other pitchers were psyched up a little bit, when they pitched against you, because of the monster crowds and all the publicity.

M. Oh, I am too! I am too! I go over and—I'm pitchin' against Tiant now, the best pitcher for Boston, in my home town. You don't think I'm *psyched?* I want to *kill* that guy. I want to walk out of there and say, Hey, I beat Tiant. Y'know?

Frank Tanana Can Say He's a
Better Pitcher than Me, but I Beat Him

T. So that brings out the best you've got, competing against a guy like Tiant?

M. Yeah! It's just like when I pitched against Frank Tanana at my home park. At the end of the game, he goes, I know I'm a better pitcher than Fidrych, but he just *won.*

T. Did he really say that? After that game in August?

M. Yeah! I said, So what? I got *my* victory, y'know? You say he's a better pitcher than me—maybe he is. Maybe if I pitched against him the second time, he woulda beaten me. But it's a one-out-of-one draw. I beat him.

T. He's cocky, he's just cocky.

M. Yeah. That's true, he's just cocky. But like, him and I see each other—Hey, how's it goin', y'know? No big deal. He just tells the press that, to keep 'em goin'. It gives 'em somethin' to write about. But yet it's not gonna bother *me,* 'cause I beat him.

T. Yeah, maybe he was just keeping the writers busy.

M. But yet, if *he* beat *me,* he wouldn't have said that. Y'know, he woulda said, Yeah, we won. But *I* coulda said it! Y'know? And he woulda taken a different *atmosphere.* But when you lose, you take it in that atmosphere. Oh, 'cause lookit, we didn't *touch* him, all the way through the whole game, man! We couldn't do nothin'. We're gettin' beat, I think, three to one. No, no, we're gettin' beat one-nothin', I think. I mean, oh, he was pitchin' a good game. And then I just kept on holdin' it, and holdin' it. And finally, don't ask me what happened, everything just *let loose!* It was like we said, You've had enough now, buddy, that's *it.* Like the team just said, Hey—I mean they, even guys in the dugout were sayin', *C'mon,* this guy is throwin' *pus,* man! Let's *get* him! He's had *enough* fun out there! And after— y'know, it just seems somethin' *clicked* on us. On the bats! Where before we were swingin' and missin', now we were hittin' the ball—*voom, voom,* three runs like that in one inning! The game was over, just like that. Tanana worked eight innings beautiful, and the game is over now. So he comes, ah, I mean he doesn't have to come out for the ninth. I had to come out for the ninth. But yet we beat him in the eighth, I think it was, or the seventh, I'm not sure.

T.   The Tigers got two off him in the sixth, one in the eighth, and won it 3–2.

M.   Three to two, right.

T.   That must have been some night. Fifty-two thousand people!

M.   It was just weird, the way everything just clicked. I mean, *voom,* a hit, then another hit, then I think a home run. That was it. It was all over, just like that. I mean, the end of the game! I mean, he worked *so* hard. And just *voom, voom, voom*—just like that, end of the game.

When I First Get Out There I'm Too Strong, but Then When I Get Tired My Arm Slows Down and the Ball Starts Moving

T.   In a lot of those games you pitched, those really tight games, the Tigers fell behind early and then came back and won late because you hung in there. Like Jason Thompson won a couple of those for you with late-inning home runs.

M.   Yeah. And Willie Bruce—I had a *lot* of games won by home runs.

T.   Right. You were holding the other team close, so the Tigers had a chance to get back. You gave your runs up early. I think you gave up more than half the runs you gave up all year in the first four innings. And then fewer runs later on in the game —until in the ninth inning, you gave up only one run all year, out of something like twenty-three ninth innings that you pitched!

M.   Really?

T.   Yeah. Meaning you were still strong.

M.   Y'see, *you* look at that. I don't know that.

T.   I mean, when you look at your record—twenty-four complete games, best in the majors, five of 'em in extra innings—that just means you're strong. It means you're strong *late,* because you're not tiring yourself out by throwing too many pitches, right?

M.   I wouldn't know.

T.   You're working fast, you're not wasting your energy on a lot of screwing around between pitches, and you're throwing maybe 75, 80 percent strikes. Throwing just strikes, so you're only throwing 100 or 110 pitches a game, where another guy's throwing 150, 160.

M.   I wouldn't know.

T.   Well, look at it this way. The Tigers were using John Hiller a lot, but he wasn't coming in on many of your games. They used him fifty-six times, bailing out starting pitchers, and I think he relieved *you* twice, maybe three times.

M.   Yeah, but you gotta look at it too. See, maybe when I first get out there I'm too strong.

T.   Throwin' over-hard?

M.   Yeah. You know what I mean?

T.   Coming up high, the ball's rising?

M.   No, no. I'm too strong. I'm throwin' it, and the ball's not movin', y'know? It's just flat, and they hit it. But then when I get tired, the arm slows down a little bit more—and now I might be just flickin' my wrist instead of before I was just, *voom,* throwin' it and lettin' it go, right? Now, the ball's *movin',* and doin' all this stuff now, where in the beginning of the game it wasn't. Where sometimes in the beginning of the game it *is*—and at the end, it *dies,* and now it get's flat, for some people. But maybe mine started movin' later—when I needed it, it started movin'. But in the beginning it was flat.

If You Want to Play the
Waiting Game, I'll Play the Waiting Game

T.   So what you're looking for every time is that little rhythm that maybe takes you half the game to find—I mean, it's like a groove thing. The whole way you work is like a groove thing

—staying in a groove, not losing that whole thing. It's like when you were talking about how that little difference in the mound at the All-Star game threw your timing off. And that broke your groove.

M. Yeah! Yeah, that's what it was. That's why a lot of managers told 'em to step *out* on me, make me wait. 'Cause they knew I was in a groove, so they'd make me wait. I'd say, I can wait, man. I'd say, You wanna play the waitin' game, I'll play the waitin' game.

T. It looked like Oakland was doing that to you in that game in Detroit in July—July 16, the one where you beat 'em 1–0 in ten innings. They were stepping out—and then Claudell Washington, who takes a lot of time up there anyway, he kept stepping out on you, so you squatted down on the mound and made *him* wait!

M. They were playin' a waitin' game. They'd say, Hey, he's goin'—he's pumpin' up too *fast*. It's like the minute they got up there—I don't let 'em dig in, y'know? The minute they got in there, they didn't get a chance, they just had to go like *that*. They didn't have a chance to dig in. Y'know, to get in their, hit their spikes, and really *dig in* and wait for the ball. All right, so you say, Go ahead! All right, go ahead, *do* that, do what you want! *I* don't care, I'll sit and wait for you. Y'know, that's what I tried to throw into my mind, 'cause I know they're tryin' to throw me off. But I just put it in my mind, Wait! You just keep—then you keep on talkin' to yourself more. You say, Hey, all right, keep that ball low, keep on throwin'. While he's standin' outside, you're just talkin' to yourself—Keep that ball low, and let's throw a strike. And *then* when he steps back in and gets his timing, you keep on talkin' and you let *him* wait a little bit now. So now *he's* standin' there waitin' tight. And right when he's standin'—*voom!* Y'know, you try to catch *him* off guard, too. It works both ways.

I Give Washington His Pay-Back for
Backing Out, and Both Our Temperaments Blow

T. So then—Washington's still up there, and you brushed him back? And he came out after you?

M. All right. He steps in. This is just an incident, man. Bruce

and I are callin' for an inside pitch. He took, he kept takin' time
. . . I mean, *C'mon,* get *in* there, man!

T.   There was a photo of you in the wire services, squatting
down like in a duck walk and pointing in at him and yelling.

M.   All right, I'm just down like this, sayin', *C'mon,* man! I
mean, how long do you *get?* Y'know? Because it got, it was gettin'
me perturbed a little bit. But that's what he wanted, so he started
eggin' on a little bit more. He said, I'm gonna stand here a little
bit more—'cause I yelled a little thing, y'know? So he's kickin'
back, lookin' at me, smilin'. I said, Fine. I said, That's it. Bruce
goes, *Inside!* He's standin' there. I just blew it right inside. Threw
it as hard as I could. That guy *flew* back! He came out at me. He
kinda—he just held his bat back, and he goes, I'll come get ya! I
said, Come out and get me. I yelled right to him—Come on out!
You want me? Come get me! I want you too. *I* ain't gonna move.
Just get back in that batter's box. Come out and get me! So then
he started walkin'. I knew my bench was gonna clear. And I knew
their bench was gonna clear. Before he even got to me. I knew
what it would be. I *knew* there was gonna be no fight. And if there
was, I had the ball in my hand, y'know, and he had the bat in his
hand. 'Cause he was gonna come at me with the bat. But if he got
close enough, then he woulda seen what he was comin' at. And
then it mighta started. But he didn't—he didn't even cross the
white line, really. He just let a lot of people push against him,
y'know? He gave it that old, *Lemme at him! Lemme at him!* So
then, *voom,* I proceeded to strike him out. With the next pitch.
But he *got* his hit off me. Y'know? But it's just that—and he
probably got his run off me, too. Y'know, he probably scored the
run, or mighta got the hit that scored a run.

T.   Well, he was 1 for 4, but you shut them out.

M.   But still, I mean people exploited that to a lot. And yet,
it was just a game, man. Just 'cause two guys' temperaments,
y'know, blew at the same time. But then he *caught* his temperament, and I caught mine, like. Y'know? Like he—

T.   He said after the game—they asked him about you. He
said, He's a hell of a pitcher!

M.   Yeah! See, he caught his temperament. He just said, Aw,
yeah, I was playing with him. So then he—y'know, he gets his

pay-back. Y'know? It's just his *pay-back.* It's just like—like when the team's winnin' ten to nothin', and a guy gets up and bunts. And if he misses it, y'know where that next pitch is goin'? Right at him! Just because—at that guy for bein' an asshole, for buntin' with ten to nothin'. Here's the pitcher out there—his team's gettin' racked, and this guy's buntin' now, to try to score a run or somethin'. If the guy bunts and gets *on,* then the next guy up's gonna get killed! And then *that* guy's gonna say, What the hell are you doin'? You're gettin' me killed for what? *Your* stupid mistake? I'll kill you personally, *they* won't have to kill you! Y'know?

T.   In that Oakland game, they were all backin' out—a lot of those guys were backin' out on you.

M.   Yeah, well they wanted to do that—to slow me down!

You've Always Got to Have a Fighting Tactic

T.   Along about that part of the year, late in the year, when you were seeing teams for the second time around, were you pitching 'em any different? Or were you just going at 'em the same way?

M.   No! I was still goin' at 'em the same. See, it works out this way—see, all right, I went out, I beat a guy, I beat a team, right? Next team I lose to, right? If I lose to this team, that's my revenge. Next time I face 'em I got a revenge for it, right? So it gives you somethin' more to thrive for. If you beat the *other* team, you've still got a revenge—y'know, you wanna beat 'em *two,* instead of lettin' 'em be tied 1–1. But then you always get that revenge. So you always got somethin' to *fight,* y'know? You always got—before you even go out there, you got a little fightin' tactic. If I don't go out there with a little fightin' tactic, I won't be the same thing—I'll just go out there and pitch. Y'know? I gotta have a little fightin' tactic in me to go out there and make it, y'know—to *make* you feel, to make you do it. Make you thrive for it, y'know?

All They Can Do Now Is Ask Me to Pitch in Their Park

T.   Sure, but they're gonna be looking for *you* now, too.

M.   They were lookin'—Hey, they were lookin' for me al-

ready! *This year* they were lookin' for me, man. They were doin'
all kinds of things to disturb me, like I told you. I mean what could
they do *next* year, throw birdseed on the mound again? What the
heck, *that* ain't gonna bother me!

T.   Yeah, like we were talking—after the pigeons, what else
could be a surprise?

M.   Yeah! Y'know, so what can they do *now?*

T.   You know what they do now? They want you to pitch
in their park—*that's* what they do now. They just hope you come,
that's all! Bring in that forty, fifty thousand!

M.   Yeah! That's like Anaheim. They asked me to sign autographs, just 'cause I never pitched in their park. You know that?
In Anaheim—that's the only reason. The guy goes, Hey, you were
supposed to pitch here, but you got rained out, so now you're not.
So could you sign autographs to bring people in our park? I said,
Fine. Y'know? It's makin' *me* money, because we get a percentage
of their gate, too! Y'know? So I said, It don't bother *me!*

T.   I bet Jim Campbell gets a lot of phone calls from the other
general managers, asking what day you're gonna pitch.

M.   Oh! oh, God, I could imagine! Y'know? People gettin'
pissed off 'cause I wasn't—like Baltimore, I was supposed to pitch
in Baltimore one time? People were pissed off. They sold the
tickets and we got rained out. They had the tickets sold, and we
got rained out. So it just got, y'know, moved up, and so we missed
Baltimore one time. But people came up to me and said, Oh, God
damn it, I'm pissed, y'know? You're not pitchin' here! It's neat.
Y'know, that gives you an incentive to really want to pitch *more,*
too.

T.   Well, it's probably more exciting to pitch when there's
fifty thousand people there than when there's about six.

M.   Yeah. Well, that's like New York, when they booed me
after I won, right? I mean, the people that knew me and all that,
were yellin'. But I heard some boos in there, right? But those boos
were *yays* really. . . . Y'know, in New York people are neat. When
they wanted an autograph, you shoulda seen 'em! They were all
there, y'know? All the kids were good. That's why I can't com-
plain about this year. Just because of the way people have treated
me.

16 The Agents Throw the Million Dollar Man in My Face

I Get $103 in the Mail

T.   So all the stuff that people sent you, you sent back, right?

M.   What stuff's that?

T.   Didn't people send stuff to you at Tiger Stadium? I heard they sent you money.

M.   Oh, yeah, I had some money. I had $103, I think it was, sent to me from, uh, Hull, Michigan. I'm not sure if it was Hull, you can't quote me on that.

T.   Believe it or not, the Tigers said it was from *Hell,* Michigan.

M.   But—and I brought it to Ralph. I mean here I am—someone sends me $103 all in one-dollar checks, y'know? Two-dollar checks, y'know, somethin' like that. And I just went, *Whoa!* I said, I can go out and get drunk tonight and have a good time! But it shocked me. I just walked over to Ralph and said, Ralph, what do I do with this? Somebody just sent me a hundred and somethin' dollars' worth of checks, here's a note with it—and Ralph read it and said, Here, return it and send it back to 'em. Send it back to that guy. And that was it. He goes, You don't need it. And he goes, It might have somethin' *conflictin'* in it. And he goes, Say you never opened this envelope, you woulda never known it. Make it like that. And I said, Okay. And I did, I sent it back. And that was the end of that.

When the Contest Was Over,
They Expected Me to Take Home All Eight Cakes

T.   Well, you got a lot of cakes and cookies.

M.   Oh, yeah! Oh, those things just went through the clubhouse. I mean I just laid 'em out on tables. Someone's bringin' in cake on my birthday? I laid it out and everyone ate it. Y'know, I never took 'em home. I had four of 'em at *home!* Y'know, I ain't about to—y'know, I had cakes up my *ass,* man! I mean, they had me a cake-eatin' contest. They wanted me to judge one, right? Eight cakes. They wanted me to take all eight cakes home. They *expected* me to take all eight cakes home! I said, *No* way. I said, You people that made the cakes can have 'em. I got so many cakes at home *now,* y'know? It was just, *whew*—I couldn't believe it. I was even givin' 'em out—I was *throwin'* 'em out, matter of fact. Y'know, I wouldn't, I couldn't tell the person that. I said, Yeah, I kept it, and maybe ate a piece out of it, but then I hadda hit the road, y'know? I hadda go on the road for a week! I froze 'em. I had a couple in the freezer, freezin'. I was just goin', *Whoa!*

In These Other Fields I Need Help, but in Baseball I Look Out for Myself

T.   But besides cakes and cookies, some bigger things started coming in after a while, didn't they? Like TV commercials and appearances and stuff—was that the point where you got together with the William Morris Agency?

M.   Yeah.

T.   And Steve Pinkus, he's like your contact there? In the future, when people want to set stuff up with you, will you be able to set it up, or will Steve do it?

M.   No. Whatever got to do with baseball, I set up. Whatever got to do with him, he sets up. That's how it is, with us. That's how I wanted it to be. I told him that in the beginning. And he said, Fine. Whatever I get for you, I get for you, if you want it. He takes 10 percent. Like, he takes 10 percent of whatever he gets, right? But I make a lot *more*—signin' autographs, sessions, and so on. And he don't get 10 percent of that. 'Cause he don't *want* 10 percent of that. He says, I don't want that stuff. He says, I want to get what I can get, too! And he goes, Just give me 10 percent. And he ain't givin' me any of that crap.

T.   I take it he's been a big help to you?

M.   I needed his kind of help. But if it had something to do with baseball, he was no longer there. But when it comes to other things, that I don't know any kind of field in—*voom!* It ain't gonna hurt me, right? Because he's just bringin' it to me. And, y'know, *voom.* But he's the one that's the—middleman that helps you. Like the wholesaler. He's a middleman. Where, when it comes to baseball, there's no middleman, no wholesaler. I get *all* the profits. Where, now, I get *some* of the profits, but I give *him* some, because I don't know the field. And he knows it, and he's helped me. I mean, he's helped me so much it's ungodly. Man, I can't *believe* how much he's helped me. Lookin' down to real— when it gets down to this kind of work. Y'know? Not to do this, not to do that. But when it gets down to it, he's helped me a lot. I mean, he—it could be Tom Jones, who knows? Y'know, for a guy. But he was the lucky man that stepped in and helped me. Where other guys wanted to help me, but they wanted to help me in *baseball.* Y'see? He didn't hit me with a baseball—he hit me with sayin', Hey, I don't want your baseball. I want what you have *after* baseball. I said, Fine. This guy don't want baseball, y'know? He ain't gonna say nothin' about baseball. But everyone else that hit me said, Baseball, baseball, baseball. And he didn't even mention baseball. He mentioned *acting.* He mentioned *commercials.* He mentioned this. He mentioned that. He just brought up a different outlook in life. I'm sayin', *Wow,* I—whaddaya mean, commercials? I said, I can't picture myself doin' commercials. But they're doin' 'em. I said, Fine. I said, *Whoa.* He said, Hey, you talk your baseball, I don't give a hang. You talk that. He said, I just want you after baseball gets over.

    T.   You were earning the major league minimum salary this year—$16,500. And then a little more than that after the new player-management agreement brought the basic wage up to $19,000. Do you figure William Morris made you as much money this year as your salary did?

    M.   Yeah, oh, yeah.

    T.   Obviously next year it'll be more. You've got an auto show job in Detroit in January, right?

    M.   Yeah.

    T.   What do you do at that, just make an appearance?

    M.   Yeah, you just sit down. You just sit down and sign

autographs for two hours. You get thousands.

T.   So there's that, plus a couple of commercials. . . . Do you know what you're making this winter?

M.   No. I just—y'know, Steve just gives me somethin'. Like I won't know how much I made this year until probably January. You know how they have to send all the W-2 forms out and all that stuff? That's when I'll find out. I mean, I already know how much I made from *baseball.* I mean, that's a set price, that's *salary.* Here I know I'm workin' for that. William Morris isn't— I mean that's just my salary, that's *work.*

I Could Have Said, Give Me a Million and I'll Play Five Years for It, but Five Years Is Kind of Long

T.   Well, getting somebody to handle your business for you was a good idea—I mean, it was just something you had to do sooner or later. But I suppose some people are going to misunderstand that. After all, you're not really interested in making ten million dollars, are you?

M.   No.

T.   Wouldn't it be more hassle for you than anything else?

M.   I think it would, for me. Just because, I can't go—

T.   Then you'd have to have *twenty* guys like Steve, man. You'd have to have twenty, instead of just one.

M.   Yeah.

T.   Handling your taxes, handling your mortgages, your investments, your appearances . . .

M.   Yeah! Mmm. I look at that, but now I think—

T.   You've got ten million dollars, and everybody's gonna call you up and say, Hey, I need some money.

M.   Yeah, but it's not that. It's just that now I go back and see my friends, y'know—*that's* where it kills you. Here I am—my buddy, y'know? I was sittin' down—Billy, y'know? And I was sittin' there. I go, Hey, I call him up—Hey, Bill, I just got a new stereo system, come on over, y'know?

T.   You put in a stereo system back in Northboro, too— besides the one in your apartment in Detroit?

M.   Yeah, I got one—maybe a two-grand one in my apartment, right? And I got a thousand-dollar one at home, almost.

And now *he* doesn't have *one* of those. And he comes over, and he goes—he goes, It must be *neat* to be rich! I go, I ain't rich. Not *yet!* And like him and I just—when I said *not yet,* him and I just laughed at each other! And we just cracked up laughin'. I mean we just—it was just somethin' funny. We just *laughed* at it, like, y'know, it's a big joke. 'Cause it *is* a joke. And that's what it was. I said, I got what I *want* man. I said, Big deal, I can own that.

T.   But nowadays all these guys are out for contracts of three million, and two million. And yet, they're—

M.   Hey! I might even get like that. They been playin' seven years, eight years! They haven't been on a winning *team* probably! Y'know? I mean when you been playin' that long and you know you're that good, if a team's gonna buy a pennant, man—they're tryin', like everyone says they're tryin' to buy a pennant. New York is tryin' to buy a pennant. And you just—you know what? They're spendin' their money, because if they don't spend it the government's gonna get it. Right? So they gotta *waste* it.

T.   Also, in that town, you can draw fifty, sixty thousand people all year long.

M.   Yeah! So it's gonna *pay* it!

T.   It's gonna come back. It's gonna come back to 'em.

M.   Yeah, but now they said they're gonna jack up the prices on the seats of the tickets. I mean that *sucks,* right then and there. If it's gonna get like that, then that sucks. But they don't *have* to jack 'em up. I don't give a shit, they don't have to. If they—if they have a winning team, a pennant team, they're gonna pack the house every night. So why do they have to jack the tickets up?

T.   Are they planning on raising prices in Detroit? I think I read that they were going to raise the $4.50 boxes to $5.00, and the $3.50 to $4.00.

M.   I don't know. If they do, they're crazy!

T.   I heard they were gonna fix up the stadium. The city's gonna give 'em some money, or the federal government I guess is giving it to the city.

M.   Yeah. Because that's all government shit, gettin' that fixed. Y'know? But you know, it's just—they jack up tickets, so now, the person that could afford a $4.50 ticket has to pay $5.00, and now he can't afford to pay $5.00, so he can't *come*. Where if you'd have kept it at $4.50, he woulda *been* there. So there's gonna be that one seat that's gonna be open. I can't see why they don't look at it that way.

T.   The *Wall Street Journal* ran a story last August saying that before the year was over you'd be making the Tigers about a million bucks. Which translates out to about sixty times what they paid you in salary. Did you see that?

M.   No. I heard about it.

T.   Yeah, well, you'd have to play five years before you got into any of that anyway, right? I mean, being a free agent, and trying to get back a little bigger cut of the money you earn for 'em?

M.   Yeah. Well, right now I'm young. Hey, shit. All right. Look, you take Butch Wynegar. I probably made more than him this year. And more than him next year.

T.   I think he signed for fifty.

M.   Oh, is that what he signed for?

T.   I think so. I saw it in the paper.

M.   Still, I'm gonna make more than him. Y'know? So what's my bitch? I got no bitch. If I wanted to make—if I wanted to make a million dollars, I coulda got a million easy this year. I *could* have.

T.   Another thing you got besides the money, you got the freedom of mind of not having to worry about it for three years.

M.   Yeah!

T.   Because if you *weren't* signed, it'd be something you'd have to live with and think about every day and every night. You'd be changin' your mind—guys'd be comin' up to you, Hey man, you can get *this,* and there's only *this* much in it for me! You know what I mean?

M.   Yeah. But, well, you look at it. If I wanted to, I *could've*. Right? I could've said, Yeah, gimme a million, and I'll play five years for it. It'd have been the same atmosphere. But, five years is kinda *long,* y'know? It's just that—I *coulda* hit 'em. People— I know I could've. Agents were comin' up to me and hittin' me with shit. They go, We're gonna hit 'em with a million and a big four-year contract, maybe five-year.

The Agents Threw the Million Dollar Man in My Face, but Jim Campbell Knew What My Mind Was Talking About

T. Agents were calling you up?

M. Yeah! I mean guys pulled me out—goin' out to eat! Can you imagine someone throwin' in your face—Hey, you're a Million-Dollar Man, as long as you do this work five years.

T. What about this guy that represents all these top free agents?

M. I don't know.

T. He never called you?

M. He probably did!

T. Kapstein's his name.

M. Kapstein? I don't remember him. He probably did, but I just didn't want to get involved.

T. How about Rusty and those guys? Do they deal for themselves?

M. Yeah. They do it themselves. Y'know?

T. I understand Rusty's got a pretty good deal.

M. Yeah. Yeah, then you get the deal that *he* wants. But now you gotta remember the agent is gonna get you—it's like, me goin' in and askin' for a million is not the same as my *agent* goin' in and askin' for a million. Y'know? He's just gonna hit 'em with all this. But still—y'know, so you avoid that. And you get what you want. And I got what I wanted. And that was it. If I—if Jim Campbell had a three-year package that had some odd amount of money on it, and if I didn't want it, I'd have said no. But he had what I wanted. It was weird. It was like we—like he already knew what my mind was talkin' about before I even got in there.

The Minute I Saw the Contract, I Just Signed It

T. So you just signed on the spot?

M. Yeah. The minute I saw the contract, I just signed it. Y'know? Then we bullshitted.

T. How long in advance did you know you were gonna go in and talk to him about it?

M. How long? Not at all.

T. You mean you just found out that day that you were

gonna talk to him about it? Did he call you up?

M.   No, he goes—well, he called me up. I went into his room, and he goes, Well, you want to talk contract now? Or later? And I said, I don't care. And he goes—he goes, Well, you gettin' an agent? I said, No. And he goes, Well, who's gonna help you? I said, My dad. And he goes, All right, tell you what. We'll fly your dad out here, right? And we'll talk this weekend. I said, Okay. Called my dad up.

T.   So this was the last weekend of the season, right? In Milwaukee—the Tigers were in Milwaukee? You signed it, and they announced it on the last day—a Sunday morning, and that afternoon you won your nineteenth game.

M.   Yeah. Called my dad up, and I said, uh, Dad, we're gonna talk contract-time now. Mr. Campbell says he'll pay to send you out here. So we did. So he came out Saturday and left Sunday. Y'know? I mean, the guy didn't *have* to pay for his ticket all the way out here. I mean, y'know, he was savin' the hassle of me just sendin' it in. Instead of talkin' to me on the phone, he wanted to talk to me in person.

T.   It makes sense to do it the way you did it. Also, it *looks* good.

M.   *I* think it does.

Who Wanted You in the Beginning?

T.   Obviously you feel some attachment to the Tigers, right? But most of these free-agent guys are only interested in the different ball clubs insofar as what money they have in the bank, what the radio-TV connections are, or what the climate is. Jim Palmer is the only other guy besides you who's come out and said, I'll play for less, but I'm staying with one club because they brought me up, I'm at home here, and I owe 'em something. He said a lot of free agents were like kids turned loose in a candy store. He said, I'm gonna stay here and play with Baltimore. I don't want to walk down the street with my kids and have people say, There goes Jim Palmer, all he thinks about is money.

M.   You know why? You know why? It's because he's *happy.* When you're *happy,* you don't have to move on. If some other guy ain't happy, then he's gonna move. It's just like havin' a job. He isn't happy—move on! Hell, after my three-year contract with Detroit—I'm just lookin' ahead now . . .

T.   Later, sure. But right now you'd be crazy to leave, when you've got a good thing going.

M.   That's right! The way Detroit has treated me? *Whoo.*

T.   If you'd come up somewhere else, who knows what'd have happened?

M.   That's right! The way I look at it, Detroit has treated me *so* well, I just say I ain't gonna move from 'em. Until they tell me to go.

T.   Three years from now you might have a different idea in your mind.

M.   That's right. All right, you have a different idea. And after three years, if you built a friendship up, but you find out— if they screw you, *that's* when you leave. Y'know, if they *have* screwed you. But after three years, fourth-year contract—if I say after the third year, Good, and he gets into this, Fine! *Voom!* Y'know, if I'm still happy. But if I'm—if they get me unhappy, then I got my choice. Y'know?

T.   What's funny is the two teams closest to where you grew up are the two teams with all the money, Boston and New York.

M.   Oh, yeah. Mm-hmm.

T.   But still, even *they* can't buy you, man. George Steinbrenner can buy anybody, but he can't buy you. I mean that's what I'm sayin', there are some limits.

M.   Like—hey, people told me, if I wanted to become a free agent, I coulda gone to New York. I coulda gone here, I coulda gone there. But I just say, Who wanted you in the beginning? And we'll see who wants you at the end.

T.   Boston was right next door to you, man. They scouted you. And they looked the other way through ten rounds of the draft!

M.   That's right.

T.   And so did the Yankees. But Detroit wanted you.

M.   And we'll see who wants you at the end. Who wanted you at the beginning, we'll see if they *still* wanted you at the end.

If They Traded Me, Detroit Might Say *Whoa*

T.   Even so, you could get traded. They could trade you tomorrow. I mean, anything can happen—Charles Manson could get elected President, you could get traded—

M.   Oh, if they did! Oh, if they had the, if they had—oh, if they did!

T.   If somebody offered 'em the Empire State Building, plus the Astrodome . . . throw in Fort Knox . . .

M.   Yeah! They'd do it! They'd say, This guy ain't *worth* that much, y'know? They'd say—that's usin' it for an example. That shows you—

T.   And then they'd want to beat your ass, the next day! Pack the house, and beat you.

M.   Mm-hmm. But that's showin' it, though.

T.   I wonder if anybody ever talked to them about that. Like the Yankees or Red Sox or anybody ever came to 'em . . .

M.   They might've. But they'd say, Wait—if we did that, we might get *shot* in Detroit! Y'know, if they traded me this year, I think Detroit might say, *Whoa,* that's it. We've had *enough* of it! But you can't say that, though. Because if the price came right—suppose they got three *great* ballplayers for me. But Detroit probably wouldn't stand—Detroit'd go, Oh, *wow,* they got rid of him! What the hell's the city gonna come to!

T.   I bet they wouldn't sell as many tickets, even if they got Catfish Hunter and Reggie Jackson for you.

M.   They wouldn't sell as many tickets. All right, they got 'em. Right? They would—in the beginning they wouldn't sell as many tickets. But if they started becomin' World Series people? Detroit would forget about me! They sold him, big deal! And *voom,* start a whole new flurry up! A whole new flower would blossom. That other flower had fallen out, and then a new one would blossom. Like if they got three players, or they got a World Series out of the deal. But if they came out the same as they *normally* did, and lost me, then they woulda said, *Whoa!* But I ain't sayin' I'm goin' *that* good. I *ain't* goin' that good. No way! But I'm just sayin', I know the people in Detroit would say they were goin' nuts. Like people in Detroit asked me, How come they're not doin' this, how come they're not doin' that? I don't know. I just look at people and say, I don't want to know. I'm just playin' the game. What other people do is what *they* wanna do, and what I do is what *I* wanna do. No guy is worried about *me!* I mean it's just as simple as that. But they won't believe that.

Dave Roberts Said, Keep On, You're Putting Money in My Pocket

T.   There must have been a lot of happy people in Detroit when you signed that three-year contract.

M.   Hey, y'know, I had a lot of guys on my team, after they found out—they let a press release out, y'know, Mark Fidrych signed his three-year contract? A lot of 'em, all they said to me was, Great, Mark! They said, It's great, but did you leave any money for me? That's all they said. But they just laughed. They knew I didn't get that much. They knew I got what I wanted. But they just—it's great. They go, We wish we were in your spot. And it opens the door for *us,* too. Kinda like, y'know? 'Cause Dave Roberts told me—he goes, Man, you keep on winnin' those games. You're puttin' money in my pocket, man! He goes, You might have a better season than me, but you're puttin' money in my pocket, too. Y'know? And I'm sittin' there goin', That's true. And it makes you—when your teammate is like that to you, y'know, you can sit there and go, *Wow!* Because you'd start—Here I am, he's been playing five years and I'm ahead of him, y'know? I'm 17 and 7. And, y'know, you're kinda lookin' at this guy— Can I *talk* to him still? Y'know? But you do. Y'know? And like he still talks to you, and he still helps you, y'know? He said, C'mon, keep winnin', man! I *wanna* see you win, y'know? Just like you wanna see *him* win. Y'know, you feel bad when he loses and you win. You just—like the air starts gettin' thick, y'know?

T.   But Roberts is a guy you could look up to.

M.   Yeah! Oh, yeah, he's been around! Y'know? And that's what I mean by those guys helped me so much this year. It's 'cause of stuff like *that.* Y'know, C'mon, you're puttin' money in my pocket, man, keep on winnin'!

When You're a Winner You're Always Happy, but
If You're Happy as a Loser, You'll Always Be a Loser

T.   Well, winning is something everybody appreciates. I mean, it's like you said about Pete Rose. It's that little gap that separates people.

M.   Maybe that's why I'm so happy.

T.   What, because of winning?

M.   Yeah.

T.   Maybe so. I think it's more *that* than money, isn't it?

M.   Yeah!

T.   Even if you were getting a million dollars—

M.   If you weren't winning, you wouldn't be happy.

T.   Well, maybe—you know how you can sometimes take two pitchers, and one guy has great stuff, great fastball, great curve, and the next guy you look at just doesn't have those things?

M.   Mm-hmm.

T.   Well, maybe when that difference isn't there, it's the guy who's more interested in winning that makes it through. Ahead of the other guy with equal skills.

M.   I wouldn't know about that. Just, when you're a winner you're always happy. When you're a loser you're not. But if you *are* happy as a loser, you're always gonna be a loser. Y'know? You *are*. I mean, why—you're not gonna change.

T.   If you can settle for that, huh?

M.   You're gonna settle for that. You're gonna always be happy. But if *I* lose, hey—don't come near me, man. Depends— y'know, if I won three in a row and I lost one, I might be able to handle that loss a little. But then I lose *two*—y'know, don't come around me any more a little bit.

T.   So like that period in the second half of the year where you lost a couple—

M.   Yeah, I was goin' *nuts!* I was talkin' to people, talkin' to 'em left and right. Oh, I *was*. I was goin' nuts. But, y'know—that was what everybody told me, it was life.

T.   Yeah, well it had to happen sometime. You weren't gonna win 29 straight, with 28 complete games—the only place *that* happens is in comic books. You came about as close to that as you could.

M. Mm-hmm.

T. I mean, nobody could have expected more than you gave them.

I'm a Bicentennial Man

M. Well, look at it this way. They exploited you. So, I ain't gonna forget this season. Even though you're supposed to. 'Cause there's no way I can explain—y'know, forget this. I cannot forget the year 1976. There's no way I could possibly forget it. Where you *should* throw it out. Just like *Bruce* ain't gonna forget it, 'cause *he* got exploited 'cause of me. Right? And 'cause of him, right? On equal points. But yet, y'know—just like Ronnie ain't gonna forget 1976. Just because he did a thirty-game hittin' streak, right? *He* did somethin' in '76, just like *I* did somethin', just like *Bruce* did somethin'. And it's just—y'know, the other ballplayers were there. But *they* won't forget '76 either. Just because they were *part* of that, right? They won't forget. Like, it's a freak, man. It's a two thou—a two-hundred-year birthday. We talked this over, man. It's a freak, y'know—*this* in 1976. The Bicentennial Year, you did this. It's just a freak. Y'know, *wow,* I—it's like, we had Bicentennial Year in our town? And we exploited it out, right? And now, Bicentennial hit. And now, I'm a Bicentennial Man!

At My Banquet in Northboro I Tell Them, Nature Calls

T. They gave you a banquet back home in Northboro after the season?

M. Yeah. Oh, that was good. They gave me free beer, for me and my buddy, and we just got drunk.

T. Did your buddies from the old days come to it? Your buddies from Northboro?

M. Oh, all my—like my friends from my town came.

T. Were there any speeches?

M. Just me and the coaches I had in high school. Y'know, the coach I had from Worcester Academy, the coach I had at Algonquin, the coach I had in Legion ball. Just those coaches, and then the people who were out there. My buddy got to talk.

T. Who's that?

M. Billy. Billy McAfee.

T. What'd he get up and say?

M. My friend? He didn't know what the hell to say! Y'know, he just got up there. And I forget what he said. But it was good, though. And like, since it was a roast, I messed around a little bit. Y'know? I just screwed around by, y'know, like when Billy was talkin' I got up and went to the john. Y'know, I *hadda* go. Right? So I just got up outa my seat and went to the john. And the moderator goes, Where you goin'? I just said, Well, Nature calls. I gotta go to the bathroom! How 'bout you? And he goes, Oh, okay, see ya later. And like we stopped the whole thing. Y'know, I didn't know what to say, how to really, y'know, get someone to laugh. So I just got up and went to the john. I mean, that's *my* way of roasting *them,* then!

I Told My Dad, It's *My* Night, I'm Gonna Do It

T. So you don't remember much of what the speakers said, like your coaches?

M. No! And then my dad, he's tellin' me, Hey, you're gettin' too drunk.

T. This is while the banquet's going on?

M. Yeah! And I'm sayin', Dad, I ain't gettin' that drunk. I'm gettin' drunk to where I want to get drunk. This guy says, Hey, here's a case of beer. Drink as much as you can. When that's done, here's another case. So—Dad, it's *my* night, right? It's *my night,* Dad. I'm gonna do it. He just shakes his head. Y'know? My buddy's gettin' just as drunk as I am. All my other friends—out there, in the audience—are gettin' just as drunk as I am. The *people* out there—this guy that I know, and his parents and stuff come up to me. And they're staggerin' up to me, goin', *Hey, that was great,* y'know? And here my dad was tellin' me *I'm* gettin' too drunk? When *they're* staggerin'? I'm sittin' there, *Whoa!*

I Do My Job for the
United Fund, but Joe Falls Cuts Me Down

T. What was the United Fund thing like? They gave you an award last month in Detroit? Sportsman of the Year or something?

M. That was—that was neat. Uh, they had like—

T. What was it, a dinner?

M. It's weird. Here you are, comin' at eleven o'clock. All right, they send you upstairs. At eleven o'clock. They got an open bar there, right? For the reporters. And you. And you have a few drinks. Y'know? But you're sayin', Well, I gotta start at eleven. I mean, everyone else'll start at eleven, I might as well start, y'know? And keep goin', till everyone leaves. And then I'll go home, and whatever happens after that, happens. Right? So you sit up there, and you start at eleven, right? No big deal. I'm goin' through—signin' autographs for everyone. And then all of a sudden this guy—a reporter—comes up. And the main guy, the main talker. I'd ask questions, people'd ask me questions. I'd, y'know, do all that stuff. Do all the work that you had to do. And then this guy cuts me down for what I *wear* to the place.

T. Who?

M. Y'know, Joe Falls. He just cut me down. Sayin', Hey, look at him, he comes with a dungaree jacket on! We gave him this award, and he comes here with blue jeans and a shirt!

T. Joe Falls writes this in the paper the next day? In his column in the *Free Press?*

M. Yeah! But yet these blue jeans and this shirt are just as much as what *he* wears, too. And I'm doin' it—but I'm doin' *work,* now, man!

I Could Do That Act, but I'd Still Stick Out

T. Well, in a case like that, I can't understand why these people don't want you to just be real. Even though at the same time they're out there earning their daily bread by writing stories about you—yet they want you to be their idea.

M. Yeah!

T. See, like what's that equation—an expensive leisure suit equals the correct amount of gratitude? You're expected to be grateful for this award? Okay, suppose you come in wearing a spiffy leisure suit, a nice Osmond brothers haircut—

M. Yeah, or whatever—

T. I mean, just for that one guy's idea of you—

M. I coulda gone that act—I coulda done that act!

T. For him?

M. If I wanted to go there in that act, I coulda done it.

T.   It's like if you wanted to walk around this hotel—like this morning we came in, you were in your cut-offs. Stare city! Like you walk around the Hilton here, five hundred executives' wives get a broken neck from checking you out as you go by!

M.   I could walk around! Y'know, if you stick out, *stick out!*

T.   But if you walked around dressed up real trim, suit and tie—go down and chat with the general managers, sign autographs—

M.   I'm gonna still stick out doin' *that!* I'm gonna stick out any way I do it.

T.   You're only going to stick out around certain people.

M.   Yeah!

T.   Around people—like, you didn't stick out this afternoon when we were over at Lance's friend's house.

M.   No! That's what's good, y'know? I sat there and got drunk, y'know?

T.   I mean, nobody there was worried about how you were dressed.

M.   No!

T.   Anyway, it was just that writer that got on you about the United Fund thing, right?

M.   But yet, like here I am signing all these autographs for everyone. Sittin' there—they said, You'll be outa there by one thirty. Yet I didn't get out of there till *two* thirty maybe. Or three, right? 'Cause I signed autographs. I coulda said, No, I don't want to do it, and just split. I did a Channel 2 interview, I did a Channel 7 interview, I did all this other stuff, right? And yet he gets on me 'cause of my dressin'. I said, What the hell, man? What the hell are you gettin' on me for—my *dressin'?* If I didn't do the work, I could see you gettin' on me for my dressin'. But I'm doin' the *work* for you, man.

17 I Get the Man
of the Year Award
And Live to Tell It

How I Pass Time in Detroit in the Winter

T.   What do you do to pass time in Detroit, like when you're there in the winter?

M.   What do I *do?* Well, I usually get up, maybe eleven thirty, twelve, right? And then I sit in my apartment and watch *Happy Days.* Right? That's probably the first thing I do, is turn the TV on and watch *Happy Days.* At twelve o'clock, that's when I'll clean the house—y'know, if it needs cleanin'. Y'know, turn my stereo system on, wash the dishes that needs it—I'll eat first, *then* wash the dishes. And then take a shower and, if I'm doin' somethin' outside, I'll just take off. Either that or just sit in the house and just relax a little bit.

T.   You been running this winter?

M.   No. I just started runnin' when I came *here* to California, y'know? But today I'll take off because I think my—I think I should.

T.   Since you're going out with Cary Grant and Frank Sinatra . . .

M.   I might as well take a day off, y'know?

T.   Well, then, what do you do now, do you shoot pool?

M.   Oh, yeah! Oh, I'll go to a—like, at night, I'll go to—there's this one bar, well, there's two bars I know of that you can go to. One's got like *six* pool tables. And then there's another place right about ten minutes from my house—a bar, right? It's good. It's got three pool tables. And if you get sick of playin' pool, all you do is go right upstairs. They got a band up there.

T.   You don't have a lot of close friends around there? You just meet people in these places?

M. Yeah, I don't have any friends in Detroit. I mean I don't have friends where they come over to my house, y'know, and just knock on the door.

I Jog on the Freeway, and
They Go, Wow, the Rookie of the Year!

T. These last couple of mornings in Los Angeles, you've been out running on the streets?

M. Not runnin', joggin'.

T. Steve says someone saw you—anyway, it got back to him somehow. I wonder who saw you?

M. I ran by someone I didn't even know.

T. Where'd you run?

M. Just around. I go around and all the way down to the expressway. And around the expressway, and all the way back up—y'know, down the hotel street? Back down on that one.

T. Down Figueroa?

M. Right. Then I take a right where, y'know, those shoe-shine guys are? The first right there, I take that, and run all the way down. And then take another right, and then take another right, and come all the way back up. And then I go back on the freeway again, and come around again. That was one time I did that. But then today I cut the freeway out.

T. So you don't know who it was who saw you? I mean, on a Monday morning on the Harbor Freeway, it could have been any one of, oh, forty or fifty thousand people!

M. Yeah! I mean that's like I said, I can't get drunk now, without anyone knowin' about it. I can't make a move without anyone seein' me. I just walked through the hall. I didn't care what I *looked* like. I just went out, man, came back all sweaty, walked up to my room, got in my hotel room—and *voom,* Steve knew about it. I never told him I ran. But people saw me. See, like that's all it takes, is one person to see you do something, and all of a sudden they exploit it out. Which ain't bad, though. Y'know? They see me runnin', they go, Wow, no wonder he's Rookie of the Year! Y'know? I felt good after I got done runnin'. Ballplayers need their time off, just like anyone else. I mean you can only play so much, then you gotta drop it. And then come back to it. Just to get you *goin'* again, to get you *refreshed.*

I Get the Man of the Year Award and Live to Tell It

T. Well, America's waiting to hear what went down at the big awards dinner.

M. Man, I just had a *whale* of a time. I met Don Rickles, Frank Sinatra, Monte Hall, Cary Grant, Pat Henry . . .

T. Where was this going on, down in the main ballroom?

M. Yeah, downstairs.

T. So what'd Cary Grant and Frank Sinatra and everybody say to you?

M. Nothin'. It was all like—it was a cut-down thing.

T. You mean they were joking?

M. Oh, they said jokes—Rickles, man? He had the people *rollin'!* You know what he said to me? He goes, I don't know, everyone talks about baseball and nuts and all that. But that Fidrych—they oughta throw him in some *house* and throw away the key! And everyone cracks up laughin'. He goes, Yeah, but then you'd see the owners of Detroit goin', *Please* let him out! *Please* let him out! Y'know? It was great.

T. Who introduced you?

M. Some guy. Just some guy. I don't know who it was.

T. Was it Vin Scully? He was supposed to be Master of Ceremonies.

M. I don't know. He just said, And now we got an award for the Man of All Times and stuff. And here it is.

T. What'd you say?

M. I got up there. I said, Uh, I'm kinda nervous. I don't know what to say, people, but uh, just in case any of you people didn't *know,* Don Rickles just walked in. Better late than never, right, Don? And then I said—what else did I say? I said, Oh, yeah, I said, Ah, when I first joined baseball, here I am during spring training and they go, You can't wear white spikes, you can't wear this—and they go Here, here's your glove, here's a pair of spikes. And they go, *We want the money.* And I said, You ain't gonna get it outa *me!* I don't know, I just—I didn't know what to say, I just, I went up there. . . . I guess

I did all right. People were laughin', y'know. If people were laughin', you hadda be doin' *somethin'* right.

T.   Stephen stopped in and told me he would tell you what to say.

M.   Yeah! Oh, yeah! He pulls me over—this is funny, man. We're up in Jim Campbell's room now, 'cause I went up to Jim's to see, y'know, if I had to be there at six. I went up to Jim's, and he goes—Steve goes, Do you know what you're gonna say now? And I said, Yeah, whatever comes into my *head!* And he pulls me into the room and he goes, Well, hey, this is what I'd like you to say. I said, Hey, Steve, see you later, I'm goin' down and say what I have to say. And walked out, y'know? No big deal.

T.   So he didn't tell you what he wanted you to say?

M.   No! Take *my* shovel? I had a good time, though, I'll have to admit.

T.   So is this—has this award that they gave you, has it ever been given before?

M.   No! It's the first award ever!

T.   The first time ever?

M.   Yeah.

T.   What does it say on it? Does it say anything? It's got a baseball diamond made of wood here on the top—it's a little rickety.

M.   I know. Well, that's 'cause it probably needs tightening. No big deal.

T.   There's two batters on here, but not one pitcher!

M.   I *got* it, man. It's gonna go right on my mantel.

T.   So you did your job, you did okay down there.

M.   I don't know. I know the people were laughin'. And I just walked—the last, the very last words I said, I said, Hey, I ain't much of an entertainer like these guys. I just—hey, I just like baseball. See you later. Thank you for everything you gave me.

I Get on Don Rickles and
Tell Cary Grant I'll Mow His Lawn

T.   Was Bowie Kuhn there, and all those guys?

M.   Oh, yeah, everyone was there. Bowie even came up to me. *Talked* to the Gipper.

T.   What'd he say?

M. Just Hi, glad to know you.

T. Do you remember what any of the speakers at the dinner said?

M. Not really, but I know they came up with some good ones. Every single one of 'em. Except like Sinatra, he didn't—he wasn't really cuttin' down. He mostly just sang, y'know?

T. What'd he sing?

M. Just some songs. And then he had one song like made up to baseball. Like to a lot of the people that were makin', y'know, people that were free agents and made some *bucks* this year. And then like, uh, who was it—Monte Hall got on Hunter somethin' *fierce,* y'know? And he was talkin' about, like the god—like, God? And then the Bible. He was takin' *pieces* out of the Bible, and then puttin' people *in* it, y'know? Different people—to cut 'em down and stuff.

T. Did Sinatra sing that song of his about baseball? Something like, There's no ballpark around here any more. . . .

M. I think that mighta been it. 'Cause he sang a baseball song.

T. And when you talked to Cary Grant, do you remember what he said?

M. Well, he goes—he just goes, I'm not much of a talker for these things, and stuff. But he had a couple of jokes that weren't bad. But I can't remember 'em. But the funniest guy was Rickles, man. Y'know, to get everyone *goin'.* I mean everyone was laughin' at everyone *else,* too, but when *he* got up, man, he just got all over people. He got all over me, just 'cause the minute he came in— like he didn't want anyone to know he was late? 'Cause he crouched down, man. He'd snuck all the way there with his head down, y'know? And like, when you look out—they got that light on you, and when you look out you can't see any of the people, y'know? So he scooted right by, *whoosh!*

T. You're up by the podium, at the head table?

M. Yeah, and you can't see. And he had scooted by every-one, y'know? It was like intermission. And I said, Ah! I don't know *what* made me think of it. But when I got *up* there, I said, Just in case no one knew, Don Rickles is here. He's just way down here, and he just got here, about two seconds ago! Better late than never, huh? And everyone just cracked up. I said, *Whoa,* I didn't think I was gonna get a good laugh here! Y'know? I didn't know. And it got me goin', a little bit.

T.   You mentioned that all these old dudes had incredible young girls with 'em.

M.   Well, Cary Grant had a *very* nice lady with him. But he told me, he goes—I go, Are you married to her? He says, No! I go, Is it your girlfriend? He goes, No, it's just a lady that takes care of me. I'm old now, y'know, and I just need someone to take care of me. Like she cooks my meals. And she does this, and she does that. And I could *see* that, y'know? But *God damn!* Can't he bring along one for me? I mean, y'know, I said to him, Man, that's the kind of girl I been lookin' for all my *life!* He goes, Well, you want to go out with her? I said, *Whoa*—Yeah! He goes, I can manage that with *ease.* He goes, Anytime you wanna go out with her—she only takes care of me. I said, God damn! I said, I'll mow your lawn!

Cary Grant Gets His Picture Taken with Me, But Monte Hall Is Probably My Highlight

T.   So it was a good time anyway.

M.   Yeah! Y'know, when I first went there, I said this is gonna be—this is gonna stink. To *me,* y'know? Because I just felt that it wasn't what I though it was—y'know, what I *wanted* it to be. Or what I thought it'd be. But then, as it was, it turned out they really treated you well. *Very* well, y'know?

T.   So did you get the feeling that that was the point of what you were supposed to be out here for? I mean, the reason they flew you out and all?

M.   Yeah. *Now,* now I got—y'know, before I said I was blank about everything, I didn't know what was goin' on? Well, after I started meetin' these guys, man—I said, *Whoa,* this is a good thing, I'm glad I came out here, y'know? I'm glad I didn't say, Nah, I can't go out there.

T.   So you were a big part of the show, in other words?

M.   Ah, a little bit.

T.   Did they give other awards?

M.   No. I don't think—Oh, they did. They gave watches out to all the—

T.   To the club executives and stuff?

M.   Yeah, like for the American League, y'know, and for A ball, Double-A and Triple-A. And they gave, y'know, different to different people.

T.   Did Rick Monday get something?

M.   Yeah, Rick Monday got somethin'. Remember that flag? Remember that incident out here with the flag? Well, he got somethin' for *that,* y'know?

T.   So you were the only two ballplayers?

M.   Mm-hmm. Like him and I sat next to each other. But these guys—I'll clue ya, these actors, man, they were neat. I just never thought it'd be that much fun. I mean, are you kiddin' me? My mother woulda went *nuts* to meet Cary Grant. And Frank Sinatra! She'd have been goin' nuts! Because that's the age that *she* grew up in, y'know? And like to me, it was just neat meetin' 'em. But my mother, oh, that woulda—it woulda been her high-light, if ever. It was a highlight to me. Like Monte Hall was probably more of a highlight to *me,* because I've *watched* Monte Hall. You know what I mean? Where Frank Sinatra, his stuff I really didn't watch too much except for if he was in a bad-ass movie, y'know? But Cary Grant, I used to see *him* a lot, y'know? But Monte Hall I'd have to say was really the guy that—y'know, 'cause they just cracked up laughin'. I said, Hey—this guy goes, Here, you wanna meet Monte Hall? I said, *Whoa,* no, don't tell me that!

T.   And Monte Hall and all these guys are baseball fans?

M.   Yeah. Oh, yeah, I guess so.

T.   Dodger fans, probably.

M.   Yeah. And like, when they showed him to me, I said, Neat, y'know? But Cary Grant—when they said, Here's Cary Grant, I looked, and said, Naw. But I looked again, I looked harder—and I could *remember,* y'know, just visionin' back. Take that white hair off, put brown hair on, a little darker hair, and the glasses. . . . I said, *Yeah, doesn't* that look like him! But, y'know, it just got to a point where—he was a neat guy, man. I mean, before they all left, right? He said, See you later, Mark. Y'know? That's what was great about it to me. And then they came up to me and said, Hey, let's take a picture together. He goes, I'd like to have a picture with you. I went, *Whoa!* I'd like to have a picture of *you,* too! Y'know, I told this photographer, Man, you better send it to me! 'Cause my mother's gonna be goin' *nuts* if I show her this!

Before They Get to Me I Go Through Thirty to a Hundred Things to Say, but I Don't Use Any of 'Em

T.   So when they gave you the award, did they say anything about why they were picking you out?

M.   Yeah, they just said, The man who's done the most for baseball this year, who's brought something—a little back of something, y'know? And like, well, while I'm sittin' there—y'know, you could kinda tell they were gettin' ready to talk to me, because Pat Henry hits me, he goes, Ha, you're next! 'Cause he was all done. Y'know, they all have things written up—all of 'em.

T.   A script?

M.   Yeah, like a script. They had all their lines written up before they get up there.

T.   All the comedian guys?

M.   Yeah, they all had their stuff. Except for Rickles.

T.   He did it ad-lib, eh?

M.   Yeah. But all the other ones had stuff written up. I could see it. I mean it was a hell of a lot easier probably for 'em, y'know, if they could read it out. I couldn't—like I told 'em, Hey, all these other people got stuff written up. But I don't have somethin' written up, because I wasn't smart enough to write, y'know? I said, When I signed for baseball, one of the reasons I signed was because the colleges didn't want me. And the only other job I had was my gas station job, or some other job, R and T Furniture, somethin' else I wanted to—y'know, somethin' to *do.* So I said, Ah, what the heck, can't lose out *here*— it's somethin' different. And everyone cracked up laughin'. But that's the *truth,* really, of why I signed. 'Cause there was no schools except if I went to New Mexico Highlands University. I got the people to laugh a little bit —that's what got *me* goin'.

T.   So you talked for a couple—for a minute or two?

M.   About—maybe five, ten minutes. Then, the one they really liked was—here I look, y'know, and I'm sittin' up there— I go, I guess I ain't goin' that bad. I guess I'm doin' better than the *management,* now. And I said, The only reason I say that is because, lookit, here I am sittin' right here—but look at those guys, they're only sittin' over *there,* y'know? Everyone's crackin' up laughin'. I said, What's so funny about that? I said, *Whoa!* I said, Pretty good, huh, Ralph? And everyone was crackin' up.

T.   What was running through your mind while they were leading up to you?

M.   Well, while they were leadin' up to me I was just—I was gettin' very sweaty in my *hands,* man, I was takin' a napkin and wipin' my hands every five seconds, or somethin' like that. I was doin' that, and I had maybe—before they got to me, I probably went through thirty to a hundred things, man, of things of how I'm gonna start it. And you know what? When I got up there I didn't use any of 'em! I didn't say *one* of those things that I was thinkin' about. You know how I said that one night I was sittin' down and thinkin' about how I was gonna do this? When I got up there, I like kinda *froze.* And I just said, Hey, I ain't much of a talker. And all of a sudden, *voom,* it just *came out,* like.

T.   Did Ralph and Jim tell you how you did?

M.   Yeah. They said I was okay. I mean, y'know, it was like —I go, Well, did I represent you guys good enough? And they said, You represented us well enough. Don't even worry about it.

T.   So they were happy with the whole event?

M.   Yeah. Oh, they were—I could have probably made a complete *ass* out of myself, and they would have probably told me I was still, y'know—You handled yourself very well. I mean, I could have—because I represented them good enough this *year.*

T.   Was John Fetzer there? The owner of the Tigers?

M.   Yeah, he was there!

T.   So did any of the Detroit people come up to you and congratulate you?

M.   Yeah, I went up to their room after and had a few beers with 'em all, y'know? And they said, Hey, you did good! After I asked 'em if I represented 'em good enough, they said, *Hell, yeah!* He goes, You probably did the smartest thing. Y'know, you weren't a comedian.

T.   Who said this?

M.   Ralph. He goes, You're not a comedian like those other people. People just want to see you, and see some of your reactions. And you played it smart by goin' up and sayin' a few words and just sittin' back down. Before you get *deep* into it, and all of a sudden you don't know what to say. But like I didn't run out of stuff, because I coulda said *a lot.* But I said, I got my couple laughs, I'll sit down now. I was happy with what happened, y'know? So I just said, Hey, I like baseball. And then just walked away. I didn't say this was—that it was the end. I just said, I just like baseball. See you later, people. Bye now!

T.   It's funny, that's the one thing it's almost hard to remember around here. That it's all about baseball!

M.   Yeah.

Hank Aaron Asks Me If I
Remember Him and Introduces Me to Linda Lovelace

T.   Well, sounds to me like you stole the show.

M.   Y'know, I really wasn't even *bored* sittin' there? Y'know how you keep on gettin' drawn out, and drawn out . . . but I didn't get that bored, y'know? And it was funny. Hank Aaron walks up to me after the thing was over. I'm downstairs, he walks up to me. And he goes, Hi, Mark! And he goes, Do you remember me? I went, *What?* I said, You gotta be kiddin' me! I said, How can you come up to me and ask me that, Hank? He goes, I just wanted to see if you remembered me, that's all. I mean, all the people you meet. . . . I said, That's true, too. You guys all look the same, and stuff. Y'know, I didn't say that to *him.* I said, I can't forget *you,* man—I struck you out! First time I faced you, men on first and second, two outs, I struck you out!

T.   Did he remember that?

M.   Yeah, *he* remembered it. And I said, You remember MacCormack, how you took him deep? He says, Yeah, I remember that. That was neat when Frank got tooken deep, though. Well, it wasn't neat, but I thought—I cracked up laughin' in the dugout, man. He wanted to strike out Aaron *so* bad! Because if he struck out Aaron, man, he woulda been on Cloud 100, man. That guy was—y'know, he gets into that kind of shit.

T.   So what else did Aaron say?

M.   Nothin'. He just introduced me to some people. Aw, he introduced me to this *person.* This was the funniest—I just sat there. Like this lady kind of read my mind, but yet she really didn't. I guess she throws this line at everyone, right? Here he is, introducin' me to a guy. Hi, how are you? And then he goes, Ah, okay, now here's the ladies. You got Linda Lovelace right here. And before she even shook my hand she said, Don't get any ideas!

T.   Is that who it *was?*

M.   Huh?

T.   Linda Lovelace?

M.   No! That was the lady's *name,* though! Y'know? It was freaky. And that's why she said, Don't get any ideas. And I just said, Whaddaya mean, get any ideas? And then I went, Oh! It clicked in my mind, goin', *Oh,* Linda Lovelace—Hi, how's it goin'? Y'know, I mean when he first announced it, I just—I mean, I wasn't thinkin' of *that.* And then, *boom,* it clicked, when she said *that.* And I just *sat* there—we were laughin' our heads off. People around her were laughin'. She said, Don't get any ideas. It mighta been Linda Lovelace!

T.   It didn't look like her, though?

M.   I wouldn't know. I wouldn't know what Linda Lovelace looked like.

T.   Hank Aaron introduced you to her?

M.   Yeah, Hank Aaron. Well, he was with a couple other people.

T.   Did she look young?

M.   Oh, yeah, she was young! I forgot to ask her if she was really *her* though.

T.   Well, that'd be an interesting combination, Hank Aaron and Linda Lovelace.

M.   Oh, no, well, he was there with—like there were four guys there, and she was with another lady. One other, two, three other—no, there was three ladies and like four guys. He's just sittin' down, one of 'em just called him over, Hey, Hank, and he knew the guys, y'know? Couple guys with him. But it was just weird, man, when she hit me with *that.*

While Mark's downstairs being wined and dined by the National Association of Professional Baseball Leagues in the main ballroom of the Hilton, I'm up in his room watching television. A bellhop arrives bearing a case of Coors for Mark, gift-wrapped, with a note on elegantly printed personalized stationery. Joni A. Mitch-

ell, the outside of the envelope reads, and there's an address in Beverly Hills. A few hours later Mark comes in, examines the note, and tells me that I've already met the sender. I am agog, all the more so because earlier in the day Mark had asked me to describe the physical appearance of the singer Joni Mitchell, whom I'd once seen perform.

The Joni Mitchell Story

M. You met her! This afternoon—she was sittin' right there.

T. *That* was her?

M. She looks a lot different, huh? That's why I *asked* you! Y'know? 'Cause I—I still didn't believe her—if she was Joni Mitchell.

T. Hey, the girl that was in *here?* No way! Joni Mitchell's tall and real thin. And has really long blond hair. Whereas *that* girl was short and kind of fat and had *black* hair . . . and was about fifteen years too young!

M. I don't think it—y'know, I never saw her in my life. So I wouldn't know.

T. Well, *that* wasn't the Joni Mitchell that sings.

M. It's a girl that liked me.

T. Yeah, but what a lot of trouble to go to. Impersonation!

M. She must have some bucks. She took me out to eat last night.

T. But this stationery—well, okay, Joni A. Mitchell. Maybe her name is with an *A.,* to distinguish it from the other Joni Mitchell's. But did she tell you she was the singer?

M. Yeah.

T. Did she talk about her singing?

M. Mm-hmm. She gave me tapes! Who do you think it was gave me those two Joni Mitchell tapes there?

T. Yeah, but those are store-bought tapes. Anybody could buy those. If she gave you those tapes, and told you that she sings, and that her name is Joni Mitchell—it's an utter con. But what —the thing is, I don't know why she would do it, because if you had ever seen Joni Mitchell you would have known immediately that this wasn't her.

M. Yeah. Well, she called me up one time when I was here. She goes, This is—I go, Who the heck is this? She says, You know Joni Mitchell? I said, No. She goes, Joni Mitchell the singer. I said, No, that doesn't ring no bell. And then I tell my roommate, and he goes, Let *me* talk to her! And he started hittin' her with things that he knew about Joni Mitchell. And she *knew* 'em!

T.   Look, when what's her name—when Joni Mitchell first called you up, was that when you were in Anaheim with the ball —club?

M. Yeah.

T.   What'd she tell you when you saw her, that when she went on stage she dyed her hair or something?

M. That's what she told me.

T.   It just means she likes you, man. The whole point is that she likes you.

M. Yeah! But, y'know, I didn't mind goin' out with her. Even though she bought me dinner.

T.   Do you think she would have got the same results if she'd told you she was Joe Shmoe's sister?

M. Hell, yeah, she would have—until I met her!

T.   Exactly!

M. We had a bet, see. When she called, in Anaheim, I said, Okay, let's make a bet now. If I ever see you in California, you have to buy *me* dinner. And if you ever come out to Detroit to see me, I'll buy *you* dinner. So—y'know, the next time I called her up was here. I said, Hey, I'm out for my free dinner, let's go!

T.   Oh, I see now, yeah.

M. When we're out to eat, she pulled—maybe three hundred dollars in fifties out of her wallet. I said, What're you *doin'*, Joni? I said, You carry all that money around with you? She goes, I don't like anyone exploitin' me. So don't tell anyone you were out with me. I said, That's cool, I understand. Y'know? But now you —*you* come in an tell me that that ain't Joni Mitchell. I just think it's a good joke now, man. Y'know, it hit—it happened, y'know? Someone pulled a deke right over my eyes. It was a *good* one. . . . But it might *not* be, though. People change!

Epilogue

Over the winter Mark continued to throw a Bird-shaped shadow, as usual without meaning to. Every week or two his name came up in the news, mostly as a figure of comparison or hyperbole. The Bird was nesting. Did he talk to snowballs? The next time I actually "saw" him was on television, where the focus is on entertaining—at the expense of history and legend. The tube managed to shrink him down from the heroically absurd dimension in which he normally exists to the more acceptable size of the merely amazing. This was February, some two and a half months after our December efforts in Los Angeles, and in the meantime Mark had undergone one physical change: His electric explosion of auburn curls, grand as a pop star's before Christmas, had been sacrificed by half its depth to a probably compulsory haircut. Otherwise, the same perpetual-motion image remained and continued to flow in its previous shapes, eccentric, unlikely, Birdian. The game itself was a joke, a National-American League all-star softball game dreamed up and telecast by CBS. In this atmosphere of farce, Mark seemed strangely serious. He did not talk to the softball. Earnest, he twirled rainbow-arc slow pitches into the jaws of the NL's sluggers. In the first inning, Johnny Bench did a Fidrych imitation, talked to his bat, and uncocked Mark's next lob over the left-field snow fence.

An inning later Mark came up to bat himself, banged a clean single over second off Tom Seaver, and then borne on a gangling flurry of arms and legs hightailed it around to third; there, he paused to goof around with Phyllis George, off camera (Phyllis's squeals from the third-base coaching box told the story better than a thousand pitchers), before coming on to score his run in a flailing, elbow-flapping dash down the base path that summoned up visions of a terrified ostrich. The sight of Mark swinging a bat and galumphing around the bases brought its own shock of recognition, carrying inklings of unsuggested abilities. Imagine The Bird swooping up to the plate as a designated hitter! Or wheeling from first to third on a drive to the outfield in Tiger Stadium— gears loose, feathers flying! Combine Harpo Marx, the Fonz, Gyro Gearloose, and Neal Cassady into one flaming package, loping into history and poetry (or third base) on the pipe-cleaner stilts of an Everglades flamingo!

Baseball couldn't stand it. Having Mark Fidrych on the field 162 times a season would be a natural excess, an embarrassment of riches, like pie and champagne for breakfast on a Tuesday—*and* Wednesday, *and* Thursday. . . .

Mark spent most of the winter in his apartment in suburban Detroit. He went home to Massachusetts over the holidays, then returned. There was work to do. "I got a phone," he said, " 'cause I needed it for business. I'm a businessman now, ain't no peon any more." Earlier in the winter he'd made an Aqua-Velva commercial in Florida, posing with Beauty and actually, as he delighted in recalling, *singing.* Now, in January, he made promotional appearances at an auto show in Michigan, for something in the four-figures-a-day range. He also took part semivoluntarily in the annual Tiger press tour around the state, with five other players, Houk, and Campbell. ("You gotta do it," Mark explained. "It's in your contract, like if they ask you—like next year I won't have to go on it.") Predictably, he was the star of the tour. Everywhere the caravan touched down in its ticket-selling itinerary, from Saginaw to Flint, from Jackson to Grand Rapids, autograph-hungry Bird fans dogged Mark's every step, Pied Piper-style, just as they had done the summer before at Tiger Stadium. The fact that Mark tooted on an old harmonica and never changed his socks made sports-page news around Michigan. In small papers up and down the state the Bird was a constant fountain of quotes, his What-Me-Worry wisdom buttering every reporter's bread. He recited

Grod's dictum ("Rome wasn't built in a day"), propounded Ralph Houk's theorem ("Ladies, but not all night"), and turned back the inevitable question about the sophomore jinx with aplomb worthy of a dugout Socrates: "What's the sophomore jinx? Made it through my sophomore year in high school, didn't I? Your hardest year is your first year that you play in the big leagues. I mean, I got nothin' to worry about. Whatever happens, happens. I can't change it, right?"

All around him, it was still happening. Kids and girls and reporters on every side. Had success changed him? "I can't see any difference at all," said Ralph Houk at one stop on the tour. Ralph could afford a comfortable smile; Mark was in good shape. "He still looks and acts the same to me." Indeed, the surprising young man who'd made the Tigers a million unexpected dollars in 1976 still looked very much like a diamond to the club officials when they looked forward to 1977. They, Mark, and everybody else knew well in advance that when the Tigers took the field for the next season's opener against the Royals at home, The Bird would be on the mound and every seat in the place would be sold out a month in advance.

For the time being, when the press tour ended, Mark went back to Detroit to wait out the country's worst winter in half a century. By phone, he told me in late January that he was "goin' nuts," killing time before baseball would begin. Early in February he went to New York, and then to Florida for the television softball. At mid-month he reported to the Tiger camp at Lakeland. On March 9 he inaugurated the major league spring exhibition season by throwing three scoreless innings at his prime 1976 nemesis, the Red Sox. It seemed to some fans appropriate that 1977's first pitches should be thrown by the player who'd recently done more to endear the game to the nation than anyone since Willie Mays—and that at a time when the game couldn't have needed the public's affection more. Knee-deep in lawsuits and lawyers, worn down by nouveau riche free agents and their envious, unfree, unhappy, and unsigned teammates, laden with failing franchises and chipped at by ever-rising costs, baseball at least had *one* positive symbol left, one chunk of mythology that still lived

and breathed and by virtue of its singularity shone out above the
ambient bullshit. There was The Bird, down in Florida among the
old men, himself a veteran now but in years still only a boy,
throwing the first pitch of the spring. It was March again, and the
smells of mustard and leather and sweat and growing grass were
in the air again, as were the soft-hard noises of ball on glove and
bat, and the casual yells of the participants and coaches, and the
polite responding applause of the crowd, and over it all the body-
relaxing sunshine promising a coming summer. At Lakeland
Mark knelt down on one knee and smoothed out the dirt around
the mound, shaping and patting until the configuration of earth
suited him. He looked in at his catcher, curled his tongue back into
the corner of his mouth, rocked twice, brought his right arm
instinctively across his uncoiling body, and fired the ancient sink-
ing fastball of Dizzy Dean and Walter Johnson, of Lefty Grove
and Christy Mathewson, into the lower half of the strike zone—
and the season was on.

The strike let loose a rush of blood in Mark's heart, and he
squawked with pleasure.

Appendix A
DETROIT TIGERS'
1976 ROSTER*

Manager: Ralph Houk. Coaches: Fred Gladding, Jim Hegan, Joe Schultz, Dick Tracewski

PITCHERS

Name	B	T	Ht	Wt	Birthdate and Place		Residence
Bare, Ray	R	R	6-2	195	4-15-49	Miami, Fla.	Miami, Fla.
Coleman, Joe	R	R	6-3	195	2- 3-47	Boston, Mass.	Lathrup Village, Mich.
Crawford, Jim	L	L	6-3	200	9-29-50	Chicago, Ill.	Palmer, Alaska
Fidrych, Mark	R	R	6-3	175	8-14-54	Worcester, Mass.	Northboro, Mass.
Grilli, Steve	R	R	6-2	170	5- 2-49	Brooklyn, N.Y.	Hauppauge, N. Y.
Hiller, John	R	L	6-0	165	4- 8-43	Scarborough, Ont.	Duluth, Minn.
Laxton, Bill	L	L	6-2	190	1- 5-48	Camden, N.J.	Haddonfield, N.J.
Roberts, Dave	L	L	6-2	195	9-11-44	Gallipolis, Ohio	Houston, Tex.
Ruhle, Vern	R	R	6-1	180	1-25-51	Midland, Mich.	Livonia, Mich.

CATCHERS

Name	B	T	Ht	Wt	Birthdate and Place		Residence
Freehan, Bill	R	R	6-2	210	11-29-41	Detroit, Mich.	Bloomfield Hills, Mich.
Kimm, Bruce	R	R	5-11	170	6-29-51	Cedar Rapids, Iowa	Norway, Iowa
May, Milt†	L	R	6-0	190	8- 1-50	Gary, Ind.	Palmetto, Fla.
Wockenfuss, John	R	R	6-0	190	2-27-49	Welch, W. Va.	Wilmington, Del.

INFIELDERS

Name	B	T	Ht	Wt	Birthdate and Place		Residence
Manuel, Jerry	R	R	6-0	155	12-23-53	Hahira, Ga.	Rancho Cordova, Calif.
Meyer, Dan	L	R	5-11	180	8- 3-52	Hamilton, Ohio	El Toro, Calif.
Rodriguez, Aurelio	R	R	5-11	180	12-28-47	Cananea, Mexico	Cananea, Mexico
Scrivener, Chuck	R	R	5-9	170	10- 3-47	Alexandria, Va.	Baltimore, Md.
Sutherland, Gary	R	R	6-0	175	9-27-44	Glendale, Calif.	Monrovia, Calif.
Thompson, Jason	L	L	6-4	200	7- 6-54	Hollywood, Calif.	Apple Valley, Calif.
Veryzer, Tom	R	R	6-1	180	2-11-53	Port Jefferson, N. Y.	Islip, N. Y.

OUTFIELDERS

Name	B	T	Ht	Wt	Birthdate and Place		Residence
Horton, Willie	R	R	5-10	205	10-18-43	Arno, Va.	Detroit, Mich.
Johnson, Alex	R	R	6-0	205	12- 7-42	Helena, Ark.	Detroit, Mich.
LeFlore, Ron	R	R	6-0	200	6-16-52	Detroit, Mich.	Detroit, Mich.
Oglivie, Ben	L	L	6-2	170	2-11-49	Colon, Panama	Southgate, Mich.
Stanley, Mickey	R	R	6-1	195	7-20-42	Grand Rapids, Mich.	West Bloomfield, Mich.
Staub, Rusty	L	R	6-2	205	4- 1-44	New Orleans, La.	Houston, Tex.

*Corrected to May 1.
†Placed on 50-day disabled list April 21.

Appendix B
Mark Fidrych's Record
in Organized Baseball

FIDRYCH, Mark Steven, pitcher
Born: Worcester, Massachusetts, 8-14-54. 6-3 175 B-R T-R. Single.
Signed by Tigers as 10th selection in June 1974 draft.

Year	Club	Class	ERA	W–L	G	GS	CG	IP	H	R	ER	BB	SO
1974	Bristol	Rookie	2.38	3–0	23	0	0	34	24	13	9	16	40
1975	Lakeland	A	3.77	5–9	17	16	10	117	111	58	49	50	73
	Montgomery	AA	3.21	2–0	7	0	0	14	15	6	5	3	11
	Evansville	AAA	1.59	4–1	6	6	4	40	27	8	7	9	29
1976	Detroit		2.34	19–9	31	29	24	250	217	76	65	53	97

Appendix C
Mark Fidrych—1976
Game-by-Game

Date	Opponent	Score	Record	Opposing Starter	Innings	Hits	Runs	Earned Runs	Walks	Strike-Outs	Time	Atten-dance
4/20	Oakland	5-6	—	Mitchell	0*	1	0	0	0	0	2:47	3,080
5/5	Minnesota	2-8	—	Blyleven	1*	2	0	0	0	0	2:20	8,317
5/15	Cleveland	2-1	1-0	Dobson	9	2	1	1	1	5	1:57	14,583
5/25	Boston†	0-2	1-1	Tiant	8	6	2	2	2	1	1:57	21,033
5/31	Milwaukee	5-4	2-1	Slaton	11	11	4	4	4	8	3:04	17,894
6/5	Texast	3-2	3-1	Blyleven	11	7	2	2	1	8	2:42	32,678
6/11	California	4-3	4-1	Ryan	9	9	3	1	0	4	2:28	36,377
6/16	Kansas City	4-3	5-1	Bird	9	5	3	2	2	2	2:08	21,659
6/20	Minnesota†	7-3	6-1	Singer	7.1	9	3	3	6	2	2:40	11,916
6/24	Boston†	6-3	7-1	Wise	9	7	3	3	2	4	2:31	26,293
6/28	New York	5-1	8-1	Holtzman	9	7	1	1	0	2	1:51	47,855
7/3	Baltimore	4-0	9-1	Cuellar	9	4	0	0	3	4	1:54	51,032
7/9	Kansas City	0-1	9-2	Leonard	9	9	1	1	1	2	2:03	51,041
7/16	Oakland	1-0	10-2	Torrez	11	7	0	0	4	6	2:26	45,905
7/20	Minnesota†	8-3	11-2	Singer	9	10	3	3	2	2	2:39	30,425
7/24	Cleveland†	5-4	—	Brown	4.1	9	4	4	1	2	2:54	37,504
7/29	Baltimore	0-1	11-3	May	9	6	1	0	1	8	1:52	44,068
8/3	New York†	3-4	11-4	Figueroa	7	8	4	4	1	3	2:21	44,909
8/7	Cleveland	6-1	12-4	Dobson	9	6	1	1	1	3	2:10	35,395
8/11	Texas	4-3	13-4	Perry	9	9	3	3	1	5	2:22	36,523
8/17	California	3-2	14-4	Tanana	9	5	2	2	1	2	2:08	51,822
8/21	Minnesota	3-7	14-5	Redfern	10	12	7	7	2	1	2:45	34,760
8/25	Chicago	3-1	15-5	Johnson	9	5	1	0	1	1	1:48	39,884
8/29	Oakland†	1-2	15-6	Torrez	11.1	7	2	2	3	1	2:42	25,659
9/3	Milwaukee	2-11	15-7	Augustine	3.2	8	9	7	3	3	2:21	32,951
9/7	Baltimore	3-5	15-8	Garland	9	11	5	2	3	2	2:19	16,410
9/12	New York†	6-0	16-8	Ellis	9	9	0	0	1	5	2:15	52,707
9/17	Boston	3-8	16-9	Tiant	2.2	7	7	6	2	1	2:09	20,371
9/21	Cleveland	5-3	17-9	Waits	9	9	3	3	2	2	2:00	7,147
9/28	Cleveland†	4-0	18-9	Bibby	9	5	0	0	1	3	1:48	3,394
10/2	Milwaukee†	4-1	19-9	Slaton	9	5	1	1	1	4	1:46	9,044

*games pitched in relief.
†Road game

Attendance	(starts only)	average
Home (18)	605,677	33,649
Road (11)	295,562	26,869
	901,239	31,077

250

Appendix D

Pitchers' Efficiency Rating System for the American League, 1976

(League leaders in bold face)

Percent Rank	Name and Team	Games	Games Started	Complete Games	Percent of Starts Completed	Innings Pitched	Innings Pitched per Start	Games Won	Bases on Balls	Innings Pitched per Base on Balls	Strike-outs	Hits	Innings Pitched per Hit	Earned Run Average	Points*
1	Fidrych, Detroit	31	29	**24**	**83**	250¹	**8.59**	19	53	4.72	97	217	1.15	**2.34**	**18**
2	Tanana, California	34	34	23	68	288	8.47	19	73	3.95	261	212	1.36	2.44	17
3	Palmer, Baltimore	40	**40**	23	58	**315**	7.88	**22**	84	3.75	159	255	1.27	2.51	14.5
4	Blue, Oakland	37	37	20	54	298	8.05	18	63	4.73	166	268	1.12	2.36	10.5
5	Ryan, California	39	39	21	54	284	7.28	17	**183**	1.55	**327**	193	**1.42**	3.36	10
6	Hunter, New York	36	36	21	54	299	8.30	17	68	4.37	173	268	1.12	3.52	9
7	Blyleven, Minn./Texas	36	36	18	50	298	8.28	13	81	3.68	219	**283**	1.05	2.87	7.5
8	Perry, Texas	32	32	21	66	250	7.81	15	52	4.77	143	232	1.08	3.24	7
9	Eckersley, Cleveland	36	30	9	30	199²	6.30	13	78	2.55	200	155	1.29	3.44	5
10	Jenkins, Boston	30	30	12	40	209	6.97	12	43	**4.86**	142	201	1.04	3.27	5

¹Fidrych pitched one inning in relief.
²Eckersley pitched one inning in relief.

*Points are determined as follows: 5 points for best performance in any of the categories listed below, 4 points for second, 3 for third, 2 for fourth, and 1 for fifth. Maximum possible points, 40.

Innings Pitched	Complete Games/Starts	Innings per Start	Games Won	ERA	Innings/BB	Innings/Hits	Strikeouts
Palmer	Fidrych	Fidrych	Palmer	Fidrych	Jenkins	Ryan	Ryan
Hunter	Tanana	Tanana	Tiant	Blue	Perry	Tanana	Tanana
Blue	Perry	Hunter	Garland	Tanana	Blue	Eckersley	Blyleven
Blyleven	Palmer	Blyleven	Fidrych	Torrez	Fidrych	Palmer	Eckersley
Tanana	Hunter	Blue	Tanana	Palmer	Hunter	Fidrych	Hunter

ROBERT C. BARTOSZ

1976 American League All-Stars. "They treated you nice at the All-Star. And then they come tellin' me that I'm gonna die, man! How bad is that?"